OXFORD ENGLISH MONOGRAPHS

Defending Poetry

Art and Ethics in Joseph Brodsky,
Seamus Heaney, and Geoffrey Hill

DAVID-ANTOINE WILLIAMS

OXFORD
UNIVERSITY PRESS

OXFORD
UNIVERSITY PRESS

Great Clarendon Street, Oxford OX2 6DP

Oxford University Press is a department of the University of Oxford.
It furthers the University's objective of excellence in research, scholarship,
and education by publishing worldwide in

Oxford New York

Auckland Cape Town Dar es Salaam Hong Kong Karachi
Kuala Lumpur Madrid Melbourne Mexico City Nairobi
New Delhi Shanghai Taipei Toronto

With offices in

Argentina Austria Brazil Chile Czech Republic France Greece
Guatemala Hungary Italy Japan Poland Portugal Singapore
South Korea Switzerland Thailand Turkey Ukraine Vietnam

Oxford is a registered trade mark of Oxford University Press
in the UK and in certain other countries

Published in the United States
by Oxford University Press Inc., New York

British Library Cataloguing in Publication Data

Data available

Library of Congress Cataloging in Publication Data
Library of Congress Control Number: 2010933181

Typeset by SPI Publisher Services, Pondicherry, India
Printed in Great Britain
on acid-free paper by
MPG Books Group, Bodmin and King's Lynn

ISBN 978–0–19–958354–6

1 3 5 7 9 10 8 6 4 2

For my mother and father

Acknowledgements

For their generous assistance at various stages of this work, it is my pleasure to acknowledge, with gratitude, Bernard O'Donoghue, Christopher Ricks, Ronald Bush, Robert Crawford, Peter McDonald, Derek Attridge, Neil Corcoran, Meir Sternberg, Norman Ravvin, Kerry McSweeny, Kathryn Murphy, Davide Cargnello, Matthew Sperling, Fiona Benson, Oliver Nash, James Womack, Mira Novek, David E. Williams, and Adèle Chené. Parts of Chapters 1 and 2 have appeared previously, in different forms, in *Yeats Eliot Review* and *Poetics Today*, respectively. Portions of this research were supported by the British Academy, the *Fonds québécois de la recherche sur la société et la culture*, Hertford College, Oxford, the University of York, Universities UK, the University of St Andrews, the Canadian Women's Club of London, and Balliol College, Oxford. My debt to my mother and father is beyond reckoning.

Heaney. Excerpts from 'Craig's Dragoons' reprinted by permission of Seamus Heaney. Excerpts from *The Triumph of Love* by Geoffrey Hill. Copyright © 1998 by Geoffrey Hill. Reprinted by permission of Penguin Books Ltd. and the Houghton Mifflin Harcourt Publishing Company. All rights reserved. Excerpts from *Canaan* by Geoffrey Hill. Copyright © 1996 by Geoffrey Hill. Reprinted by permission of Penguin Books Ltd. and the Houghton Mifflin Harcourt Publishing Company. All rights reserved. Excerpts from *New & Collected Poems, 1952–1992* by Geoffrey Hill. Copyright © 1994 by Geoffrey Hill. Reprinted by permission of the Houghton Mifflin Harcourt Publishing Company. All rights reserved. Excerpts from *Collected Poems* by Geoffrey Hill. Copyright © 1985 by Geoffrey Hill. Reprinted by permission of Penguin Books Ltd. Excerpts from *Speech! Speech!* by Geoffrey Hill. Copyright © 2001 by Geoffrey Hill. Reprinted by permission of Penguin Books Ltd. and Geoffrey Hill. Excerpts from *The Orchards of Syon* by Geoffrey Hill. Copyright © 2002 by Geoffrey Hill. Reprinted by permission of Penguin Books Ltd. and Geoffrey Hill. Excerpts from *Scenes from Comus* by Geoffrey Hill. Copyright © 2005 by Geoffrey Hill. Reprinted by permission of Penguin Books Ltd. Excerpts from *Collected Critical Writings* by Geoffrey Hill. Copyright © 2008 by Geoffrey Hill. Reprinted by permission of Oxford University Press.

The following are reprinted by permission of Farrar, Straus and Giroux, LLC, and Faber and Faber Ltd.:

Excerpts from 'Less Than One', 'To Please a Shadow', 'A Commencement Address', 'A Poet and Prose', and 'Catastrophes in Air' from *Less Than One* by Joseph Brodsky. Copyright © 1986 by Joseph Brodsky. Excerpts from 'Altra Ego', 'How to Read a Book', 'An Immodest Proposal', 'Homage to Marcus Aurelius', 'Collector's Item', 'Letter to Horace', and 'In Memory of Stephen Spender' from *On Grief and Reason* by Joseph Brodsky. Copyright © 1995 by Joseph Brodsky. Excerpts from *Preoccupations: Selected Prose 1968–1978* by Seamus Heaney. Copyright © 1980 by Seamus Heaney. Excerpts from *The Government of the Tongue: Selected Prose 1978–1987* by Seamus Heaney. Copyright © 1989 by Seamus Heaney. Excerpts from *The Redress of Poetry* by Seamus Heaney. Copyright © 1995 by Seamus Heaney. Excerpts from 'Digging', 'Toome', 'The Tollund Man', 'Traditions', 'Broagh', 'Bog Queen', 'Triptych III', 'The Badgers', 'September Song', 'Away from it All', 'Station Island', 'Terminus', 'The Mud Vision', 'The Golden Bough', 'Seeing Things', 'The Journey Back', 'Mycenae Lookout', 'An Invocation', 'Cassandra', 'Weighing In', 'The

Flight Path', 'Requiem for the Croppies', 'A New Song', 'Bone Dreams', 'Glanmore Sonnets III', 'Song', 'The Skylight', 'Crossings xxviii', 'Tollund', and 'M.' from *Opened Ground: Selected Poems 1966–1996* by Seamus Heaney. Copyright © 1998 by Seamus Heaney. Excerpts from 'Glanmore Eclogue', 'Montana', 'Vitruviana', 'The Bookcase', 'On His Works in the English Tongue', 'Audenesque', and 'Electric Light' from *Electric Light* by Seamus Heaney. Copyright © 2001 by Seamus Heaney. Excerpts from *Finders Keepers: Selected Prose 1971–2002* by Seamus Heaney. Copyright © 2002 by Seamus Heaney. Excerpts from 'Midnight Anvil', 'The Tollund Man in Springtime', and 'Nonce Words' from *District and Circle* by Seamus Heaney. Copyright © 2006 by Seamus Heaney. Excerpts from *Stepping Stones: Interviews with Seamus Heaney* by Dennis O'Driscoll. Copyright © 2008 by Dennis O'Driscoll.

Contents

List of Abbreviations

BOOKS BY T. S. ELIOT

SW	*The Sacred Wood* (1920, rpt. 1928)
SE	*Selected Essays* (1932, rpt. 1951)
UPC	*The Use of Poetry and the Use of Criticism* (1933)
NDC	*Notes Towards the Definition of Culture* (1948)
OPP	*On Poetry and Poets* (1956)
CP	*Collected Poems 1909–1962* (1963)

BOOKS BY JOSEPH BRODSKY

JBSP	*Joseph Brodsky Selected Poems* (1973)
LTO	*Less than One* (1986)
GR	*On Grief and Reason* (1996)
CPE	*Collected Poems in English* (2001)

BOOKS BY SEAMUS HEANEY

DN	*Death of a Naturalist* (1966)
DD	*Door into the Dark* (1969)
WO	*Wintering Out* (1972)
N	*North* (1975)
FW	*Field Work* (1979)
P	*Preoccupations: Selected Prose 1968–1978* (1980)
SI	*Station Island* (1985)
HL	*The Haw Lantern* (1987)
GT	*The Government of the Tongue: The 1986 T. S. Eliot Memorial Lectures and Other Critical Writings* (1989)
CT	*The Cure at Troy: A Version of Sophocles's Philoctetes* (1990)
ST	*Seeing Things* (1991)
CR	*Crediting Poetry* (1995)
RP	*The Redress of Poetry: Oxford Lectures* (1996)

SL	*The Spirit Level* (1996)
B	*Beowulf* (1999)
EL	*Electric Light* (2001)
FK	*Finders Keepers: Selected Prose 1971–2001* (2002)
DC	*District and Circle* (2006)
SS	*Stepping Stones* (2008)

BOOKS BY GEOFFREY HILL

GHCP	*Geoffrey Hill: Collected Poems* (1985)
C	*Canaan* (1996)
TL	*The Triumph of Love* (1998)
SS	*Speech! Speech!* (2000)
OS	*The Orchards of Syon* (2002)
SC	*Scenes From Comus* (2005)
WT	*Without Title* (2006)
CCW	*Collected Critical Writings* (2008)

OTHER ABBREVIATED TITLES

| OED2 | *The Oxford English Dictionary*, 2nd edn (1989) |
| OED3 | *OED Online*, additions series and draft entries (1989–) |

1

Ethics, Literature, and the Place of Poetry

τοῦτ᾽ ἄρα ἔσται καὶ ὁ τραγῳδοποιός, εἴπερ μιμητής
ἐστι, τρίτος τις ἀπὸ βασιλέως καὶ τῆς ἀληθείας
πεφυκώς, καὶ πάντες οἱ ἄλλοι μιμηταί.

And the tragic poet is an imitator, and therefore, like all other
imitators, he is thrice removed from the king and from the truth.

Plato, *Republic*, 390 BC

The common idea that the artistic and the ethical belong to isolated
branches of experience is a recent one. In philosophy, it arises from one
stream of interpretation of Immanuel Kant's tripartite division of
philosophical inquiry into pure reason (epistemology and metaphysics),
practical reason (ethics/morals), and judgement (aesthetics). Within the
English literary and critical tradition it is an even younger categorical
separation, taking hold only around the turn of the twentieth century,
its Kantian origins mediated by Romanticism and secular humanism.
With universal religious faith long dissipated as the principle of harmo-
nization between the self and its surrounding world, the failure on this
count of religion's supposed successors, the Romantic emotive-expres-
sive principle and the humanistic rational principle, left no higher order
within which ethical and aesthetic ways of understanding could be
reconciled. Nor could one be suffered to supplant the other. In the
early years of the century, T. S. Eliot immunized poetry against the
substitutive function promoted by Matthew Arnold, saying, 'nothing in
this world or the next is a substitute for anything else; and if you find
that you must do without something, such as religious faith or philo-
sophic belief, then you must just do without it' (UPC, 113). For others,
art was too subjective a thing from which to derive moral guidance, a
view confirmed by the defining historical narratives of the century: the

stories of Nazi Germany and totalitarian communist empire. Not only was art small succour during these emergencies, it seemed also at times to offend all decency. Theodor Adorno's much-abused dictum, 'to write poetry after Auschwitz is barbaric',[1] sums up this view: the Holocaust presented the world with the bare and hideous fact that, in George Steiner's way of putting it, 'a man can read Goethe or Rilke in the evening...and go to his day's work at Auschwitz in the morning'.[2] Corroboration of the suspect link between politics and culture came from the Soviet Union, where the reigning ideology called art to its service. Socialist Realism, which demanded that art represent reality 'in its revolutionary development', asserted that 'the truthfulness and historical concreteness of the artistic portrayal should be combined with the ideological remoulding and education of the toiling people in the spirit of socialism.'[3] Taken together, these examples showed both sides of the coin: that high culture does not necessarily give rise to a moral society, and that a stable political system cannot guarantee a healthy culture. On the contrary, the integrity, not to say the wholesomeness, of art culture would appear to depend at least to some degree on its autonomy from such worldly concerns, on its self-interested and self-regarding attitude—an existence determined outside the instrumental demands of any ethics, politics, or other social theory.

It is hard to disagree. Nevertheless, with full knowledge of the twentieth century's evil, often with direct experience of it, and never with disregard for it, some poets have continued the long tradition of apologia, or poetic defence. In this book I examine attempts at the ethical defence of poetic art by three of the most important poet-critics of the past fifty years. In their essays and lectures, at times also in their poetry, Joseph Brodsky, Seamus Heaney, and Geoffrey Hill have engaged intensely with what it means to write in the lyric mode, what the potential of language may be when wrought in this way, what dangers it may pose, and what help it may offer. They have done so amid a predominant tendency—in the popular imagination as much as in the

---

[1] Theodor W. Adorno, *The Adorno Reader*, ed. Brian O'Connor (Oxford: Blackwell, 2000), 210.

[2] George Steiner, *Language and Silence: Essays on Language, Literature, and the Inhuman* (New York: Athenaeum, 1967), ix.

[3] A. A. Zhdanov, in an address to the Union of Soviet Writers Congress, August 1934. Reprinted in Maxim Gorky et al., *Soviet Writers' Congress, 1934: The Debate on Socialist Realism and Modernism in the Soviet Union*, trans. and ed. H. G. Scott (London: Lawrence and Wishart, 1977), 21.

academy—to view literature either as an artefact of prevailing power systems to be judged mainly on political criteria or as a purely aesthetic artefact with no attestable significance beyond the singular moment of enjoyment. Both of these reductions are repeatedly challenged by the poets treated here. The result is a set of poetic theories which, in their various contentions, hold that the madeness of wrought language is the only appraisable quality of poetry, that its aim and orientation is primarily the aesthetic qualities of its linguisticity, while acknowledging that the good and bad of human potential, our history and our future, are bound up in language, are represented in language, and may sometimes be affected by language.

THE CASE AGAINST

There have been three important lines of objection to the joining of aesthetic and ethical inquiry, which can broadly be categorized as arguments from (1) inefficacy, (2) corruption, and (3) injury. For those who deny the moral efficacy of poetry, its ability to affect human circumstances directly and for the better, to effect changes in and among societies, W. H. Auden's saying that 'poetry makes nothing happen' is frequently to hand.[4] Richard Posner reaches for it in defence of what he calls the 'aesthetic tradition'. Arguing that 'immersion in literature does not make us better citizens or better people',[5] Judge Posner builds a credible case against the central claim of the didactic school: that literature, by presenting us with imaginary characters negotiating their imaginary circumstances, makes available rich and various models of virtuous and vicious behaviour, all the while exercising our moral faculties in their regard. Posner's refutation of this claim is both commonsensical and empirical:

the moral dilemmas depicted in canonical literature are for the most part remote from current ethical concerns; above all, there is no evidence that talking about ethical issues improves ethical performance.[6]

---

[4] W. H. Auden, *The English Auden: Poems, Essays and Dramatic Writings 1927–1939*, ed. Edward Mendelson (London: Faber and Faber, 1977), 242.
[5] Richard Posner, 'Against Ethical Criticism', *Literature and Philosophy* 21:1 (1997), 1–27, 2.
[6] Ibid. 12.

However, Posner does not merely dismiss the 'edifying school' as an innocuous result of category confusion; the fact that 'English majors are no more moral in attitude or behavior than their peers in other fields' is only one part of the story.[7] The insertion of moral norms into literary analysis is, for Posner, antithetical to the aims and aspirations of a liberal society:

The separation of culture and the state, of what is properly private and what is properly public, is menaced by the didactic school. By assigning to literature the function of promoting sound moral (including political) values, it associates literature with public functions, such as the inculcation of civic virtue. By doing this it makes literature an inviting candidate for public regulation and thus contracts the private sphere.[8]

In other words, the incursion of literature into the public sphere is essentially and aggressively anti-democratic, a simultaneous attack on collective progress and on individual autonomy, the two competing values that democracy promotes and seeks to balance.

The ensconcing of democracy as the favoured mode of political organization has perforce reunited politics with ethics—the prevailing rhetoric of democracy promotes it as the agent simultaneously of individual autonomy and of collective interest, of human and of humanity. The modern ideology of freedom, historically the basis of democratic movements, is at once political and ethical, and naturally prefers politics as the means of achieving its ethical objectives. Politics concerns itself with the organization of power and the administration of collective resources, including their redistribution, and so is suited to addressing most directly the moral challenges society sets for itself: crime, inequality, poverty, and so on. Comparatively, art has little purchase on action. The role of the poet as bard, as society's interpreter of its own potential, or, in Shelley's grandiose phrasing, as the 'hierophants of an unapprehended inspiration',[9] feels outmoded for precisely the same democratic reasons that political activism is favoured. On the one hand there is poetry's absence from public discourse, from corporate balance sheets, parliamentary Hansards, stock market tickers, and television transcripts—seemingly from all points of contact with the public sphere. As early as the 1830s

---

[7] Ibid.
[8] Ibid. 8.
[9] Percy Bysshe Shelley, 'A Defence of Poetry', in *Shelley's Poetry and Prose*, ed. Donald H. Reiman and Neil Fraistat (London: Norton, 2002), 509–35, 535.

Alexis de Tocqueville, comparing American democracy to European aristocracies, commented on the 'anti-poetic...life of the man of the United States', where the goal of imaginative attention is almost always 'to conceive of what may be useful, and to represent the real'.[10] All of this flows into a powerful argument, not only against the 'relevance' of poetry to modern civic institutions, but also in favour of Posner's claim that the yoking of ethics and aesthetics offends the 'values of openness, detachment, hedonism, curiosity, tolerance, the cultivation of the self, and the preservation of a private sphere—in short, the values of liberal individualism'.[11]

On the other hand, and also stirring up feelings for democratic egalitarianism, the suspicion persists that poetry is an amusement of the educated elite, a legacy not only of Shelleyan declamations but also of T. S. Eliot's high-culture associations and the cult of literary and theoretical opacity of the late twentieth century. United States Poet Laureate (1997–2000) Robert Pinsky distinguishes between intellectual and social egalitarianism when he writes—guardedly, but ultimately with approval—about the American 'freedom to judge the art of poetry itself as a consumer, intimidated by the art's difficulty but not by its social prestige or authority'.[12] To subscribe to this view, 'for good or ill', as Pinsky says, is to prepare a space for poetry within democracy, but the cost may be higher than Pinsky anticipates. If we accept that poetry can or ought to be consumed like other products of the democratic-capital- istic economy, must we not also submit to the judgement of the market? And on this count, would not what we now call poetry be even shorter in supply, or higher in cost—truly a luxury, like foie gras and truffles?

For those who enjoy a little poetry with their foie gras, the populism of Pinsky's analysis is likely to ring alarm bells. Complementing the efficacy argument of social theorists is the charge from the literature side of corruption or debasement, the subordination, as Charles Altieri puts it, 'of what might be distinctive within literary experience to those frameworks and mental economies that are attuned to modes of judg- ment shaped by other nontextual, and (usually) less directly imaginary,

---

[10] 'On ne saurait rien concevoir...de si anti-poétique, en un mot, que la vie d'un homme aux États-Unis.' 'L'imagination...s'adonne presque exclusivement à concevoir l'utile et à représenter le réel.' Alexis de Tocqueville, *De la démocratie en Amérique*, vol. 2 (Paris: Gallimard, 1993), 108, 94.

[11] Posner, 'Against Ethical Criticism', 2.

[12] Robert Pinsky, *Democracy, Culture and the Voice of Poetry* (Princeton, NJ: Princeton University Press, 2002).

worldly demands'.[13] Eliot stated axiomatically (and with unacknowl-
edged Kantian undertones) that the work of art is 'autotelic' (SE, 30),
defined by its self-regarding, self-interested character, and on this basis
the 'New' and other formalist critics tend to disqualify approaches to
literature that have extraliterary ends in view. These critics also refer us
to Auden, or else to one of Oscar Wilde's prefatory statements to *The
Picture of Dorian Gray:* 'there is no such thing as a moral or an immoral
book'; 'An ethical sympathy in an artist is an unpardonable mannerism
of style'; 'all art is quite useless'.[14] Though art for art's sake, in its first
counter-Romanticism incarnation, precedes the rise of theory in the
academy by almost a century, of late its tenets have been redeployed in
the resistance to theory. Helen Vendler draws a sharp line between the
function of a text and its literary merit, claiming that 'theory that is
interested in the social function of literature . . . refuses precedence to
the "imaginative arts" . . . of language, and puts writing that exhibits
poesis on the same footing as all other "texts"'.[15] She deplores, for
instance, Columbia University's 'tendency with literary texts, which is
to fasten on the political and the moral over the erotic or aesthetic or
epistemological', because 'such an emphasis is a standing invitation to
correctness or incorrectness, since it steers discussion, willy-nilly, toward
currently agitated political and moral questions'.[16] Vendler's ordering
of erotic, aesthetic, and epistemological considerations admits, against
its own grain perhaps, that there is more to art than just beauty, that
beauty might even be a medial or transitional state between desire and
knowing, or between pleasure and understanding, but in opposing the
moral to the epistemological, Vendler drastically reduces the field of
epistemological enquiry (not to mention of erotic enquiry) to its most
technical and self-reflexive dimension. Despite her anti-reductive
stance, she replaces the criterion of relevance with the criterion of the
'aesthetic tradition', whose tenet is that 'In literature, one earns one's
place by writing memorably, not by expressing agreeable attitudes that

---

[13] Charles Altieri, 'Lyrical Ethics and Literary Experience', in Todd F. Davis and
Kenneth Womack (eds), *Mapping the Ethical Turn: A Reader in Ethics, Culture, and
Literary Theory* (Charlottesville: University Press of Virginia, 2001), 30–58, 31.
   [14] Oscar Wilde, *The Artist as Critic: Critical Writings of Oscar Wilde*, ed. Richard
Ellmann (New York: Random House, 1969), 236.
   [15] Helen Vendler, *Soul Says: On Recent Poetry* (Cambridge, MA: Harvard University
Press, 1995), 196.
   [16] Helen Vendler, 'The Booby Trap', *The New Republic* 215:15 (7 October 1996),
34–40, 37.

will wear as well in 1991 as in 1300, or that can be forgiven by an "understanding" reader',[17] or, as in Posner's less pointed and more abstract formulation, that 'the proper criteria for evaluating literature are aesthetic . . . authors' moral qualities or opinions should not affect our valuations of their works'.[18]

If arguments from inefficacy and corruption seek to insert a mutually salutary barrier between the aesthetic and ethical modes, the argument from injury proceeds from the ethical position that in certain (and for some, in all) circumstances, art is *un*ethical practice, inimical to our ethical selves. Despite its apparent extremism, this is arguably the position with the longest, most intricate, and most rigorous intellectual history: in its current forms it can be traced through divergent and even clashing philosophical traditions. Its roots are tangled in the beginnings of moral philosophy, with Plato's expulsion of the poets from his imaginary ideal republic. Plato assails not only poets, but all workers of language: in the *Phaedrus*, he cautions against speech-writers; in the *Gorgias*, rhetoricians; in the *Ion*, rhapsodes, unless their performances be divinely inspired. In *Laws*, Plato places poets under the strict watch of judges. Finally, literary critics (especially those who discuss poetry) come into disrepute in *Protagoras*.[19] Artistic crafting—*poiēsis* (ποίησις—'fabrication')—is inherently suspect to Plato because, depending on the skill and intent of its maker, it has the power to deceive and to persuade, but more fundamentally because its main technique is *mimēsis* (μίμησις—'imitation'), which is by nature a corruption of the true form of things. Whatever their intention, professional imitators, poets not the least of them, are in Plato's famous phrase, 'thrice removed from the king and from the truth'.[20]

The relationship between truth and ethics is an elemental question for philosophy, and how one conceives of it has important consequences for many of its other branches. The implications for aesthetics, and specifically for literary aesthetics, will be considered below. For now it is enough to point out the minimal position that for ethical concepts such as 'justice', 'respect for the other', and, more generally, 'the (moral)

---

[17] Ibid. 36.

[18] Posner, 'Against Ethical Criticism', 2.

[19] See Plato, *Republic*, [595a]–[608b]; *Phaedrus*, [277b]–[278d]; *Gorgias*, [463a]–[466a]; *Ion*, [533d]–[535a]; *Laws*, [659b]–[660e]; *Protagoras*, [347c].

[20] Plato, *Republic*, [597e]. This translation from *Dialogues of Plato: Translated into English with Analyses and Introductions by B. Jowett*, 4th edn, trans. Benjamin Jowett (Oxford: Clarendon Press, 1953).

good' to be meaningful, it is desirable, and may be necessary, to posit a truth of the matter to which the ethical self may (or may not) accede. At least for a universalist like Plato, whatever interposes itself between our understanding and ethical truths is an impediment to ethical self-real-ization. Whatever theme the poet may be treating, whatever lesson his poem means to impart or enact, what he offers are mere simulacra, leading away from instead of towards the truth.

What Plato is really defending against art, however, is not the truth per se, but reason, the means of access to truth that Plato holds to be supreme. Whereas in the pre-Socratic period, philosophy concerned itself with the problems of natural science, and poetry (epic and drama-tic) investigated and expounded ideas of morals, justice, and divinity,[21] after Plato theory founded on reason is the one authorized approach to truth in all spheres of knowing. There is no doubt an ulterior, practical dimension to this: Eric Havelock has described the *Republic* as an extended attack on the Greek educational system, dominated by poets at the time of Plato's writing,[22] and in many places Plato's trenchant debating supremo Socrates does seem to function as an advertisement for a good Academy education. But the philosophical divergence is not to be minimized—in its celebration of multiplicity and individual instantiation, in its reliance on arbitrary formal conventions, even in its attention to the acoustics of words and phrases along with their significations, poetry frustrates the Platonic hierarchy of universal and particular. The exile of the poets—or at the very least the circumscrip-tion and strict management of their activities—is therefore a necessary step in the consolidation of the theoretical method as the preferred mode of access to truth.

In twentieth-century criticism it is possible to recognize traces of this position in theory-driven critiques of literature, though their proximate derivation is from German phenomenology, not ancient philosophy. For instance, the reassessment of the so-called 'Western

---

[21] For a useful discussion of pre-Socratic ethics, see, for instance, Chapter 2, 'The Prephilosophical History of "Good" and the Transition to Philosophy' of Alasdair MacIntyre, *A Short History of Ethics: A History of Moral Philosophy from the Homeric Age to the Twentieth Century* (London: Routledge, 1998), 5–13, as well as Chapters 2 and 3 of MacIntyre, *Whose Justice? Which Rationality?* (Notre Dame, IN: University of Notre Dame Press, 1988), 12–46.

[22] See especially Chapter 1 of Eric A. Havelock, *Preface to Plato* (Cambridge, MA: Harvard University Press, 1963), 3–19. When Plato's *Republic* is read as such, Havelock argues, 'the logic of its total organisation becomes clear' and 'the successive critiques of poetry fall into place' (13).

canon', acrimoniously pursued on political as much as pedagogical grounds during the sixties, seventies and eighties, arises from the suspicion that texts (and other 'narratives') encode prevailing power systems (i.e. systems of inequality) and in so doing propagate and reinforce them, a suspicion that will not be assuaged by any evidence of authorial intention. The shift of moral valence from the author's intent to the narrative itself, its ways and means, in effect places all literature out of trust. The vocabulary of the 'other' comes to replace that of objective and eternal truths, but the basic position is the same: that *mimēsis* fails on its own account to represent accurately, or faithfully, or ethically; that the aesthetic sense of 'representation' exists in permanent tension with its democratic sense. As it was for Plato, the preferred method of inquiry for practitioners of theory is not the aesthetic but the rational theoretical mode, which they call 'critique'. It is only when paired with the continuous critique of texts, with the constant deconstructing of them and disclosing of their inscribed violence to the other, that these texts can be permitted on political grounds. Understood this way, the ethical value of literature is realized negatively in the exposing of its own natural corrupting force, the uncovering of the self's ineluctable tendency to subsume the other.

This is one way of coming to terms with Adorno's dictum, which, even as it appears to reject the possibility of ethical poetry, is a critique of poetry that is fundamentally ethical. To penetrate into Adorno's argument, instead of leaving his words to stand aphoristically for art's inability to answer suffering, is to understand that for him poetry and critique are the elements of culture that are necessary to uncover the barbarism within culture. 'Auschwitz', the first and already the primary synecdoche for the yet-unnamed Holocaust, is the major crisis in which the traditional dialectic of culture and barbarism, of culture set against barbarism, collapses. With the realization that culture is itself barbaric—actually only a partial realization, which is itself contaminated (Adorno says 'corroded') by this very barbarism—emerges a new state of affairs, a post-dialectical aporia in which the impossibility of truly ethical art-creation is permanently set against the enduring ethical necessity of art-creation.

Sooner or later the art of literature, existing principally as a vehicle of aesthetic enjoyment and arising primarily from the imagination, must come face-to-face with the enduring non-fictions of human suffering, and for poets writing after 1950, the Holocaust is the most intense and challenging locus of this encounter. Steiner asks whether, after the

Holocaust, 'the poet should speak or be silent ... whether language is in a condition to accord with his needs'.[23] And Primo Levi, plausibly the greatest writer of the Holocaust, nevertheless articulates a fundamental impediment to its representation when he writes that 'our language lacks words to express this offence, the demolition of man'.[24] This is one way to understand the barbarism of poetry after Auschwitz: poetry as dumb speech, language permanently unequal to its theme, unable to do justice to its subject, language that on one hand falls short of useful explanation or sufficient condemnation of the offence, and on the other fails to attain the high level of care and respect that human victims demand—a language, in short, that is incommensurable with the ethical requirements of subject matter such as the Holocaust. Yet struggling counter to this sense of language's inadmissibility, its incommensurability, is a sense of its necessity. Levi's statement on language's deficiency must be taken together with his literary achievement, and his later reformulation of Adorno's dictum: 'after Auschwitz, one can only write poetry on Auschwitz.'[25]

The Nazi extermination project, in particular its realization in the Jewish Shoah, stands as the ultimate challenge to the capacity of writing to constitute ethical practice. The Hebraic proscription of images has made the debate especially vexed within Jewish Holocaust scholarship, where the imperative to 'always remember', compounded by a strong religious obligation towards the dead, exists in tense misalignment with the commandment against figurative representation. It is fitting that Emmanuel Levinas, a central figure both to contemporary Jewish philosophy and to continental French philosophy, inflicts the century's most uncompromising attack on literature. Since for Levinas the other remains eternally unavailable to the self—to 'understand' the other is to subsume him into the ontology of the self—almost all literature is killing. This is just as true, and perhaps even especially true, of literature that claims to speak the part of the other, or on behalf of the other, to give voice or representation to the other. Thus even the kinds of un- or

[23] Steiner, *Language and Silence*, 53.

[24] Primo Levi, quoted in Irving Howe, 'Writing and the Holocaust', in Berel Lang (ed.), *Writing and the Holocaust* (New York: Holmes and Meier Publishers, 1988), 175–99, 186.

[25] 'In quegli anni, semai, avrei riformaluto le parole di Adorno: dopo Auschwitz, non si può più fare poesia se non su Auschwitz.' Primo Levi, 'Levi: l'ora incerta della poesia', interviewed in *Corriere della Sera* (28 October 1984), 3.

anti-canonical writing promoted by other-oriented ethical or political positions fail to overcome the high standard of Levinasian ethics.

Apart from their particular framing in Jewish philosophy and theology, the questions raised by debates over Holocaust representation are central to the injury argument against ethical literature and to the wider problem of the relationship between writing and suffering. The Holocaust concentrates and intensifies these questions, so much so that, as Paul Ricoeur writes, its victims, because of their intense and vivid presence in our memory, can act as reminders of other victims from other times.[26] It is victimization and the suffering it inflicts that in the general case pose the ethical challenge to writing. Joseph Brodsky, for instance, has no compunction about adapting Adorno's specific reference to 'Auschwitz': 'one familiar with Russian history can repeat the same question by merely changing the name of the camp' (GR, 55) to that of one in Stalin's gulag archipelago, he says. Seamus Heaney, who contemplates more the suffering experienced under communist dictatorship than under Nazi occupation, can also feel the conflict between art and suffering locally. During the early Troubles in Northern Ireland, he reports 'experiencing, at a most immediate and obvious level, [the] feeling that song constituted a betrayal of suffering... to have sung and said the poems in those conditions would have been a culpable indulgence' (GT, xii). For Geoffrey Hill, himself the victim of no regime, it may be that literary activity is eternally unjustified, or unjustifiable. He has lamented modern culture's 'neglect of the dead'[27] while remaining deeply suspicious of the capacity of a 'fallen' human language to effect any atonement for society's sins.

THE 'ETHICAL TURN'

Lately it has been the vogue to speak of a 'turn to ethics' in literary studies, and a corresponding 'literary turn' in disciplines more usually

---

[26] 'Les victimes d'Auschwitz sont, par excellence, les délégués auprès de notre mémoire de toutes les victimes de l'histoire.' ('The victims of Auschwitz are, par excellence, representatives in our memory of all of history's victims.') Paul Ricoeur, *Temps et récit*, vol. 3 (Paris: Seuil, 1985), 273.

[27] Geoffrey Hill, interview with Carl Phillips, 'The Art of Poetry LXXX: Geoffrey Hill', *Paris Review* 154 (Spring 2000), 272–99, 298.

associated with ethics, principally philosophy, theology, and law.[28]
Within literature, at least, one should really refer to a '*return* to ethics',
since in its two most common forms, current 'ethical criticism' revisits
and adapts well-established critical categories, displaced during most of
the twentieth century by aestheticist and formalist critical movements.
Both approaches to ethical criticism start from the conviction that
literature, as an art rooted in language, concerned in the main with
social and individual situations and experiences, and straddling the
division between private and public activity, cannot escape involvement
in ethics.

The first approach, which stresses the function of the exemplary in
the development of the moral self (what Posner calls the 'edifying
school'), can claim an intellectual tradition reaching back to the ancients.
Broadly characterized as 'neo-Aristotelian', this kind of ethical criticism
emphasizes the didactic role of literature, starting from the observation
that moral education, historically and currently, is overwhelmingly

---

[28] In an early concentration on the question, *New Literary History* published a
'Literature and/as Moral Philosophy' issue (Autumn 1983), bringing together thinkers
from a range of mostly non-literary disciplines, including Martha Nussbaum (philosophy, classics), Hilary Putnam and David Sidorsky (philosophy), Richard Kuhns (law),
and Nathan A. Scott Jr. (theology). The question of the literary within the ethical, and
vice versa, has since received intense attention in each of these disciplines. In law,
Nussbaum, Richard Weisberg, and Robin West argue, against Posner, that literature
provides a necessary ethical education for lawyers and judges. In the various subfields of
philosophy, issues of narrative, identity, and society are central to, among others, Paul
Ricoeur, Charles Taylor, Alasdair MacIntyre, and Hannah Arendt. Prominent among
philosophers either arguing for or actively participating in an engagement with literary
texts are Nussbaum, Bernard Williams, Richard Rorty, Stanley Cavell, and members of
the 'radical orthodoxy' school of Cambridge theologians. A preliminary bibliography
would highlight Martha Nussbaum, *Poetic Justice: The Literary Imagination and Public
Life* (Boston: Beacon Press, 1995) and *Love's Knowledge: Essays on Philosophy and
Literature* (Oxford: Oxford University Press, 1990); Richard Weisberg, *Poethics and
Other Strategies of Law and Literature* (New York: Columbia University Press, 1992);
Robin West, *Narrative, Authority, and Law* (Ann Arbor: University of Michigan Press,
1993); Paul Ricoeur, *Temps et récit* (Paris: Seuil, 1983–5); Charles Taylor, *Sources of the
Self: The Making of the Modern Identity* (Cambridge: Cambridge University Press, 1989);
Alasdair MacIntyre, *Whose Justice?*, Hannah Arendt, *Between Past and Future: Eight
Exercises in Political Thought* (New York: Viking, 1968); Bernard Williams, 'The
Women of Trachis: Fictions, Pessimism, Ethics', in R. B. Louden and P. Schollmeier
(eds), *The Greeks and Us* (Chicago: University of Chicago Press, 1996); Richard Rorty,
Contingency, Irony, and Solidarity (Cambridge: Cambridge University Press, 1989);
Stanley Cavell, *Disowning Knowledge in Six Plays of Shakespeare* (Cambridge: Cambridge
University Press, 1987); John Milbank, *The Word Made Strange: Theology, Language,
Culture* (Oxford: Basil Blackwell, 1997); Catherine Pickstock, *After Writing: on the
Liturgical Consummation of Philosophy* (Oxford: Basil Blackwell, 1998).

transmitted through literature—from the stories of the Bible to secular cautionary tales, children's stories, nursery rhymes, plays, novels, myths, fables, and parables. Long before the ancients invented moral philosophy, their poets—from Homer to the Athenian tragedians—were exploring the central moral question of how to conduct one's life. In the modern period, to include within 'literature' other narrative forms is to extend the field to histories, documentaries, news reports, films, comedic, dramatic, and 'reality' television programmes, internet blogs, and so on. The ethics of literature from this point of view is in its exemplariness—its ability to represent characters in situations, and in so doing to provide a model for decision and action in the real world. Wayne C. Booth's idea of stories as virtual 'friends', companions to which (whom?) we turn in moments of ethical decision,[29] emerges from his empirical claim that we 'are at least partially constructed, in our most fundamental character, by the stories we have heard, or read, or viewed, or acted out in amateur theatricals: the stories we have really *listened* to'.[30] For Martha Nussbaum, omnipresent protagonist of the literature-and-philosophy debates, the necessity of literary experience to ethical reflection is the result of a gap between the depth and range of representation possible in literature and what can be achieved with 'conventional philosophical prose': 'there may be some views of the world and how one should live in it—views, especially, that emphasize the world's surprising variety, its complexity and mysteriousness, its flawed and imperfect beauty', Nussbaum writes, that can only be represented 'in a form that itself implies that life contains significant surprises, that our task, as agents, is to live as good characters in a good story do, caring about what happens, resourcefully confronting each new thing'.[31]

If the 'edifying school' is primarily 'self'-regarding, concerned in the main with the education and improvement of the self through the rich examples supplied in literature, the second stream of ethical criticism produced by the 'turn to ethics' is chiefly other-oriented. The direction of this turn is outwards as opposed to inwards, the result of an ethics conceived not as the Aristotelian pursuit of *eudaimonia* (εὐδαιμονία—the 'good life', 'human flourishing'), but in terms of responsibility. This

---

[29] Wayne C. Booth, *The Company We Keep: An Ethics of Fiction* (Berkeley: University of California Press, 1988).

[30] Wayne C. Booth, 'Why Ethical Criticism Can Never Be Simple', in Davis and Womack (eds), *Mapping the Ethical Turn*, 16–29, 18–19; original emphasis.

[31] Nussbaum, *Love's Knowledge*, 3.

kind of ethical criticism, with roots in continental philosophy and drawing on techniques in phenomenology, semiotics, and deconstruction, is constructed either positively or negatively. Richard Kearney exemplifies the former method when he writes that '*Qua* dialogue which opens us to foreign worlds . . . narrative imagination functions as a precondition for the "representative" subject. It transfigures the self-regarding self into a self-for-another, the *moi* into a *soi*.'[32] It is more usual to construct other-oriented ethical criticism negatively, by acknowledging and exposing the inherent violence of narration, its inevitable tendency to subsume into its selfness the otherness it claims to represent. This realization, once had, leads ethical reading down what Lawrence Buell calls the 'via negativa of rigorous undecidability',[33] taking ethical writing with it. Instead of 'speaking of and for the marginalized or silenced Other', James Meffan and Kim Worthington argue, the ethical writer (as opposed to the political writer—J. M. Coetzee is their subject) will seek to 'encourage the reader to self-critique in the performative process of the act of imagination that is reading and from this basis to suggest the political possibilities of an ethical respect for alterity'.[34] This approach, because it places the emphasis not on 'representation' of the other but on awareness of the self's violence against the other, also clears a path for Levinasian ethics to enter literary criticism. As a result of the 'turn to ethics', Levinas has gained in popularity among literary critics, who invoke him with various intentions, and corresponding degrees of plausibility.[35] If

---

[32] Richard Kearney, *Poetics of Modernity: Towards a Hermeneutic Imagination* (Atlantic Highlands, NJ: Humanities Press, 1995), 105–6.

[33] Lawrence Buell, 'What We Talk about When We Talk about Ethics', in Marjorie Garber, Beatrice Hansen, and Rebecca L. Walkowitz (eds), *The Turn to Ethics* (New York: Routledge, 2000), 1–14, 6. Buell is following Barbara Johnson's identification and discussion of 'rigorous unreliability' as an underlying evaluative principle of deconstruction in Paul de Man. See Chapter 2 of Johnson, *A World of Difference* (Baltimore: Johns Hopkins University Press, 1987), 17–24, and Paul de Man, *Allegories of Reading: Figural Language in Rousseau, Nietzsche, Rilke and Proust* (New Haven, CT: Yale University Press, 1979).

[34] James Meffan and Kim L. Worthington, 'Ethics Before Politics: J. M. Coetzee's *Disgrace*', in Davis and Womack (eds), *Mapping the Ethical Turn*, 131–50, 147.

35 The more difficult and valuable work has been done in philosophy and French studies, notably by Jill Robbins in *Altered Reading: Levinas in Literature* (Chicago: University of Chicago Press, 1999) and on more limited scales in Seán Hand, 'Shadowing Ethics: Levinas's View of Art and Aesthetics', in Seán Hand (ed.), *Facing the Other: The Ethics of Emmanuel Levinas* (Richmond: Curzon, 1996), 63–90; Norman Ravvin, 'Have you Reread Levinas Lately?', in Andrew Hadfield et al. (eds), *The Ethics in Literature* (London: Macmillan, 1999); and Edith Wyschogrod, 'The Art in Ethics:

anything, the invocation of Levinasian responsibility, with its rejection of the humanistic self and its refusal to entertain a practical or normative ethics, demonstrates how far this 'turn to ethics' has taken criticism from politically oriented theory of earlier decades.

The reaction to this movement has at times been furious. Compounding the general resistance to ethical criticism, characterized above in terms of inefficacy, corruption, and injury, within the academy there has been additional resistance, drawing on all three arguments, from those who view the 'turn to ethics' as a renunciation—in disgust or despair—of the various political roles that the theory movement conceived for literature and criticism. 'The turn to ethics is a turn away from the political',[36] writes John Guillory, vocalizing a concern that becomes a conspicuous theme of the Garber et al. collection of essays on ethics and literature. Judith Butler, for instance, worries there that the turn to ethics has meant not only an 'escape from politics' but also a regression of critique towards mere moralism.[37] In the same volume, Chantal Mouffe argues that the 'current infatuation with . . . ethically good causes' represents the 'triumph of a sort of moralizing liberalism that is increasingly filling the void left by the collapse of any project of real political transformation',[38] in other words that ethics, at least in its current 'fashionable' practice, is an empty politics, a politics eviscerated

Aesthetics, Objectivity, and Alterity in the Philosophy of Emmanuel Levinas', in Adriaan T. Peperzak (ed.), *Ethics as First Philosophy: The Significance of Emmanuel Levinas for Philosophy, Literature and Religion* (New York: Routledge, 1995), 138–48. Prominent monographs on Levinas and literature include Andrew Gibson, *Postmodernity, Ethics and the Novel: From Leavis to Levinas* (London: Routledge, 1999), and Michael Eskin, *Ethics and Dialogue in the Works of Levinas, Bakhtin, Mandel'shtam, and Celan* (Oxford: Oxford University Press, 2000). Strategies deployed from within English studies have been on the whole less convincing, despite—or perhaps on account of—their growing abundance: a third of the essays in the Davis and Womack collection invoke Levinas, the same proportion in the Garber et al. collection. Recent essay collections suggest we are in the midst of a period-by-period rereading of English literature through the Levinasian lens: see Ann Astell and Justin Jackson (eds), *Levinas and Medieval Literature: The Difficult Reading of English and Rabbinic Texts* (Pittsburgh: Duquesne University Press, 2009) and Donald Wehrs and David Haney (eds), *Levinas and Nineteenth Century Literature: Ethics and Otherness from Romanticism through Realism* (Newark: University of Delaware Press, 2009).

[36] John Guillory, 'The Ethical Practice of Modernity', in Garber et al. (eds), *The Turn to Ethics*, 29–46, 29.

[37] Judith Butler, 'Ethical Ambivalence', in Garber et al. (eds), *The Turn to Ethics*, 15–28, 15.

[38] Chantal Mouffe, 'Which Ethics for Democracy?', in Garber et al. (eds), *The Turn to Ethics*, 85–94, 85–6.

of its instrumentalism only to be stuffed up with high (but impotent) ideals. Writing in another collection, and from an opposing assessment of the value of political writing, Altieri nevertheless comes to a similar conclusion, that 'literary criticism has to be able to idealize ethics now that it has manifestly failed to affect politics'.[39]

POETRY AND ETHICS

By 'poetry' I do not mean, here, the obsolete broad sense recorded in the OED as 'Imaginative or creative literature in general' (OED3, †1). As late as the third (1973) edition of his *Philosophy of Literary Form*, Kenneth Burke felt he could employ the word in this way,[40] and, uncoincidentally, it is a usage especially typical of philosophical works on aesthetics, where it is often extended even further to refer to the artistic in general.[41] So liberally defined, or undefined, it means too much and too little, as Shelley sensed but did not adequately realize. By 'poetry' I mean 'poems': *Gedichte*, to make use of a convenient lexical distinction in German, not *Poesie*. The main emphasis in what follows will be on the lyric poem, a category Eliot disputed in his 1953 essay 'The Three Voices of Poetry', where he pointed to the OED's broadening definition of 'lyric' as evidence of a growing semantic fuzziness: 'Now used as the name for short poems (whether or not intended to be sung), usually divided into stanzas or strophes, and directly expressing

---

[39] Altieri, 'Lyrical Ethics and Literary Experience', 30.

[40] 'I here use the term [poetry] to include any work of critical or imaginative cast.' Kenneth Burke, *The Philosophy of Literary Form*, 3rd edn (Berkeley: University of California Press, 1973), 1.

[41] So, for instance, Kant divides the 'arts of speech' into only rhetoric (*Beredsamkeit*) and poetry (*Dichtkunst*); Friedrich Schlegel says, 'A painter must be a poet' and talks about the 'poetic inspiration' of Dürer and Raphael; Martin Heidegger, while carving out a narrow sense for *Dichtung*, also employs it in a wide sense, saying 'the essence of art is poetry', and even 'Language itself is poetry'; and Levinas refers to the 'poésie de Dickens', though clearly he means his prose. The tendency probably has roots in Plato, who took *poiēsis* to mean the making of anything, even when he was singling out the maker of tragedy as *poiētēs*. See Kant, *Critique of Aesthetic Judgement*, trans. James Creed Meredith (Oxford: Clarendon Press, 1911), §51; Schlegel, *The Aesthetic and Miscellaneous Writings of Frederick Von Schlegel*, trans. E. J. Millington (London: Bohn, 1849), 70; Heidegger, 'The Origin of the Work of Art', in *Off the Beaten Track*, trans. Julian Young and Kenneth Haynes (Cambridge: Cambridge University Press, 2002), 47, 46; and Levinas, 'La réalité et son ombre', *Les Temps Modernes* 38 (November 1948), 771–89, 785.

the poet's own thoughts and sentiments' (OED2, 1).[42] Eliot refers instead to 'poetry of the first voice', which he memorably defines as 'the voice of the poet talking to himself—or to nobody' (OPP, 96, 89). Even if the OED entry leaves much to be desired, a lexical definition can never match a theoretical one. In any case, other dictionaries split the sense more carefully, and native speakers can easily accord the term the kind of polysemy our language handles well—a lyric is a kind of poem (characterized, if not defined, by meditative as opposed to discursive or narrative language) and also the words to a song. Our sense is newer and derives from the other, and because of this is less fixed, its ostensive instances more open to dispute and reclassification. Without making sub-generic claims in favour of the lyric (and conceiving it broadly, as opposed to the epic or the dramatic poem), focusing on it here retains the emphasis of the poets treated, and indeed of the mainstream of modern and contemporary English verse. And focusing on the lyric— while taking into account the fact that poetry takes and has taken various forms, from the postmodern prose-poem to the ancient elegy—also brings into relief what I take to be the principal characteristic of poetry, though there may well be others: its self-regarding preoccupation with linguistic inventiveness within established, though ultimately violable, formal strictures.

Considering first that, in the Western tradition, poetry has stood at the centre of ethics-and-aesthetics debates, not to mention the rest of literary production and its attendant criticism, from antiquity until at least the nineteenth century, and second that the lyric has been the default poetic genre since perhaps the mid-eighteenth,[43] its lack of status within the revival of ethical criticism is conspicuous. Characterizing poetry as self-regarding, as I have, or defining it in Eliot's terms as a poet talking 'to himself—or to nobody' goes some way towards understanding this lacuna. How can something fundamentally self-regarding display or induce a regard for others? How can something written for nobody be of any use to anybody? While holding out hope for other kinds of poetry, Donald Davie has attacked the lyric specifically for its 'overweening' personal 'I', which he says grants immunity to the poet while

---

[42] Cf. OPP, 97. Eliot abridges this definition when quoting it.

[43] M. H. Abrams, in *The Mirror and the Lamp: Romantic Theory and the Critical Tradition* (New York: Norton, 1958), traces the rise of the lyric to the high renown of Abraham Cowley's *Pindarique Odes* in the 1650s. Certainly by the time of John Stuart Mill's two essays on poetry in 1833, the lyric had surpassed the epic and dramatic modes as the 'poetic norm' (see Abrams, 84–8).

absolving the reader from 'taking his poet's sentiments to heart'.[44]
Many writers on the ethics of literature simply ignore poetry and the
poetic altogether: if the neo-Aristotelian didactic and the responsibility-
oriented deconstructive streams of ethical criticism share anything, it is
that both rely on broad theories of narration, which is to say they regard
real or imagined human actions, consequences, and fates (usually)
within social situations. It is the narrative components of novels, stories,
dramas, etc. that are discussed and debated over, not, usually, their
formal effects. Leaving aside the pervasive yet contestable psychological
and philosophical assumption that people understand themselves and
their worlds primarily in narrative terms,[45] it is unclear where narrative-
dependent ethical criticism leaves poetry, especially lyric poetry. At-
tempts to account for an ethics of poems are often perforce drawn back
to narration: Susan Gubar, in discussing recent Holocaust poetry,
ultimately locates its ethics in its ability 'to counter the numbing
amnesia inflicted on its casualties by traumatic injury and on their
descendants by our collective overexposure to widely circulated narra-
tives of atrocity'.[46] In other words, poetry's ethicity depends on the
extent to which its narratives can replace or refresh old, worn ones.
Unsurprisingly, Gubar's analysis never lingers on anything non-narra-
tive, formal, or even 'poetic' in the poetry she treats.

Plato teaches that the good must be achieved through rational phil-
osophizing, not through creative imagining. Aristotle teaches that the
good comes from proper self-realization, and that art can present good
and bad examples of this through mimesis. Kant teaches that the good is
a duty to others, and that aesthetic experience must be disinterested.
Most modern ethics discourses ask questions about how to live and
what to do, what personal or national policies to adopt in the face of the
prevailing conditions. Very little in the mainstream of philosophical
ethics literature, much less in the popular mainstream, refers to the
kinds of things that poetry depends on: linguistic imagination, concep-
tual inventiveness, formal virtuosity, aesthetic response. In short, it is
little wonder that the ethical turn in literary studies has revolved mainly

[44] Donald Davie, *Czeslaw Milosz and the Insufficiency of the Lyric* (Cambridge:
Cambridge University Press, 1986), 29.
[45] For the counter-narrativity argument, see Galen Strawson, 'Against Narrativity',
Ratio 18:4 (4 December 2004), 429–52.
[46] Susan Gubar, 'Poets of Testimony: C. K. Williams and Jacqueline Osherow as
Proxy Witnesses of the Shoah', in Davis and Womack (eds), *Mapping the Ethical Turn*,
165–91, 185.

around issues raised in narratives, where there are actors and actions, situations and exemplars—in other words, where concepts and categories in traditional philosophy can be applied without much additional theoretical groundwork.

Yet, some difficult groundwork has been laid. Writing in the early decades of the twentieth century, Martin Heidegger found that in order to account for the essence of art, it would be necessary to revise nothing less than the idea of truth established and promoted by almost all philosophy since the ancients. Instead of basing truth on objective correspondence between proposition and thing in the world, Heidegger rethinks truth as *alētheia* (ἀ-λήθεια—'unhiddenness', 'unconcealment'; Heidegger says *Unverborgenheit*), the 'uncovering' of the 'ontological condition for the possibility that assertions can be true or false—that they may uncover or cover things up'.[47] For the early Heidegger, 'true art' was only possible in ancient times, but his philosophy of Greek art has nonetheless opened the way for responses to truth-based critiques of current literature that do not depend on the traditional (and problematic) distinction between the apophantic and non-apophantic rhetorical modes.[48] Robert Eaglestone contends that understanding the 'truth of art'—including even the art of today—in terms of Heideggerian *alētheia* allows 'a different and more profound sense of what the ethics of literature might be: something that is, at least, not reducible to axioms or to instrumental use' but which instead shows how ethics, metaphysics, and aesthetics can be, as in Wittgenstein's formulation, 'one and the same'.[49] Also following Heidegger, Andrew Bowie writes that understanding truth not as the correspondence to an objective state of affairs, but instead as the disclosure of 'ways of seeing', 'begins to suggest good theoretical reasons why "literature" might continue to be a major source of the ways in which we make sense of the world'.[50] Understanding

---

[47] 'die ontologische Bedingung der Möglichkeit dafür, daß Aussagen wahr oder falsch (entdeckend oder verdeckend) sein können.' Martin Heidegger, *Being and Time*, trans. John Macquarrie and Edward Robinson (Oxford: Blackwell Press, 1967), 269 [H. 226].

[48] This distinction, the *locus classicus* of which, at least in English literature, is Philip Sidney's claim, in refutation of Plato, that the poet 'nothing affirmeth and therefore never lieth', originates with Aristotle's classification of poetry, in *On Interpretation*, within the non-apophantic (i.e. non-assertive, non-propositional) mode of speech. For a discussion of the implications Aristotle's distinction has had for ethics in literature, see Michael Eskin, 'On Literature and Ethics', *Poetics Today* 25:4 (Winter 2004), 573–94.

[49] Robert Eaglestone, 'One and the Same? Ethics, Aesthetics, and Truth', *Poetics Today* 25:4 (Winter 2004), 595–608, 606.

[50] Andrew Bowie, *From Romanticism to Critical Theory* (London: Routledge, 1997), 18.

truth this way has the advantages of incorporating and accounting for variability in experience: not only is the structure of 'seeing-as' the 'basis of how the contents of our inner and outer world become articulated', it is also 'historically variable, in ways which cannot be circumscribed by a definitive scientific description of what the thing "really is"'.[51] The displacing of objective correspondence as the settled determiner of truth in favour of something like 'disclosing', 'uncovering', or 'seeing-as', offers up ways of returning ethics to art through its relation to truth. Though this approach does nothing to rule out an ethics of narrative art, it makes irrelevant the presumption of correspondence underlying narrative-centred ethical criticism, that in the relevant respects characters resemble real people and stories resemble possible events in lives of readers.

Michael Eskin has similarly described an ethics of poetry by reaching beyond traditional aesthetic and ethical categories. Eskin's investigation congregates Levinas and Mikhail Bakhtin with Osip Mandel´shtam and Paul Celan to foreground the role of dialogue both in poetry and in ethics. Eskin's ambitious collation of these two philosophers and two poets flows from his view that because poems display their 'dialogic constitution both materially and thematically', poetry 'provides a particularly unobstructed view of the complex enmeshment of the dialogic and the ethical'.[52] His method, what he calls his 'poethics',[53] centres on what he believes to be 'the inseverability of dialogue, ethics, and poetry'.[54] Eskin brings Levinas's idea of dialogue as originary (and therefore representative of the ethical) into contact with Bakhtin's metalinguistics (the study of a text as dialogic utterance, as opposed to purely linguistic textual study), in order to investigate the ethical conditions and implications of Celan's 'dialogic' translations of Mandel´-

---

[51] Ibid. 18.

[52] Michael Eskin, *Ethics and Dialogue in the Works of Levinas, Bakhtin, Mandel´-shtam, and Celan* (Oxford: Oxford University Press, 2000), 1–2.

[53] The neologism has multiple seemingly independent origins. It appears first to have been used by Joan Retallack in a series of essays dating back to the 1980s, some of which are collected in *The Poethical Wager* (Berkeley: University of California Press, 2003). Since, the word has also been used by Richard Weisberg in *Poethics and Other Strategies of Law and Literature* (New York: Columbia University Press, 1992). However, the meaning of the term is still far from fixed. Each of these authors uses it to signify something different: Eskin as a hermeneutic approach to reading the poetry of Celan and Mandel´shtam, Weisberg as a tool for lawyers reading and arguing cases, Retallack as a technique for 'reading' ethical systems revealed in experience. Seamus Heaney coins 'po-ethics' in his poem on Auden in 'Ten Glosses' (EL, 55).

[54] Eskin, *Ethics and Dialogue*, 2.

shtam's poetry, as well as his continuing 'dialogue' with the Russian poet in *Die Niemandsrose*.

Others have recently attempted, not a specified ethics of poetry, but a broader literary ethics that recognizes the lyric as paradigmatic of linguistic art. Charles Altieri writes that emphasizing the lyric's 'centrality for literary experience allows us to stress modes of ethos capable of challenging the models of agency that dominate moral discourses'.[55] For Altieri, the power of the lyric lies in its ability 'to explore the limitations of all judgmental stances by requiring complex blends of sympathy and distance and hence eliciting our fascination with extreme states of mind while complicating any possible grasp of how one might put such states into the categories of commensurability on which ethical judgment may ultimately depend'.[56] An appreciation for the 'intensities' concentrated in and by the lyric leads Altieri into a Nietzschean analysis, rejecting the current practices of ethical criticism in favour of a theory that starts from the observation that 'In our experiences of the lyrical at least, the will often emerges less through an interpretation of what is true or good about the text than as an attachment to what is powerful within it'.[57] Though this does not foreclose the possibility of ethical reading, it does relocate the site of response from that of *pathos* and *logos* (which are constitutive of the narrative mode) to that of *ethos* constructed through specifically linguistic means: a poem's 'specific efforts at articulation provide a sense of discovery or sharpen what we thought we knew'.[58]

Derek Attridge has also sought to overcome the limitations of the traditionally conceived encounter between ethics and aesthetics—the boundaries of 'instrumentalism' and of the 'aesthetic tradition'—by proposing 'a mode of attention to the specificity and singularity of literary writing as it manifests itself through the deployment of form'.[59] Attridge's approach, drawing on elements of Adorno, Levinas, Jacques Derrida, and Maurice Blanchot, views literature as a 'performance' in which 'the authored singularity, alterity, and inventiveness of the work as an exploitation of the multiple powers of language are experienced and affirmed in the present, in a creative, responsible reading'.[60] Attridge's theory can account as well for the lyric as it can

---

[55] Altieri, 'Lyrical Ethics and Literary Experience', 31.   [56] Ibid. 32.
[57] Ibid. 53.
[58] Ibid. 53.
[59] Derek Attridge, *The Singularity of Literature* (London: Routledge, 2004), 13.
[60] Ibid. 136.

for the narrative because attention is not to plot or character but to the linguistic and formal 'inventiveness' of authorship and the reciprocal 'staging' of the literary event's 'otherness' in the mind of the reader, which, 'while it inevitably strives to convert the other into the same, strives also to allow the same to be modified by the other'.[61] Thus, for Attridge, 'responsible' reading—reading which is open to the otherness of the text, which affirms its singularity, which is disinterested (in the Kantian sense) but which is prepared to be responsive—is always ethical reading.

As the investigations undertaken by Eaglestone, Eskin, Altieri, and Attridge suggest, an ethics of literature that accounts for the lyrical mode necessarily invokes, even if it does not always originate, a broader theory of language. With their different emphases—unhiddenness, dialogue, intensity, singularity—these attempts to theorize poetry's ethicity make claims about how language functions when wrought artistically. A narrative-based ethical theory, though it may make reference to the uses of language, does not require a theory that is linguistic per se, as the inclusion of non-literary forms (such as film, or television, or classical ballet) within the broad category of narration indicates. The lyric is, pre-eminently, a concentration of language and on language. Depending on its scope and purpose, an ethics of language may or may not make reference to the lyric, but an ethics of the lyric is necessarily a specified ethics of language.

DEFENDING POETRY

This belated (and still provisional) turn towards the genre of poetry among ethics critics in the academy only underscores the degree to which writing about literature's ethics really represents a *return*. Unlike the fable or the novel or the drama or even the song lyric, poetry has had an attendant tradition of defence, or apology, ever since Plato first attacked it. This is as much the case in the English tradition, where it is the question of poetry's ill or good that begins and sustains the tradition of defence. When Harry Bailly informs Chaucer's pilgrims that they will compete to tell 'Tales of best sentence and moost solaas',[62] he is taking up Horace's dictum that good poetry should 'benefit' and

---

[61] Ibid. 124.   [62] Geoffrey Chaucer, *The Canterbury Tales*, I.798.

'delight'.[63] That was narrative verse, to be sure, but Bailly is as concerned with the tellers' skill in poetry as he is with their storylines, as his harsh censure of Chaucer over the Tale of Sir Thopas amusingly conveys.[64] Sir Philip Sidney posthumously inaugurates the tradition proper in 1595 with his witty *Defence of Poesie*, but his achievement is synthetic, not original—by the time of its writing he is supremely well furnished with precedent and authority. Among a few dozen lesser thinkers, Sidney invokes Gower, Chaucer, Thomas More, and Edmund Spenser; Juvenal, Lucretius, Cicero, Horace, Ovid, Virgil, Plutarch, Boethius, Dante, Petrarch, and Boccaccio; Homer, Hesiod, Solon, Thales, Pythagoras, Pindar, Herodotus, Parmenides, Empedocles, Euripides, Xenophon, Demosthenes, Plato, and Aristotle; and Holy Scripture. Sidney's work is often remembered for its hybrid definition of poetry, cobbled from Plutarch and Horace: 'A speaking Picture, with this end to teach and delight.'[65] The good mix of philosophers and historians among the poets in Sidney's list of authorities (there is also at least one politician and at least one theologian, and most wear many hats) points to the underlying, more significant point, adapted from Aristotle. Whereas the philosopher deals abstrusely in universals, and the historian irrelevantly in particulars,

Now doth the peerless Poet perform both, for whatsoever the Philosopher saith should be done, he gives a perfect picture of it by some one, by whom he presupposeth it was done, so as he coupleth the general notion with the particular example.[66]

---

[63] Horace, *The Art of Poetry*, ed. Burton Raffel (Albany: SUNY Press, 1974), 57. The original Latin is '*aut prodesse volunt aut delectare poetae | aut simul et iucunda et idonea dicere vitae*' ('Poets wish either to benefit or to delight or to say things that are simultaneously pleasing and applicable to life').

[64] Chaucer, *Canterbury Tales*, VII.919–35. The irony is deeper and more significant than the bare fact of Chaucer's character Harry Bailly telling (Chaucer's character) Chaucer the pilgrim that 'Thy drasty rymyng is nat worth a toord!' (930), for the Tale of Sir Thopas mimics the rhyme and metre of the popular romance poetry of the time, as Benson's notes relay, and the Prologue metrically resembles the prim, pious stanzas of the foregoing Prioress's Tale. Chaucer appeases Bailly by switching into prose, and also by finding a less entertaining, more edifying tone and topic for the Tale of Melibee. This in turn foreshadows the prologue to the Parson's Tale, where once again verse is deprecated in favour of prose on moral grounds.

[65] Philip Sidney, 'A Defence of Poetry', in *Miscellaneous Prose of Sir Philip Sidney*, ed. Katherine Duncan-Jones and Jan Van Dorsten (Oxford: Oxford University Press, 1973), 80. See also Plutarch, *Morals* II.58: 'poetry is vocal painting and painting silent poetry'; and v.624: 'Simonides calls painting silent poetry, and poetry speaking painting.'

[66] Sidney, 'A Defence of Poetry', 85.

And the poet does this so sweetly and so accessibly that he 'is the food for the tenderest stomachs . . . the right popular Philosopher',[67] according to Sidney.

Though in an obvious way Sidney's *Defence* begins the tradition of apologia in English literature, it also represents the end of one *kind* of defence of poetry. Sidney's thorough rehearsing of Classical and medieval aesthetics in support of the Horatian dichotomy leaves little room for development. In Percy Shelley's *Defence of Poetry*, which parallels Sidney's work in more than just the title, one can take measure of roughly twenty-three decades of intellectual advancement. The English Enlightenment and the Romantic movement have intervened, so that while Shelley's Horatian didacticism is of a feather with Sidney's, Shelley has recourse to the social theory of Locke and Hume (whom he mentions) as well as a theory of the interior life of man developed by Wordsworth and Coleridge (whom he does not mention). Linking these two theories is a notion of language as both a public and a private thing, a shared social possession as well as a means of personal expression.

This emergent attention to the social conditions of linguistic expression is already present in Wordsworth, who in 1802 describes his *Lyrical Ballads* (1798) as 'a selection of language really used by men'.[68] The 'plainer and more emphatic language' of the 'Low and rustic life' is the most suitable for poetic composition, Wordsworth asserts, because 'being less under the influence of social vanity', the language of the common man 'is a more permanent, and a far more philosophical language, than that which is frequently substituted for it by Poets'.[69] This open provocation would draw criticism, notably from Wordsworth's friend, neighbour, and occasional collaborator. Coleridge was right to expose Wordsworth's primitivist protosociology for nonsense in the *Biographia*,[70] even if the social theory he opposes to it is no more compelling a way of thinking about the relations between class, diction, and poetry. Wordsworth was searching for a poetic idiom which would

---

[67] Sidney, 'A Defence of Poetry', 87.

[68] William Wordsworth, 'Preface to *Lyrical Ballads*', in *Lyrical Ballads, and Other Poems, 1797–1800*, ed. James Butler and Karen Green (London: Cornell University Press, 1992), 743.

[69] Ibid. 743–4.

[70] Chiefly in Chapter XVII. See Samuel Taylor Coleridge, *Biographia Literaria II*, in *The Collected Works of Samuel Taylor Coleridge*, vol. 7, ed. James Engell and W. Jackson Bate (Princeton: Princeton University Press, 1983), 40–57.

gain permanence by achieving true expression of the poet's recollected emotions. This expressive function, gradually overcoming the mimetic function which had traditionally been supposed to define poetry, would assign to poetry a greater importance to the social and spiritual life than had previously been contemplated. Coleridge believed that the poet's expressive language, relying on imagination, constituted the best means of discovering and conveying connections amongst things and ideas—of philosophizing, in other words. Like Sidney before him and Shelley after, he counts Plato among the greatest of poets by way of special pleading—the quality of his prose is sufficient proof that one need not write in verse to be called a poet.[71] 'No man was ever yet a great poet', according to Coleridge, 'without being at the same time a profound philosopher.'[72] Perhaps Shelley's notorious ascription of the role of 'unacknowledged legislators of the world' was intended for him: Coleridge planned to write an 'Essay on the Elements of Poetry' which 'would in reality be a *disguised* System of Morals & Politics'.[73]

Both Wordsworth and Coleridge can make excited noises about the nature and functions of poetry, but in this respect it is Shelley who takes the cake:

A poem is the very image of life expressed in its eternal truth.

Poetry is a sword of lightning, ever unsheathed, which consumes the scabbard that would contain it.

Poetry ever communicates all the pleasure which men are capable of receiving: it is ever still the light of life;

A great poem is a fountain forever overflowing with the waters of wisdom and delight;

Poetry, and the principle of Self... are the God and Mammon of the world.

---

[71] Meleager of Gadara includes several poems attributed to Plato in his anthology of Greek poetry, and as late as the early nineteenth century their authorship is a matter of debate among commentators, including Charles Merivale, who meekly defends the ascription in his new edition of the *Greek Anthology* (1833). In any case, it is evidently not these writings that are the objects of the Romantic poets' praise. See Coleridge: 'The writings of PLATO ... furnish undeniable proofs that poetry of the highest kind may exist without metre, and even without the contradistinguishing objects of a poem' (*Biographia II*, 14); Sidney: 'I have ever esteemed most worthy of reverence; and with good reason, since of all Philosophers he is the most Poetical' ('A Defence of Poetry', 107); Shelley: 'Plato was essentially a poet—the truth and splendour of his imagery, and the melody of his language, are the most intense that it is possible to conceive' ('Defence', 514).
[72] Coleridge, *Biographia II*, 25–6.
[73] Samuel Taylor Coleridge, *The Collected Letters of Samuel Taylor Coleridge*, vol. 1, ed. Earl Leslie Griggs (Oxford: Clarendon Press, 1966), 356; original emphasis.

Poetry is indeed something divine. It is at once the centre and circumference of knowledge; it is that which comprehends all science, and that to which all science must be referred.

It is at the same time the root and blossom of all other systems of thought. . . . It is the perfect and consummate surface and bloom of all things; it is as the odour and the colour of the rose to the texture of the elements which compose it.[74]

To the final two declarations, we might compare, respectively, Wordsworth's that poetry is 'the impassioned expression which is in the countenance of all Science',[75] and Coleridge's that it is 'the blossom and the fragrancy of all human knowledge, human thoughts, human passions, emotions, language'.[76] Two things may be remarked about these characteristically extravagant Romantic assertions. The first is that in their extravagance they are themselves highly poetic, relying heavily both on metaphor and on cadence (controlled both by metre and alliteration: 'a fountain forever overflowing') for strength. The second is that they are self-consciously yet unironically so. The idea that poetic thought is paradigmatic of ideal human thought so permeates the Romantic defence that it characterizes even the prose conceived to expound it. What can appear either windy and immodest or else unendearingly naïve actually rests on an ambitious philosophical project with serious intentions.

But Coleridge failed to provide what he had promised in the *Biographia*—a rigorous philosophical account of the imagination to explain the proper relationship between poetry and philosophy—and according to one popular interpretation, that spelled the end of philosophical engagement within English-language literary studies until theory reintroduced us to German philosophy as French philosophers had understood and developed it in the second half of the twentieth century. This is overstated, but it is true that while Coleridge's successes were imitated by his successors, his failures were not reattempted. Coleridge's method of practical criticism is retained and enhanced in the Victorian period by Matthew Arnold, but the philosophical justification for the reading and writing of poetry is reduced in Arnold to a vague Wordsworthian claim to poetic truth. Arnold was thinking of Wordsworth when he held that 'Without poetry, our science will appear incomplete; and most of what now passes with us for religion and philosophy will be replaced by

---

[74] Shelley, 'Defence', 515, 520, 522, 528, 531, 531, 531.
[75] Wordsworth, 'Preface', 753.
[76] Coleridge, *Biographia II*, 25–6.

poetry',[77] and similarly was Wordsworth on his mind when he expanded that thought:

> It is important, therefore, to hold fast to this: that poetry is at bottom a criticism of life; that the greatness of a poet lies in his powerful and beautiful application of ideas to life,—to the question: How to live.[78]

At times we are tempted to forgive Eliot his churlish, impatient remark on Arnold that 'in philosophy and theology he was an undergraduate; in religion a Philistine' (UPC, 105). Arnold knew enough to observe that 'Morals are often treated in a narrow and false fashion; they are bound up with systems of thought and belief which have had their day; they are fallen into the hands of pedants and professional dealers; they grow tiresome to some of us',[79] but he was not wise enough to realize the implications of this for his own judgements, for instance that 'Burns's world of Scotch drink, Scotch religion, and Scotch manners, is often a harsh, a sordid, a repulsive world' over which Burns had to 'triumph' (and often did) in order to produce poetry of the best kind.[80] Wordsworth, and Coleridge especially, had made courageous, ambitious attempts at a morals based on the poetical mode of thought; with Arnold, too often poetical thinking is subjected to small Victorian moralizing.

Eliot's attack on Arnold is often thought of as clearing away the remnants of Romantic claims for poetry's rights over other spheres of human mental activity—over science, philosophy, religion, and ethics. Those for whom this development was a positive one could, after Eliot, engage in Coleridgean practical criticism without encumbering themselves with Coleridgean philosophical investigation. Yet, despite first being translated to the Victorians by Arnold and then overtly rejected on behalf of modernity by Eliot, it is important to note how much of the Romantic defence of poetry survives in twentieth-century poetry and criticism. It is furthermore instructive to note that, as it happens, often it is Eliot who, sometimes covertly—or else unconsciously—can be found transmitting these ideas. To Wordsworth's protosociology we must compare Eliot's protoanthropology, and flowing from it, his approving words about 'a rural people whose speech is naturally poetic'

---

[77] Matthew Arnold, 'The Study of Poetry', in *The Complete Prose of Matthew Arnold*, vol. IX: *English Literature and Irish Politics*, ed. Robert Henry Super (Ann Arbor: University of Michigan Press, 1973), 161–88, 161–2.

[78] Matthew Arnold, 'Wordsworth', in *Complete Prose* IX, 36–55, 46.

[79] Ibid. 46.

[80] Arnold, 'The Study of Poetry', 182.

(OPP, 77). Eliot violently deprecates Shelley, but Shelley's claim that poets who 'affected a moral aim' diminished their work 'in exact proportion to the degree in which they compel us to advert to this purpose'[81] accurately anticipates Eliot's later warning that 'confusing poetry and morals' leads to a deplorable 'disturbance of our literary values' (UPC, 116). A final example may tell the most: Eliot charges Coleridge with paying more attention to his own emotions than to 'the data of criticism' (SW, 13), but the main thrust of Eliot's earliest and most influential prose—his insistence on poetic 'impersonality', conceived of as anti-Romantic and anti-Victorian—is already present in Coleridge's agreement with Aristotle 'that poetry as poetry is essentially *ideal*, that it avoids and excludes all *accident*'.[82]

T. S. ELIOT AND THE MODERNIST DEFENCE

Modernism was, like all movements, a reaction as well as a renovation, a backward as well as a forward motion. Just as Romanticism found an antidote to Enlightenment rationalism in medieval symbology, modernism drew on a classical ideal to shore itself against Romantic sentimentality. Also in common with other movements, modernism was a creation of hindsight: the term itself, like 'romanticism', was initially used pejoratively by a cultural rearguard, only later to be accepted and adopted by the writers it was meant to put down.[83] But more than Romanticism, and perhaps more than any comparably influential literary movement, modernism was also highly self-fashioned, with its own self-made terminology and critical apparatus: its leading members styled themselves as neo-classical, or late Symbolist(e), or else Imagist(e), or again as Vorticist, and aggressively—and publicly—promoted the precepts they believed would nourish the necessary revolutions in artistic style.

In the area of literature, Eliot was the member of this extended circle who would achieve lasting influence, but it was Ezra Pound, and to a

---

[81] Shelley, 'Defence', 518.

[82] Coleridge, *Biographia II*, 45–6.

[83] See the earliest quotations in OED2, 'romanticism' 3 (1823: 'polluted by the dramatic heresy of romanticism') and OED3, 'modernism' 4, and 'modernist' 4 (1879: 'The fanatical realists and modernists'). By 1940 Eliot was being publicly introduced as 'one of the greatest living poets and critics...Modern of the moderns'. See 'Poetry of W. B. Yeats; Mr Eliot's Critical Assessment', *The Irish Times* (1 July 1940), 6.

lesser degree T. E. Hulme, who set the early tone of what would come to be known as the modernist movement. This was a polemical tone of contrarian judgement on principle, authoritative endorsement and de-nunciation, pithy credo and catchphrase, theoretical apparatus and attendant nomenclature. It was pursued largely in prose form, via essays and manifestos in literary publications, some of which were founded specifically as organs of the cause, others of which had to be taken over for that purpose. Hulme, Pound, and Eliot attacked the Romantic cult of self-expression, especially as indulged in by the Victorians. The result was an *ars poetica* characterized by censorious pronouncements on Romantic or Victorian category confusions balanced by endorsements and recommendations so high and dry as to seem either oracular (as they were received by disciples) or pious (as later generations have at times judged).

But even as the early modernists deprecated their predecessors for confounding aesthetic, ethical, social, and spiritual criteria in a miasma of contingent personality, in their advocacy for new ways of writing they could sound alarmist in a way that imbued seemingly aesthetic princi-ples with the kind of human urgency usually reserved for issues of moral or social consequence. So, writing for the *New Freewoman* (soon to be renamed the *Egoist*), Pound receives the baton of apologia gingerly and with rhetorical detachment: 'It is curious that one should be asked to rewrite Sidney's *Defence of Poesy* in the year of grace 1913', he writes, adding, 'I think one work of art is worth forty prefaces and as many apologiae.'[84] Nevertheless, he revises Sidney with gusto, challenging the idea that the poet neither asserts nor lies with a Platonesque argument, based on truth-telling recast in the language of authenticity, which is to say textured by positive ideals of subjectivity and individuality: 'This brings us to the immorality of bad art. Bad art is inaccurate art. It is art that makes false reports.'[85] The corollary is that 'good art can NOT be immoral', no matter how or whether it corresponds to the prevailing social mores: 'By good art I mean art that bears true witness, I mean the art that is most precise.'[86] And, just as the literary manifesto is itself a deliberate act of public speech, it happens that for Pound the poetic telling of truths or falsehoods involves an explicitly social dimension, even if it is expressed in specifically antisocial language:

[84] Ezra Pound, *Literary Essays*, ed. T. S. Eliot (London: Faber and Faber, 1954), 41.
[85] Ibid. 43.   [86] Ibid. 44.

If an artist falsifies his report as to the nature of man ... in order that he may conform to the tastes of his time, to the proprieties of a sovereign, to the conveniences of a preconceived code of ethics, then that artist lies.[87]

Modernist writers tended to think of themselves as a vanguard, a righteous minority of forward-facing artists rejected and despised by the established tastes of society. The latent ironic potential of this pose would realize itself gradually over subsequent decades.

Eliot was actively and generously promoted by Pound, and the younger poet felt a personal debt to the older that would endure a divergence of critical interest, political affiliation, and public reputation. He turned out to be a finer thinker than his patron and a more careful critic, though in the early days of his career he was no less censorious on the periodical pages. From 1917 until the mid-1920s, Eliot advanced his *ars poetica* there, insisting that poetry's integrity was being threatened by current practices of 'personal' poetics and 'impressionistic' criticism. In his preface to the second edition of *The Sacred Wood*, he reflects on the early impact of those essays. He describes them as each dealing with some aspect of 'the problem of the integrity of poetry, with the repeated assertion that when we are considering poetry we must consider it primarily as poetry and not another thing' (SW, *viii*). The word 'integrity' is carefully chosen, and is used in the early sense of 'wholeness' or 'completeness', being in an 'undivided or unbroken state' (OED2, 1–2). Yet it is difficult for the reader to shake off the moral resonance of the term (OED2, 3) when it is deployed so consciously and conspicuously as a theme for Eliot's assertions and exhortations. The antonym 'corruption', which can reverse both the early 'wholeness' and later 'moral' definitions of 'integrity' (OED2, 2, 3), illustrates how easily the word can slip in and out of its ethical dimension. The adamant style of Eliot's writings on 'integrity' only reinforces this association—the reader's impression is constantly that there is a wrong being done, that somewhere (if not everywhere), poetry is being violated and corrupted, and requires our defence. That the site of this assault is the arena of social, moral, and religious values cinches it—even if Eliot is clear that his subject matter is literature, the effects of the battle over culture are felt far beyond the literary sphere.

The antonym for 'integrity' in the Eliotic lexicon is not in fact 'corruption', but 'dissociation', a term that appears first in 'The Metaphysical

---

[87] Ibid. 43–4.

Poets' (1921), receiving subsequent elaboration in *The Use of Poetry and the Use of Criticism* (1933). 'Dissociation' refers to the splintered consciousness of the modern age, the separation of human interests and pursuits into independent spheres of knowledge—science, philosophy, theology, morality, art, and so on. Though he regrets the 'dissociation of sensibility' that accompanies the Age of Enlightenment, what Eliot challenges most vehemently is the post-Enlightenment reaction to this dissociation, especially among the Romantic poets and the critics that follow them. For Eliot, the problem is one of 'religious faith and its substitutes' (UPC, 125). In the crisis provoked by the loss of religion as an ethical and spiritual unifier of the various spheres of knowledge, Eliot reacts against the elevation of art in general, and poetry in particular, to the role of harmonizing principle. 'The decay of religion', he writes, 'and the attrition of political institutions, left dubious frontiers upon which the poet encroached . . . for a long time the poet is the priest' (UPC, 26). Eliot reads this and all substitutive attempts as wishful nostalgia for an unfractured pre-modern world. Arnold's assertion that 'Poetry is the reality, philosophy the illusion' is, according to Eliot, 'dangerous and subversive' (UPC, 113). Eliot's preferred view of the place of poetry is tight-laced: 'nothing in this world or the next is a substitute for anything else; and if you find that you must do without something, such as religious faith or philosophic belief, then you must just do without it' (UPC, 113). Far from returning culture to a prelapsarian state of harmony, any substitutive or synthetic attempt is to be seen as a further corruption of the integral ideal—not only is consciousness fractured into a multitude of independent spheres, but the spheres themselves lose their wholeness, their integrity, and eventually any particular use or significance they may have.

This description of the state of modern culture arises from a basic concern for the continued viability of the ethical and religious processes of society, even if these must operate independently of each other, and independently of society's other many processes (of economy, say, or of politics or science). Eliot may only bring the question of ethics in society to the fore so that he can set it aside, but in making the point that poetry is no substitute for ethics, he does not make the ethical question disappear. Instead it recedes, only to form a continuous background to Eliot's discussion of poetry's place in society. When he pauses to affirm that his subject is not the serious spiritual and moral consequences of substituting art for religion, but 'the disturbance of our *literary* values' (UPC, 116; emphasis added), he makes a show of adhering to his own principle of integrity, taking literary matters separately from spiritual, social, and moral matters. But in referring to the 'deplorable moral and religious effects of confusing poetry and morals' (UPC, 116), even to reserve the topic for later discussion, he impresses on his audience the broader implications of the subject at hand. Eliot's discourse on poetic integrity is from the very beginning set against a scene of social—meaning civic, moral, and religious—degradation. Clearly, respecting the integrity of each field helps to shore up the others. What is unexpected, and what textures and complicates Eliot's original formulation, is how in his later prose work he uses the same principles of poetic integrity to argue on behalf of poetry's social function, its tangible effects within and among cultures.

This turn owes a good deal to Eliot's proto- or pseudoanthropology, which grows from an early interest in the emergent social sciences,[88] and which feeds a pluralistic social theory not often emphasized by commentators. As a result of Eliot's later-life standing as literary grand old man and his reputation for conservatism of the classicist, royalist, Anglo-Catholic variety, the exhortation of the 'dead master' in 'Little Gidding' (1942) to 'purify the dialect of the tribe' is often characterized as a stuffy condescension. In their introduction to *The Penguin Book of Poetry from Britain and Ireland Since 1945*, for instance, Simon Armitage and Robert Crawford invoke the passage to contrast Eliot with more 'local' or 'regional' poets:

Where T. S. Eliot, nicknamed 'the Pope of Russell Square', had pronounced *ex cathedra* in 'Four Quartets' on the poet's mission 'to purify the dialect of the tribe', more and more post-war poets delighted in the impure 'mud flowers of dialect', as Heaney called them.[89]

In fact, Eliot's call for purification of dialect implies neither a rejection of it nor the filtering out of its local, 'tribal', or primitive elements. On the contrary, it is the presence of dialect in poetry that is seen as the guarantor of vibrant language. In placing the emphasis on 'purify'

---

[88] On Eliot's engagement with Émile Durkheim and Lucien Lévy-Bruhl, see Marc Manganaro, '"Beating a Drum in a Jungle": T. S. Eliot on the Artist as "Primitive"', *Modern Language Quarterly* 47:4 (December 1986), 393–421. Eliot's interest in the social sciences and related theories of evolution dates back to his undergraduate days at Harvard College. Robert Crawford's *The Savage and the City in the Work of T. S. Eliot* (Oxford: Clarendon Press, 1987) documents Eliot's earliest encounters with these currents of thought and traces their influence on him.

[89] Simon Armitage and Robert Crawford (eds), *The Penguin Book of Poetry from Britain and Ireland since 1945* (London: Viking, 1998), xxi.

instead of 'dialect' and 'tribe', glossators ignore Eliot's 1933 analysis of Mallarmé's original phrase, in which he insists that 'this purification of language is not so much a progress, as it is a perpetual return to the real'.[90] What must be smelted from the language is not the evidence of its tribal filiation but the insidious clichés of modernity—the 'mumbling. . . jargon' of the 'inarticulate'.[91] It is clear as early as 1926 that it is the tribal emphasis of Mallarmé's expression, *'donner un sens plus pur aux mots de la tribu'*,[92] which is most important to Eliot. Writing in a French periodical, Eliot says of Mallarmé's poetry that it 'insists on the primitive power of the Word', and he goes on to praise 'The effort towards restoring the power of the Word' which is manifest there.[93] Behind Eliot's recurrent analysis of Mallarmé is an insistence on linguistic return, restoration, and renewal, which keeps an 'auditory image' of the primitive, or savage, at the centre of its renovating project.

If Eliot saw fit in the darkening days of 1932 to tell a Harvard University audience that poetry represents the 'highest point of consciousness' of a people, and that 'The people which ceases to produce literature ceases to move in thought and sensibility' (UPC, 15), he also sensed that there was much that was unconscious—or subconscious—in poetry, and that poetic inspiration inhabits the feral forgotten protohistory of a culture as much as it uplifts and advances that culture. The accompanying statement that 'The people which ceases to care for its literary inheritance becomes barbaric' (UPC, 15) casts its eye in both directions, looking back on inheritance to ensure future progress, safeguarding the past to prevent a return to a state which has no past. The progenitor of that line of inheritance is the 'savage' who, in beating out a rhythm, performs a seemingly brutish act which is really a first attempt to impose pattern on noise, to make music of cacophony: 'Poetry begins, I dare say, with a savage beating a drum in a jungle, and it retains that essential of percussion and rhythm' (UPC, 155). Eliot may have been recalling an earlier observation that 'an unoccupied person,

---

[90] T. S. Eliot, *Varieties of Metaphysical Poetry*, ed. Ronald Schuchard (New York: Harcourt Brace, 1993), 290. The quotation is from Eliot's Turnbull Lectures.
[91] Ibid. 290.
[92] Literally, 'to give a purer meaning to the words of the tribe'. See Stéphane Mallarmé, 'Le tombeau d'Edgar Poe', in *Œuvres complètes: Poésies* (Paris: Gallimard, 1998), 38.
[93] 'insiste sur la puissance primitive du Mot'; 'L'effort pour restituer la puissance du Mot'. T. S. Eliot, 'Note sur Mallarmé et Poe' (French trans. Ramon Fernandez), in *Nouvelle revue française* 15:158 (November 1926), 524–6, 526. The above are my re-translations from the French, the original English text never having been published.

finding a drum, may be seized by the desire to beat it; but unless he is an imbecile he will be unable to continue beating it... without finding a reason for so doing'.[94] From the beating comes rhythm; from rhythm comes order; from order comes ordered thought, reason, and so on. The beating of a drum, like poetry, is at the same time primal and civilizing: it draws out of the past to elevate the future. In Eliot's defence of literary tradition as a cultural safeguard against 'barbarism' we discern a vital element of the ethical turn which he is about to make. By forging links through his poetic anthropology among the 'consciousness' of a people, their shared history, and the art they produce, Eliot lays the ground in *The Use of Poetry* for his subsequent consideration of the relationship between the poet and the people whose culture he represents.

The theoretical culmination of Eliot's early interest in the primitive as a foundation for the modern is his memorable description of the reader's grasp of a poem's patterns and their underlying meaning as the function of an 'auditory imagination', a concept whose name unites sound, image, and idea:

What I call the 'auditory imagination' is the feeling for syllable and rhythm, penetrating far below the conscious levels of thought and feeling, invigorating every word; sinking to the most primitive and forgotten, returning to the origin and bringing something back, seeking the beginning and the end. It works through meanings, certainly, or not without meanings in the ordinary sense, and fuses the old and obliterated and the trite, the current, and the new and surprising, the most ancient and the most civilised mentality. (UPC, 119)

Foreshadowing the synthesis of 'time present', 'time past', and 'time future' in *Four Quartets*, Eliot envisions the fusion of the 'current', the 'old', and the 'new' in language. The sound qualities to which Eliot attributes the agency of this fusion are syllable and rhythm. The first makes up a word or a subcomponent of a word, the second emerges from a sequence of words. A feeling for these verbal sub- and superstructures leads to a related understanding of the poem's component parts—the complex of associations, ranging from the distantly primitive to the contemporary, which informs it and which it evokes—as well as the poem's place in the larger order, the way it leads the literature forward into the 'new and surprising', just as a reader is led forward by the rhythm of a line. Eliot is describing a kind of linguistic archaeology as well as a

---

[94] T. S. Eliot, 'The Beating of a Drum', *The Nation and The Athenaeum* 34:1 (6 October 1923), 11–12.

programme for advancement, an evocation of those forgotten elements of language and culture which persist in traces—below the level—but which can be heard by the attentive and imaginative ear. Being alive to this syllabic and rhythmical music in poetry does not simply recall the ancient, but in seeking both the beginning and the end, brings the beginning back to be reincorporated into the end, continuing a cycle of replenishment that rejuvenates both the language and the collective consciousness of those who use it. In this way the modernist programme of 'making language new' is effected by recycling its oldest components. It is an acoustic archaeology that feeds an anthropology which will later ground a fuller sociology. Eliot's late social theory of poetry develops the linguistic principles established and investigated here.

A DUTY TO LANGUAGE: THE EXAMPLE OF ELIOT

Despite the success of his early prose efforts—or perhaps because of that success—for Eliot the problem of the integrity of poetry was already much diminished in importance by the time of the second edition of *The Sacred Wood*, where in a new preface he pleaded with the reader to treat the collection as an 'introduction to a larger and more difficult subject' (SW, viii). This subject, 'that of the relation of poetry to the spiritual and social life of its time and of other times' (SW, viii), would occupy Eliot to the end of his writing career. The second element of this relation, Eliot's ideas on the 'spiritual and social life' of this and other times, is a matter of considerable contention—and much production—in recent Eliot scholarship. If the savage beating a drum represents the lost root of common culture with which the culture must commune, then all that is antithetical to this in contemporary modern culture is personified in what Eliot once referred to as the 'free-thinking Jew'.[95] Eliot's writings are full of contradictions and inconsistencies, but perhaps none as blameworthy as this: his social theory, which values cultural exchange and interchange, diversity of opinion and expression, and freedom from the cultural autarky of privileged classes (which may be constituted nationally, regionally, socioeconomically, or demographically) refuses a place at the table to the intellectual and cultural traditions

---

[95] T. S. Eliot, *After Strange Gods: A Primer of Modern Heresy* (London: Faber and Faber, 1934), 20.

of secular Judaism, and worse, takes these traditions as paradigmatically inimical to the project. In this respect Geoffrey Hill's judgement on Pound at first seems more palatable a stance to take in relation to Eliot: 'The moral offence of his vicious anti-semitism does not call into question the integrity of his struggle; neither does the integrity of the struggle absolve him of responsibility for the vulgar cruelty' (CCW, 164). Yet the matter is not as categorical as that: Eliot's anti-Semitism, though no less a vice, was certainly less cruel than Pound's; his 'struggle',[96] to re-enclose Pound's fascistic lexis in inverted commas, was not against a cooked-up 'opposition' of tyrants, plutocrats, and Jews, but rather in favour of a framework for inter- and intracultural development based on literary production and interchange. In one sense this greatly damages the integrity of Eliot's position, since he allowed a particular set of social preferences to limit the scope of application of his general theory. But we need not accept or endorse the particulars of Eliot's vision of culture to approve the framework, just as we need not make excuses for, nor even forgive, his anti-Semitism to learn from the example he set promoting poetry as a public good. Such a stance does not seek to sequester the personal vice from the integrity of a public struggle, nor from the intellectual robustness of a theory, nor from the aesthetic achievement of a poem, as Eliot's sympathetic and unsympathetic critics alike have tried at times to do—in many cases the bad and the good consort darkly. It only states that taking Eliot as an example need not commit one to every aspect of his thinking. The poets treated in the next chapters, each in his own way, have taken freely from Eliot in some areas while at the same time reproving or repudiating him in others.

Eliot's early influence was already a kind of living legacy by the mid-1930s. C. Day Lewis, in *A Hope for Poetry* (1934), was both giving him centre stage and hurrying him off it when he called Eliot, along with Gerard Manley Hopkins (d. 1889) and Wilfred Owen (d. 1918), one of 'our immediate ancestors'[97]—in fact Eliot had more than thirty years to live and much left to say, in poetry and about poetry. But for Day Lewis

---

[96] Ezra Pound, interview with Donald Hall, 'The Art of Poetry V: Ezra Pound', *Paris Review* 28 (Summer–Fall 1962), 22–51. Pound's answers to Hall are frequently couched in terms of 'struggle', a term which he uses positively. In addition to the instance Hill quotes—'the struggle not to sign on the dotted line for the opposition' (48)—Pound writes about the struggle 'for orthodoxy' (36), 'against one's ignorance' (37), 'to keep the value of . . . a particular culture in this awful . . . avalanche toward uniformity' (43), 'for individual rights' (48).

[97] C. Day Lewis, *A Hope for Poetry* (Oxford: Blackwell, 1947), 3.

and other writers of the 1930s, Eliot's early influence had to be taken in a new, much more publicly active and overtly political direction than Eliot could endorse. *A Hope for Poetry*, which was already in its fourth printing by the time Eliot's contemporaneous *The Use of Poetry and the Use of Criticism* reached a second, was a highly popular account of the ethical and aesthetic obligations a poet might feel—there would be eight printings in all in the space of thirteen years. Day Lewis's idealistic defence of a progressive public poetry, punctuated by exemplary MacSpaunday verse (the 'Mac', unusually in this case, standing for MacDiarmid as well as MacNeice), bravely negotiates between Eliotic poetic integrity and a communist desire for social revolution. But in his envoi we can sense both the ambition and the precariousness of the balance Day Lewis is trying to achieve:

Between the two ideals of poets to-day, social justice and artistic integrity, a foundation should be laid for a poetic future not unworthy of the traditions we have inherited and the society some of us hope for and are fighting for.[98]

'Some of us' is a telling if necessary concession to the contingencies of the political, a contrast to 'traditions', which cannot but retain its imperturbable Eliotic monumentality. This unconscious and counter-intentional bias in the argument—which is betrayed by nothing more culpable than a simple kind of honesty—would quickly rise to the surface. It was only 1943 when Day Lewis wrote 'Where are the War Poets?', a short, grim poem that ends in the kind of pessimism that passes for realism: 'It is the logic of our times, | No subject for immortal verse— | That we who lived by honest dreams | Defend the bad against the worse.'[99] In his cynicism over the 'logic of our times', Day Lewis is yet idealistic enough to lodge a protest, but both the hope and the fight have gone out of his argument. This is not the good kind of poetic propaganda he had pretended was possible in *A Hope for Poetry*,[100] but rather a sad protestation at the passing, in the all-consuming prosecution of the Second World War, of the example of Owen, the kind of writer who had 'emotionally experienced a political situation and assimilated it through his specific function into the substance of poetry'.[101]

---

[98] Ibid. 98.
[99] C. Day Lewis, *Collected Poems* (London: Jonathan Cape, 1954), 228.
[100] 'Yet the bourgeois critic must remember that there is no reason why poetry should not also be propaganda.' Day Lewis, *A Hope*, 49.
[101] Ibid. 56.

The development of Eliot's thoughts and interests, at least by contrast, follows a linear progression. Not having ventured very far into that kind of politics, there was little from which to retreat, and even those positions which he came to regret he preferred to think of as distractions or dead ends rather than errors. In his thinking about the social function of poetry, Eliot combines his early linguistic pseudoanthropology with his principle of poetic integrity to inform the new concept of a 'duty to language', which, in its socially disinterested execution, could also be of use to society. It is in an essay published in 1945 called 'The Social Function of Poetry' that Eliot most clearly enunciates this tenet:

We may say that the duty of the poet, as poet, is only indirectly to his people: his direct duty is to his language, first to preserve, and second to extend and improve. (OPP, 20)

Later Eliot reformulates this idea of 'duty', writing, 'the great master of a language should be the great servant of it'.[102] In bringing 'the language' into a triangular relationship with author and audience, Eliot attributes social utility to the poet without giving him an explicitly civic role. With language, not souls, as the immediate locus and focus of his duty, the poet can pursue his work with professional indifference to its social effect and yet achieve a social good. Neither does Eliot limit the good that a poet does to the individual moment of revelation, learning, or pleasure that he affords his reader. Because language is a shared public thing laden with cultural and historical resonances peculiar to the people who speak it, the beneficiaries of the poet's work in language include all members of his society whether they are readers or not:

[Poetry] may effect revolutions in sensibility such as are periodically needed; may help to break up the conventional modes of perception and valuation which are perpetually forming, and make people see the world afresh, or some new part of it. (UPC, 155)

In performing his duty to language (both preserving and developing it) the poet is 'changing the feeling by making people more aware of what they feel already, and therefore teaching them something about themselves' (OPP, 20).

Feelings of duty and responsibility are naturally amplified in times of civil emergency, which also concentrate feelings of cultural identity, whether these be national, regional, racial, or religious. Threat moves

---

[102] T. S. Eliot, *To Criticize the Critic* (London: Faber and Faber, 1965), 133.

the citizen to question his role in the defence of the collective, however construed. For poets, immediacy of human suffering has long posed a challenge to their choice of profession. In his own reflections on poetry's social significance during conflict, Seamus Heaney quotes a low point in Eliot's wartime morale—a letter written to E. Martin Browne in October 1942:

In the midst of what is going on now, it is hard, when you sit down at a desk, to feel confident that morning after morning spent fiddling with words and rhythms is justified activity....And on the other hand, external or public activity is more of a drug than is this solitary toil which often seems so pointless. (GT, 107)

It is reassuring, if incongruous, to catch the publicly Olympian Eliot in so human a moment of private self-doubt. Incongruous, especially in light of the industrious way in which he went about his literary business throughout the War years: in addition to 'fiddling with words and rhythms' (he wrote three of the *Four Quartets* as well as several minor poems), Eliot published more than seventy short pieces of expository prose during the War, and kept up a full schedule of radio talks and public lectures, even making the journey to Dublin in 1940 amid increasingly strict travel bans to deliver the inaugural Yeats lecture there, and travelling throughout neutral Sweden in 1942 to wage 'cultural warfare'[103] under the auspices of the British Council. In the midst of this crisis, where no less was at stake than the 'legacy of Rome, Greece, and Israel' (NDC, 123–4)—in other words the continuance of two millennia of European culture—Eliot launched a broad campaign of 'public activity' to defend the role of culture generally, and poetry specifically, in society.

Typical of his activities was 'Social Function', which Eliot delivered in 1943 as a lecture to the British-Norwegian Institute, a *kulturfront* organization established in London's Norwegian refugee circles. Eliot tells this deracinated audience that a poet writing out of a duty to language can be of use beyond his immediate circle of audience. He presents the matter as one of immediate and practical importance:

---

[103] This is Eliot's term, in a letter to his brother dated 1 June 1942, in which he details his schedule of lectures and readings, which have taken him to Uppsala, Gothenburg, Lund, and Stockholm. T. S. Eliot Papers (MS Am 1691). Houghton Library, Harvard University.

For I think it is important that every people should have its own poetry, not simply for those who enjoy poetry . . . but because it actually makes a difference to the society as a whole, and that means to people who do not enjoy poetry. I include even those who do not know the names of their own national poets. (OPP, 18)

Eliot's 'nationalistic' approach to the use of poetry descends from the early primitivist essays in *The Dial* and *The Athenaeum* via the 'auditory imagination'. Because 'the structure, the rhythm, the sound, the idiom of a language, express the personality of the people which speaks it' (OPP, 19), poets have a special role both in the crafting and in the representation of that personality. This role, faithfully executed, results in a poetry which has particular importance to his community. This community he variably calls a 'people', 'race', 'tribe', 'culture', 'society', and 'nation'. It is almost everywhere constructed historico-linguistically, as a group of people sharing a common tradition of language, and possessing a group identity which is reflected in the component qualities of that language.

Because languages belong only to 'the people of the poet's race', Eliot writes, 'no art is more stubbornly national than poetry' (OPP, 18–19). Though we might now prefer a term like 'culture' to 'race', in any case it is clear that Eliot's notion of the British 'race' is not homogeneous but, like his related notion of the English language, is 'an amalgam of systems of divers sources' (OPP, 29)—Anglo-Saxon, Celtic, Norman French, etc.—and draws strength and vigour from this fusion of pluralities. Thus it stands squarely against the competing nationalisms and internationalisms of the time, which, loosely speaking, were founded on the monistic totems of racial purity (Nazism) or global ideology (communism). Eliot's culturally oriented nationalism (perhaps it is more correct to call it a nationally oriented culturalism), anchored in the vernacular and represented to itself and to others in poetry, confers a double social role on poetry. On the one hand poetry is a vehicle for social development and improvement; on the other it is a means of preservation, a defence against external forces of change.

The first role of poetry as stimulator of social development stems from Eliot's statement in *The Use of Poetry* that 'The people which ceases to produce literature ceases to move in thought and sensibility.' But the consequences of literary stagnation are not simply a matter of cultural or intellectual inferiority. 'Social Function' relates cultural limitation to political weakness, asserting that unless people 'go on producing great authors, and especially great poets, their language will deteriorate, their culture will deteriorate and perhaps become absorbed in a stronger one' (OPP, 21). When Eliot gives the talk in 1943, the Blitz has ceased, Allied armies have control of North Africa, and German forces have finally been turned back at Stalingrad. However, Europe from France to Poland remains under Nazi dominion. Britain, nearly having succumbed under furious pressure, has emerged the lone survivor against what had seemed an unstoppable force. London is also in 1943 the seat of the Norwegian government in exile, and the fact that the paper is delivered at a meeting of the British-Norwegian Institute is significant: what the audience had foremost on their minds was the ongoing occupation of Norway. In the 'Notes on Contributors' section of *The Norseman*, where 'Social Function' first appears in print, the editor's gloss makes that connection explicit: 'In the article published in this number... Mr. Eliot states the alternative which civilization offers to the view that cultural domination can be imposed by propaganda and the sword.'[104] The accompanying articles in the journal are more directly concerned with the fight against German occupation in Nordic countries. The back cover's 'mission statement' describes the cultural struggle it has undertaken to parallel the military struggle:

[In *The Norseman,*] Norwegians who have succeeded in making their way out of their besieged and fettered country... are able to voice in the free world the values and ideals which their countrymen in Norway are struggling to preserve, and indeed are rediscovering in their hard and inarticulate fight against the powers and ideologies of modern barbarism. The aim of *The Norseman* is to maintain the continuity of our best traditions so that the threads may be taken up again in Norway when the day of liberation arrives.[105]

It is in this context that Eliot tells his audience that, 'if I were told that no more poetry was being written in the Norwegian language I should feel an alarm which would be much more than generous sympathy' (OPP, 25), offering them a cultural formula for resistance. Despite the 400,000 German troops stationed in occupied Norway, the Norwegian people can retain a measure of independence through their poetry, which keeps their language alive and properly 'theirs'. Making a distinction between speaking in a language and feeling in a language, Eliot argues that though the former activity can be suppressed by force, the latter will persist as long

---

[104] Dr Jacob S. Worm-Müller (ed.), 'Notes on Contributors', *The Norseman: An Independent Literary and Political Review* 1:6 (November 1943), 480.
[105] The back cover text is adapted from the journal's inaugural editorial, by Dr Jacob S. Worm-Müller (ed.), in *The Norseman* 1:1 (January 1943), 5–6.

as poetry is being written. The practice of poetry, resulting in the preservation of language and linguistic feeling, is therefore directly related to the welfare of a people, the safeguarding of its independence and identity. As if to underscore the hope that poetry can bring, *The Norseman* follows 'Social Function' with a chorus from *Murder in the Cathedral*:

> For the blood of Thy martyrs and saints
> Shall enrich the earth, shall create the holy places.
> For wherever a saint has dwelt, wherever a martyr has given blood
>   for the blood of Christ,
> There is holy ground, and the sanctity shall not depart from it
> Though armies trample over it. . . .[106]

It is not too fanciful to think that the minds of *Norseman* readers substituted for a short time the occupied Royal Palace of Oslo for the play's violated Canterbury Cathedral.[107]

However far poetry may go to preserve a culture from the trampling hordes, poetry's social role is not to be understood only as a protective barrier to intrusive alien forces. Eliot is careful to distinguish his view from cultural isolationism, which he knows can breed dangerous forms of nationalism. Eliot is at pains to assert that he does not mean to imply that poetry only separates speakers of different languages, 'for I do not believe that the cultures of the several peoples of Europe can flourish in isolation from each other' (OPP, 23). On the contrary, while poetry as a cultural flag-bearer can stave off the forcible imposition of one culture upon another, it also can foster reciprocal, fruitful intercourse between cultures. Eliot says it is cultural '*autarky*' that poetry prevents by keeping language alive and developing. The 'hope of perpetuating a culture', he continues, 'lies in communication with others' (OPP, 23) and it is poetry that facilitates this goal of intercultural communication, precisely because it is so 'stubbornly national'.

Just before the end of the War Eliot takes up these themes in an address to the Czecho-Slovak Institute. 'Cultural Diversity and European Unity', later published in *The Adelphi*,[108] begins by identifying three

---

[106] T. S. Eliot, 'A Chorus', *The Norseman* 1:6 (November 1943), 458.

[107] It is unlikely to be a coincidence that this chorus is placed between 'Social Function' and 'The Conscience of the State' (Bjarne Höye), an article which promotes the role of the Norwegian Church in resisting the Nazis. In any case the 'Chorus' makes a suggestive segue from the function of poetry to the function of religion in wartime.

[108] T. S. Eliot, 'Cultural Diversity and European Unity', *The Adelphi* 22:4 (July–September 1945), 149–58.

types of international relationships: the political, the economic, and the cultural. Of these, Eliot says, it is the cultural that is the most important, since 'without good cultural relations—which means, not merely respect or admiration, but mutual influence—two peoples simply cannot understand each other'.[109] Without fruitful cultural intercourse and understanding, countries are always in danger of falling into bad economic and political relations, the extreme form of which is war. To an audience intimately acquainted with political union in a culturally diverse context—many of its members would have witnessed both the unification of their home nations in 1918 and their subsequent forced disassociation in 1939—Eliot repeats his earlier conviction that the preservation and advancement of culture on the most local scale is integral to the preservation and advancement of greater cultural, social, and political institutions. The mosaical accretion of vibrant cultural units also fosters political harmony amongst the more broadly constituted groups:

My conception, or ideal, of Europe as an organic unity of cultures, each one of which will itself be an organic unity of cultures ... is one which I think would make for peace.[110]

With an Allied victory in Europe only weeks away, Eliot is already looking towards a post-war programme of reconciliation and reconstruction. If a stable and productive Europe is to emerge, Eliot implies, the victors will have to abide by his principles of cultural diversity. The military and political conquest of Germany cannot license a concomitant cultural supremacy. And as victory becomes more and more probable, Eliot's literary pronouncements tend more and more to the conciliatory, proposing a literary path to social recovery. For example, Michael Coyle has noted that in his BBC Radio address of 5 June 1944, one day after the liberation of Rome, instead of a victory speech Eliot delivered a literary talk: he 'insisted on the spiritual kinship of all Europeans and submitted, meditatively and with an eye to the future, that the bonds among Europeans had been forgotten in peace before they were broken in war'.[111] In their moment of triumph, the Allies would have to reaffirm with 'humility and piety ... the legacy of the writers and poets of Rome'.[112]

---

[109] Ibid. 149.   [110] Ibid. 155.
[111] Michael Coyle, '"This Rather Elusory Broadcast Technique": T. S. Eliot and the Genre of the Radio Talk', *ANQ* 11:4 (Fall 1998), 32–42, 36.
[112] Ibid. 36.

After the War Eliot continued to promote intercultural exchange as an instrument of spiritual rehabilitation, often focusing his radio addresses on the subject of the cultural recuperation of Europe.[113] In March of 1946 he delivered a series of radio addresses in German for the BBC's German service. In 'Reflections of an English Poet on European Culture',[114] Eliot returns to the ideas he has been expounding to home audiences, refugees, and resistance groups. He tells his defeated German audience that though culture and politics are interrelated manifestations of a people, in international relations we are wrongly much more interested in the politics of foreign nations than we are in their culture (NDC, 118). Exchange, diversity, and organic unity are all promoted as essential to the re-establishment of the social peace. Pointing to English as an example of a language made rich by contact with others, Eliot cites its Germanic, Scandinavian, Norman, Latin, and Celtic influences, and makes the following observation about the rhythms of English poetry:

Each of these languages brought its own music.... And even to-day, the English language enjoys constant possibilities of refreshment from its several centers: apart from the vocabulary, poems by Englishmen, Welshmen, Scots and Irishmen, all written in English, continue to show differences in their Music. (NDC, 111)

The rich interplay of the diverse sources of English—its many musics—becomes a microcosmic example of intercultural interplay. Just as the Irish writer, to use Eliot's example, draws in varying measure both from the common English-language sources and the Celtic sources which are proper to a more local cultural sphere, 'the possibility of each literature renewing itself . . . depends on two things. First, its ability to receive and assimilate influences from abroad. Second, its ability to go back and learn from its own sources' (NDC, 113). Aware of the

---

[113] Ibid. 38.

[114] This is the title Coyle supplies, with the added information that the series formed part of a segment called 'Famous Contemporaries' (ibid. 38). Here a bibliographic correction appears to be in order. Though Coyle points to the publication of the second talk in *Adelphi* (Gallup A523b) and the entire series in *Die Einheit der Europäischen Kultur* (Gallup A46) he does not refer to the subsequent publication of all three German radio addresses, under the English title 'The Unity of European Culture', as an appendix to Eliot's *Notes toward the Definition of Culture* (London: Faber and Faber, 1948), 110–24. Since *Notes* is the most currently accessible of the above-mentioned publications, parenthetical references refer to it, though the reader should bear in mind its original context.

'local' qualities which make poetry 'more stubbornly national' than other forms of art, Eliot also insists that there exists an 'international fraternity of men of letters' (NDC, 118) whose duty it is to probe the common sources which link the European cultures—the Greek, Roman, and Hebrew legacy—and to promote contemporary exchange. But the exchange must be mutual, and Eliot is careful to emphasize the importance of reciprocity. The osmosis of foreign culture, without reciprocal contribution to that culture, is as damaging to both as the culture which only imposes itself on another without receiving anything in exchange (NDC, 121).

Speaking in a reconciliatory tone to a vanquished people, Eliot makes just one direct reference to the War, characterizing it primarily as a violation of this ideal of reciprocity in cultural exchange: 'An error of the Germany of Hitler was to assume that every other culture than that of Germany was either decadent or barbaric. Let us have an end of such assumptions' (NDC, 118). The consequence of this assumption was a literary Germany increasingly self-centred and isolated, a manifestation of the cultural autarky Eliot abhors in 'Social Function'. In his final years as editor of the *Criterion*, Eliot had come to believe, very much against his hopes, that the newer German writers were retreating more and more from the wider European context, that they had begun to write a literature which 'could be understood, if understood at all, only in German' (NDC, 117). Now that this monistic aesthetic and the ideology that fostered it have been defeated in war, Eliot sees the imperative to return to the common sources for the common good, and to produce, together, 'those excellent works which mark a superior civilization' (NDC, 123). Eliot is thinking once again of the poet's duty to language, and once again the subtext confirms its use beyond the literary sphere. The 'superior civilization' that results from the execution of this duty lies in sharp contrast to the war-broken Europe of 1946. Ahead lies the task of reconstruction and reconciliation. Eliot ends the talk by insisting on 'what matters':

What matters is that we should recognise our relationship and mutual dependence upon each other. What matters is our inability, without each other, to produce those excellent works which mark a superior civilisation. . . . We can at least try to save something of those goods of which we are the common trustees; the legacy of Greece, Rome and Israel, and the legacy of Europe throughout the last 2,000 years. In a world which has seen such material devastation as ours, these spiritual possessions are also in imminent peril. (NDC, 123–4)

Twenty years after he had begun to think seriously about 'the relation of poetry to the spiritual and social life of its time and of other times', Eliot can now call works of literature the 'spiritual possessions' of European society. It is by serving the end of cultural enrichment that the poet also serves the end of social advancement. The production of 'excellent works' is achieved by reaching back both to the peculiar and the common sources of the language, and by sharpening one's awareness and appreciation of the other literatures of the time.

LEARNING FROM ELIOT

Within the academy, Eliot's critical and theoretical legacy has largely been coterminous with the preoccupations of his early prose essays. The shift in concern that occurred around the time of the second edition of *The Sacred Wood* left many early followers of Eliot cold: gone, it seemed, was the fresh, revolutionary vision for poetry proclaimed in the pages of *The Dial* and *The Athenaeum*. For several of these critics, it was the moral and religious inflection of Eliot's later work that disabled it. M. D. Zabel, writing in 1925, said that Eliot had 'perplexed his readers by a slow reversion . . . to the moral absolutism of which the Hippopotamus was an inverted parody'.[115] One *TLS* reviewer wrote that Eliot's new 'attitude' was 'to-day no longer a vital one'.[116] Echoing this, F. W. Bateson later accused Eliot of having 'signed up with the English establishment', complaining that 'We, who had been the most ardent admirers both of the poems . . . and of almost all the literary criticism, felt ourselves let down.'[117] In place of their 'lost leader', as Bateson calls him, early followers of Eliot formed a prosperous critical school based on the principles he had articulated in the late teens and early 1920s.

Some of these critiques have found a recent reincarnation in Geoffrey Hill's strongly negative appraisal of Eliot's late poetry and critical prose.

---

[115] M. D. Zabel, 'T. S. Eliot in Mid-Career', in *T.S. Eliot, 'Prufrock', 'Gerontion', 'Ash-Wednesday' and Other Shorter Poems: A Casebook*, ed. B. C. Southam (London: Macmillan, 1978), 71–80, 71. Originally published in *Poetry* 36:6 (July 1930), 330–7.

[116] Anonymous [Geoffrey West], 'Mr Eliot's New Essays', *Times Literary Supplement* (6 December 1928), 953.

[117] F. W. Bateson, 'Criticism's Lost Leader', in *The Literary Criticism of T. S. Eliot: New Essays*, ed. David Newton-de Molina (London: Athlone, 1977), 1–19, 3.

Hill finds in *Four Quartets* a tiresome serving up of 'spiritual platitudes from the credo of the Church of England',[118] and considers Eliot's prose from the 1930s onwards a 'dereliction of the critical imagination' (CCW, 562). 'Dereliction' is a loaded term, especially since (Hill thinks it an irony) this was the period during which Eliot energetically set about not only describing the poet's duty, but also executing that duty as he conceived it. Hill glosses it: 'Dereliction: "the action of leaving or forsaking (with intention not to resume)", "the condition of being forsaken or abandoned"; "a morally wrong or reprehensible abandonment or neglect"' (CCW, 562–3). Hill is too young ever to have considered Eliot a 'leader' in Bateson's sense, though Eliot was certainly an early exemplar for him. Bateson's phrase from Hill's pen would have retained much more of the early moral and spiritual sense of 'lost' (OED2, 1a). Hill admires the early modernist polemic not least for the strength of its articulation and its sense of being righteously at odds with contented conventional society. Accordingly, Pound is the more prominent figure for Hill, especially in Hill's early essays. Part of what he finds reprehensible about Eliot's late writings is the ease with which Eliot allies himself to the social, civic, and religious institutions of England:

> The deepening failure of Eliot, both as a poet and critic, to focus his powers, I attribute to his increasing inability—and it begins fairly early, in the late 1920s—to contemplate the heavy cost of being, of becoming, radically, irretrievably, alienated. (CCW, 556)

Late in his own career, Hill is effectively deploying early Eliot's integrity principle against late Eliot. He thinks Eliot's later poetry and prose show him to be insufficiently at odds with society to form a credible voice within the polis. But Hill's idea of alienation is bifold: on one hand it entails keeping one's distance from the 'vast apparatus of Opinion' (CCW, 173) that presumes to dictate value in a plutocratic and anti-intellectual society, but it also means artistic self-distancing, the matter of a strange 'genius of language' alienating the artist from his own work, and from itself (CCW, 565). In this second sense of alienation it is worth returning to an essay Hill singles out as an example

---

[118] Geoffrey Hill, interview with Anne Mounic, 'Le poème, "moulin mystique": Entretien avec Geoffrey Hill' (19 March 2008); http://www3.sympatico.ca/sylvia.paul/ghill_interview_by_AnneMounic.htm, accessed 31 May 2010.

of Eliot's late dereliction (CCW, 557), proof of his 'inane' late speechi-fying (CCW, 573). In 'The Three Voices of Poetry', Eliot describes the writer of poetry as being 'haunted by a demon, a demon against which he feels powerless, because in its first manifestation it has no face, no name, nothing; and the words, the poem he makes, are a kind of form of exorcism of this demon' (OPP, 98). Early in his prose writings Hill was drawn to what Eliot says in the same paragraph about the feeling of annihilation the poet gets when a poem is finally written (CCW, 4). In his late writings, he might have acknowledged in Eliot's description of artistic 'exorcism' a metaphor closely allied to his second sense of alienation, and perhaps even have recognized a disconcerting conso-nance between his early attraction to this page of Eliot's late writings and his late criteria for rejecting them.

I have been trying to show, against the thrust of Hill's critique, that one of the achievements of Eliot's late career was to expand his early idea of the 'integrity of poetry' without vitiating it, allowing it to be nourished first by his long interest in the audible historical-cultural signatures in language, and eventually by his experience of severe cultural and civil breakdown, the quick and apparently complete foundering of the still newly modern European society. This idea of integrity, first constructed to barricade poetry within purely literary criteria of appreciation and analysis, remains in place as Eliot moves in the direction of a socio-ethical theory of poetic use. By triangulating poet, language, and society, Eliot maintains poetry's literary and linguistic integrity while claiming a vital role for literature in the social and spiritual life of a people.

This foundation for an apologia that might meet the ethical demands of the twentieth century while resisting, with twentieth-century scepti-cism, both the didactic and aestheticist demands of previous centuries is the third and perhaps the most enduring way in which Eliot has been an example in our time. Eliot's early example, though it was widely followed, had been abandoned by Eliot himself as early as 1928, and in due course his followers abandoned him. His late example, in which he strove to lead by example as a public man of letters, attracts as much ridicule as awe—Cynthia Ozick's caustic essay on the occasion of Eliot's centenary and Hill's accusations of dereliction represent two very different ways of opposing that same bugaboo, the 'Pope of Russell Square'.[119] But for those who have found themselves as much in

---

[119] Ozick is memorably cutting in her call to 'disclaim the reactionary Eliot', whom she considers, among other things, a 'considerably bigoted fake Englishman'. See

agreement with Eliot that a poet's 'direct duty is to his language', as with his insistence on the responsibilities towards people that this duty implies, Eliot's long meditation on poetry's value is an important and lasting example. This group would include Hill, who acknowledges his debt, and perhaps even Ozick, who does not.

In the chapters that follow I present three different ways in which the relation among poets, language, and people has been conceived and elaborated by strong-minded poet-critics of the past half-century, each of whom thinks the primary duty of the poet is a linguistic one—to write well. In their thinking about the ethical demands and obligations on the writer, each develops a different aspect of Eliot's broad theory, guided by versions of the integrity principle. For Joseph Brodsky, integrity means valuing and defending the creative product above all other social artefacts. 'Aesthetics is the mother of ethics', Brodsky says, which dictum leads him to a social ethics of literary-linguistic primacy founded on a personal ethics of aesthetic encounter. For Seamus Heaney, Eliot's linguistic anthropology, especially his idea of the auditory imagination, chimes with Heaney's own sense of literature's sociohistorical resonance, its value to the cultural and social life of historically and regionally constructed identities. Eliot's theory of poetry's function within and among societies is taken up in Heaney's literary ethics in a way which reflects the duality of the Eliotic picture, though for Heaney this is expounded dichotomously, or at least diachronically— his early defences of poetry raise ethically protective cultural barriers, whereas in his late work Heaney seeks to transcend these barriers to create a more inclusive and incorporative literary and ethical space. For Hill, who as a young poet too readily accepted Eliot's proscriptions against overly 'personal' poetry without understanding 'the qualifications that Eliot himself would have entered',[120] the question of integrity is one of constant struggle against what Eliot called the 'natural sin of language',[121] what Hill calls (after Richard Baxter) its 'natural "pondus"' (CCW, 362), even in the face of that struggle's impossibility. All three of these poets have rejected demands for a socially relevant poetry,

---

Cynthia Ozick, 'T. S. Eliot at 101', *The New Yorker* (20 November 1989), 119–54, 154, 121. Hill is both more responsible and more charitable in his critique.

[120] Hill, 'Art of Poetry LXXX', 282.

[121] Anonymous [T. S. Eliot], 'The Post-Georgians', *The Athenaeum* 4641 (11 April 1919), 171–2.

just as they have continued to think deeply about how poetry can be socially relevant in and of itself.

T. S. Eliot, Joseph Brodsky, Seamus Heaney, Geoffrey Hill. Of these four poets, three came of age in the period following the Second World War, as humanity was coming into a new consciousness of its own potential for evil. Three were Nobel winners, representing native lands and adopted ones in Stockholm and attesting to the value of their art form there. Three are major contributors to the corpus of English-language poetry. Three wrote in the midst of major civil crises in which family or acquaintances were terrorized, imprisoned, or killed. To take only the post-war poets, two were good friends and sometimes collaborators, two cultivated dedicated minority audiences and courted literary controversy, and two now frequently appear in British second-ary school and university syllabi and are routinely anthologized on both sides of the Atlantic. That many things in common leave out one of these poets, and each time a different one, is an indication both of their uniqueness and of their interrelatedness. None of their readers, even if one admired separately their individual corpora, would think they formed a natural poetic group, or school, or movement.[122] But each poet has written lengthily and at times with urgency on the social and spiritual function of poetry, despite a prevailing countertrend in critical theory and in the public imagination, and each has invested consider-able personal resources of time and energy publicly expounding his ideas on the subject. Moreover, in each poet the inclination to explain and argue for the value of poetry appears to have grown as his experience of life and literature has grown. They have continued the tradition of apologia inaugurated by Plato's challenge, adapting their poetic

---

[122] Recent studies have, however, established important lines of influence. Strongest in arguing for Eliot's formative influence on Heaney is Michael Cavanagh, in *Professing Poetry: Seamus Heaney's Poetics* (Washington, DC: Catholic University of America Press, 2009). Hill's relationship to Eliot is better known than Heaney's, but perhaps less understood, a situation Christopher Ricks attempts to redress, in part, in *True Friendship: Geoffrey Hill, Anthony Hecht, and Robert Lowell under the Sign of Eliot and Pound* (New Haven, CT: Yale University Press, 2010). The recent edition of interviews by Valentina Polukhina about Joseph Brodsky provides useful information about his relationships with his English-language contemporaries, including Heaney. See especially volume 2 of her *Brodsky through the Eyes of His Contemporaries* (Boston: Academic Studies Press, 2008). Finally, in a highly original argument, Stephen James points to instances of Hill's influence on Heaney in *Shades of Authority: The Poetry of Lowell, Hill and Heaney* (Liverpool: Liverpool University Press, 2007).

defences to the ethical imperatives and aesthetic preferences of the current age.

My aim in the following chapters will be to explicate writings by Brodsky, Heaney, and Hill on the ethical, social, and spiritual value of their art, keeping Eliot's example in mind, as they do. Subtending this effort are two related claims, which by now will be apparent: first, that attention to the ethics of literature profits our understanding of literature, that critical interest in the ethical concerns of writers and their works need not, *pace* Vendler, refuse precedence to the 'imaginative arts' nor put crafted language 'on the same footing as other "texts"'. Second, that such critical attention should account for poems and the writings of poets on poetry at least as well as it accounts for narrative literature. The poets treated here make special ethical claims for 'writing that exhibits poesis', claims they do not make for other kinds of 'text'. This is because each combines a view of poetry as a pre-eminently linguistic accomplishment, the pre-eminent accomplishment of language, with an ethics—be it inflected personally, sociologically, or theologically—that acknowledges the force of language in the social and spiritual life of man. In other words, the modes of literary ethics described below are attendant to a belief that language is more than mere communication, that it is charged, positively or negatively, with humanity's hopes and disappointments, its potential and its actuality, the possibilities of its future and the realities of its past. When immersed in the medium of language, when one's work is in it and on it, one is continuously creating small discharges of this energy, discharges that *mean something*, in both senses of that phrase.

*

Before moving on to study the ethical defences of poetry conceived, pursued, and promoted by these three poet-critics, let us return with a little more background to the words of Auden—'poetry makes nothing happen'—written at the brink of war, now so often and so casually invoked by those who would deny the ethics of verse. Auden's poem for Yeats has always struck me in its entirety as both a deeply felt and a deeply ethical account of the art of poetry. In the first place it does not diminish or ironize its status as elegy, taking up a position of utter sincerity in its desire to honour its subject and to convey grief at his loss. What strikes me about the second section in particular is not only its own timbre of sincerity, but the effort it makes on behalf of the sincerity, indeed of the integrity, of poetic enterprise. Though a poet may be 'hurt into poetry' by circumstance, poetry is not something like

retaliation or reaction. Circumstance, whether a political or a meteorological one—Ireland's 'madness and weather' both in some way the result of topography or geography, both somehow national, both perhaps inevitable and unalterable—may be a site of poetry but is not the concern of poetry. Auden figures poetry as a river, shielded, perhaps even hidden at the source, but flowing down the river bed of common human experience, flowing, as the stressed rhymes in penultimate lines do, from 'griefs' to 'believe' ('live' ghosting the line), on through 'die' to 'survives', so that the phoneme /aj/ of 'die' is woven into the initial /iv/ and /if/ rhyme by the consonance of /ajv/ in 'survive'. The elegiac topos, that the work outlasts the poet, that through the poetry, the man 'survives', is a common one. But how and where and in what ways poetry is imagined to survive makes gestures that are at once aesthetic and ethical: certainly poetry survives interiorly, privately, and individually, but in its surviving it also links together the private existence with the social existence, the lonely ranches with the populated towns. The image ends, not with a closing-in of the tamper-proof defences of poetry, but an opening out of poetry into the world, the river mouth also the mouth of poetry, a source to draw from.

2

Joseph Brodsky: A 'Peremptory Trust in Words'

I hear it was charged against me that I sought to destroy
institutions,
But really I am neither for nor against institutions,
(What indeed have I in common with them? Or what with
the destruction of them?)

Walt Whitman, 'I Hear it Was Charged Against Me', 1860

Nur wahre Hände schreiben wahre Gedichte. Ich sehe keinen
prinzipiellen Unterschied zwischen Händedruck und Gedicht.
Only truthful hands write true poems. I cannot see any principal
difference between a handshake and a poem.

Paul Celan, in a letter to Hans Bender, 18 May 1960

The story of Joseph Brodsky's life is told in two short chapters. The first, which he lived out mostly in Soviet Leningrad, lasts a difficult thirty-two years. In his early teens Brodsky abandoned school to work a string of jobs in factories and on surveying expeditions, none of which held his interest for more than a few months. At about the age of twenty, he began to move in the literary circles of Leningrad, where he met Lev Losev, Efim Etkind, Anna Akhmatova, Marina Tsvetaeva, and others. He worked for a few years without attracting much notice, writing poems and taking on a large amount of translation work in English, Cuban, Polish, and Serbian poetry. By many accounts Brodsky was a prodigious writer and a formidable reader of poetry, but he did not join any writers' collective and so was mostly unknown outside his immediate circle. Then in 1964 he was arrested, tried, and convicted of 'social parasitism', a crime for which he was sentenced to five years' labour in high subarctic Arkhangel'sk. Within months of the verdict, a secret transcript of Brodsky's trial had reached Western publications,

eventually appearing in German, Polish, and English translation.[1] By
the time his sentence was commuted eighteen months later, Brodsky
had acquired not only national and international celebrity but also the
aura of integrity and moral authority often accorded to the unjustly
punished. For the next seven or so years Brodsky continued to write
poems, circulating them mostly in *samizdat* within Leningrad but also
enjoying sporadic publication in the West. In May 1972, the rise in
Jewish emigrations from the Soviet Union to Israel provided authorities
with a pretext for getting rid of Brodsky for good. One day Brodsky
received in the post a *vyzov* (вызов—an official letter of invitation)
from a purported Israeli relation. As befell hundreds of other contented-
ly settled Russian Jews in the early 1970s, Brodsky had his passport
stamped and was told it would be better for him to leave the country as
soon as possible. 'Think it over, Brodsky,' said the colonel at Visas and
Registrations, 'but decide now.'[2]

The second chapter of Brodsky's life begins less than three weeks
later, when, after landing in Vienna, he opts not to board the connect-
ing flight to Tel Aviv. Instead he is met by his friend Carl Proffer, a
professor at the University of Michigan, and together they go driving
into the Austrian countryside. In Kirchstetten, northern Austria, they
meet Wystan Auden at his country home, and he takes Brodsky in.
Thus the Russian exile whose poor conversational English embarrassed
him began his association with the great and good of English-language

---

[1] See n. 30, below.

[2] Alan Levy, 'Think it Over Brodsky, but Decide Now', *Saturday Review* (8 July
1972), 6–8, 6. The widely circulated story of Brodsky's expulsion has recently been
challenged or qualified by some of his Russian contemporaries, several of whom contend
variously that Brodsky wished to emigrate or actively pursued emigration. The truth is
probably as complicated as anyone's feelings towards a repressive homeland are likely to
be. See especially interviews with David Shrayer-Petrov, Edward Bloomstein, and
Genrikh Steinberg in Valentina Polukhina, *Brodsky through the Eyes of his Contempor-
aries*, vols. 1 and 2 (Boston: Academic Studies Press, 2008). Fuller accounts of Brodsky's
early experiences in Russia can be found in Efim Etkind, *Notes of a Non-Conspirator*,
trans. Peter France (Oxford: Oxford University Press, 1978); ibid, *Процесс Иосифа
Бродского (Protsess Iosifa Brodskogo)* (London: Overseas Publications Interchange,
1988); ibid, *Brodski, ou, Le Procès d'un Poète* (Paris: Librairie Générale Française,
1988); Solomon Volkov, *Conversations with Joseph Brodsky: A Poet's Journey through
the Twentieth Century*, trans. Marian Schwartz (New York: The Free Press, 1988);
Liudmila Shtern, *Бродский: Иосиф, Осиа,, Joseph (Brodskii̐: Iosif, Osia, Joseph)* (Mos-
cow: Izd-vo Nezavisimaia Gazeta, 2001), revised and translated by the author and
published as *Brodsky: A Personal Memoir* (Fort Worth: Baskerville, 2004); and Lev
Losev, *Иосиф Бродский: Опыт литературной Биографии (Iosif Brodskii̐: Opyt
literaturnoĭ Biografii)* (Moscow: Molodaia gvardiia, 2006).

poetry, an association that would also bring him close to Stephen Spender, and later to Derek Walcott and Seamus Heaney. Brodsky emigrated to the United States to take up a teaching post in Ann Arbor, and later he held lecturing positions at Mount Holyoke in Massachusetts, and Queens College and Columbia University in New York. He became a US citizen and won a Nobel prize. In 1991, he was named Poet Laureate Consultant in Poetry to the Library of Congress, officially concatenating the epithets 'American' and 'poet', though he continued to emphasize his identity as a 'Russian poet'. While he continued to write poetry mostly in Russian, his subject matter naturally shifted in the direction of America, and he added many translations and co-translations of his own work to the small amount of English verse he composed. However, Brodsky's major contribution to the tradition of English poetics, also his most substantial output in English, is his two collections of personal and critical essays.

In his personal relations, professional appointments and offices, and critical corpus, and to a lesser but not insignificant degree in his poetic corpus, Brodsky bestrides the English and the Russian literary traditions. Heaney, for whom Brodsky is a model of artistic and personal integrity—and an example of how these can be one and the same—places him 'in filial succession within two great poetic traditions', while also describing his 'intimate, face-to-face relationship' with a 'whole pantheon of the classical and vernacular literatures of Europe and the Americas'.[3] These two relational tropes—the parent-child succession, and the face-to-face relationship—have their own special ethical significance in Brodsky's poetics, a feature which will be taken up in the fourth section of this chapter. In Heaney's description they both particularize and universalize Brodsky, at once claiming him as a brother poet and according him a status that would transcend the contingencies of period, language, and nationality. The fact that Brodsky *did* transgress two of these boundaries meant among other things that he would become, despite himself, repeatedly politicized—once persecuted for writing politically suspect poetry, latterly honoured and celebrated by a rival politics as a dissident with a (presumably) allied ideology. But if Brodsky had an ideology, it was inseparable from his poetics, which rejects the very instruments of social or civic coercion that were responsible for his early incarceration and late elevation. In addition to being a

---

[3] Seamus Heaney, 'Brodsky's Nobel: What the Applause Was About', *The New York Times* (8 November 1987), BR1.

powerful if idiosyncratic thinker about the value of poetry to people and to society, Brodsky is himself an incarnation of some of the most vexed battles over that very question.

PLACING BRODSKY

Brodsky's biography is a good story: romantic, even heroic. But Brodsky himself avoided talking much about his life in Russia, especially about his rough encounters with the State. At times he seemed vaguely embarrassed by, or else affected complete disinterest in, the facts of his persecution, deflecting or dismissing the curiosity of interviewers.[4] Before his death he formalized this antipathy, legating a ban on any official biography for fifty years.[5] The most autobiographical thing that he wrote begins with a rhetorical disclaimer: 'I remember rather little of my life and what I do remember is of small consequence' (LTO, 3–4). When an audience member at a reading asked him, in 1978, what he thought about Solzhenitsyn and the legend that had grown up around him, Brodsky advised: 'As for legend . . . you shouldn't worry or care about legend, you should read the work.'[6]

Part of the reason Brodsky's legend still tends to frame critical treatments of his work—at least in English—may be that the work poses some real difficulties for commentators. Brodsky's poetry has not been especially well received in the English-speaking literary and academic circles that championed him at the time of his exile.[7] As for the prose, readers often struggle to make sense of the strong ethical position they intuit there. Brodsky's gnomic utterances—such as the maxim he frequently repeated, 'aesthetics is the mother of ethics' (GR, 49, 208)— have an aura of authority, but on reflection can sound philosophically

---

[4] See, e.g. interviews in *Joseph Brodsky: Conversations*, ed. Cynthia L. Haven (Jackson: University Press of Mississippi, 2002), 34, 40–1, 51, 115, 142–3.

[5] See Polukhina, *Brodsky through the Eyes of his Contemporaries*, vol. 2, vii.

[6] Haven (ed.), *Joseph Brodsky: Conversations*, 52.

[7] There were early detractors of Brodsky's poetry, led by Christopher Reid and Craig Raine. But even sympathetic commentators, such as Sven Birkerts and Andrew Kahn, have acknowledged a decline in Brodsky's literary reputation since his death. See Reid, 'Great American Disaster', *London Review of Books* (8 December 1988), 17–18; Raine, 'A Reputation Subject to Inflation', *Financial Times* (16 November 1996), Book 19; Birkerts, 'A Subversive in Verse', *The New York Times* (17 September 2000), 7.10; and Kahn, 'First Person: The Great Brodsky', *Times Literary Supplement* (4 May 2007), 3.

casual.[8] The biography, it seems, is both more compelling and more tractable, and can act as a guarantor of Brodsky's literary merit or ethical seriousness, despite the objections that Brodsky would surely have raised against the reliance on history or psychology as a ground for literary study.

Many of those who knew Brodsky in Leningrad take pains to reframe the discussion of his life, especially as it concerns his persecution, in terms of his literary style. The offence he committed in his pursuit of poetry, they say, was not political but stylistic: he deviated from the aesthetic tenets of Socialist Realism. Fellow poet Yunna Moritz qualifies her characterization of Brodsky as 'apolitical' by asserting that 'all his stylistics, the entire level of his linguistic, intonational thinking, was loathsome to [Soviet] literature, which had created its own style and defended its own style with a bayonet and grenades'.[9] Lev Losev, latterly also a poet in exile and an early Brodsky scholar, writes that 'the polity sensed something subversive in the very linguistic matter of his verse even before he introduced any political themes'.[10] A third Leningrad friend, Solomon Volkov, explains it this way: 'Brodsky's poetry wasn't "civic"—in this sense—at all. It wasn't anti-Soviet so much as it was un-Soviet, ignoring the regime utterly and refusing to enter into any kind of dialogue with it.'[11] Brodsky's mistake was believing that anyone could remain, contra the regime's expectations of its citizens, not anti- but un-Soviet in Khrushchev's, and later Brezhnev's, Soviet Union.

There is a question as to whether this indifferent temperament corresponds in some way to what Svetlana Boym has called Brodsky's 'art of estrangement'.[12] That is, one could argue for the literary relevance of Brodsky's biography on the grounds that his art-creation is

---

[8] The philosopher Marcia Muelder Eaton, one of very few writers who have tried to come to terms with this statement, points out in 'Aesthetics: The Mother of Ethics?', *Journal of Aesthetics and Art Criticism* 55:4 (Fall 1997), 355–64, 355, that the 'history of philosophy does not offer many theories in which aesthetics is prior to ethics'. Eaton, though she calls Brodsky's maxim 'enthralling', ultimately finds she must reject it.

[9] Elisabeth Rich, 'Joseph Brodsky in Memoriam: The Russian Perspective', *South Central Review* 14:1 (1997), 10–31, 28–9.

[10] Lev Losev (as Lev Loseff), 'Politics/Poetics', in Lev Losev and Valentina Polukhina (eds), *Brodsky's Poetics and Aesthetics* (London: Macmillan, 1990), 34–55, 35. The 'political themes' Losev refers to he traces back only as far as Brodsky's post-Arkhangel'sk writing, e.g. 'A Halt in the Desert' (1966).

[11] Volkov, *Conversations*, 12.

[12] Svetlana Boym, 'Estrangement as Lifestyle: Shklovsky and Brodsky', *Poetics Today* 17:4 (Winter 1996), 511–30, 532.

readable as a product of this constitutional indifference. Boym gets her term directly from Brodsky:

> it occurred to me that Marx's dictum that 'existence conditions consciousness' was true only for as long as it takes consciousness to acquire the art of estrangement; thereafter, consciousness is on its own and can both condition and ignore the existence. (LTO, 3)

The art of estrangement, Boym says, 'became a dissident art; in the Soviet artistic context of the 1960s, estrangement represented a resistance to sovietization'.[13] This statement is true on a certain reading, but it exacerbates an unfortunate ambiguity in Brodsky's text. The temptation to interpret 'art' as 'artwork(s)', or as one of the various fine arts, must be resisted: these are not the kinds of thing that the consciousness can 'acquire'; Brodsky means 'skill', or 'knack'. But 'the art of estrangement', decontextualized, suggests that Brodsky's idea of poetry is created from or is otherwise imbued with the same psychological indifference that he expressed towards the State. To equate it with 'dissident art' reinforces, however subtly, a spurious connection between Brodsky and the movement of unofficial (usually visual) artists who thought of their work specifically in opposition to official State art—that is, who understood art as one of many sites of political resistance. So, while it may be true that Brodsky's practised indifference to the polity was in a sense one of the skills a dissident might acquire, that is far from saying that he was committed to a poetics of estrangement. Boym is more correct in her recent revisiting of the question of art, politics, and estrangement: 'The "art of estrangement" in Brodsky's quote is no longer an aesthetic device but a tactic of dissent, a form of alternative self-fashioning, a survival strategy.'[14]

Strictly speaking, of course, Brodsky was no dissident, though he was a survivor. He did not produce, promote, or distribute dissident art. He did not disagree. He ignored. The estrangement he practised was in relation to politics and to history. Brodsky could estrange himself from art, but only from ersatz, State-sponsored art, such as the portraits of Lenin and Stalin ubiquitous in the Soviet Union of his youth: 'I think that coming to ignore those pictures was my first lesson in switching off, my first attempt at estrangement' (LTO, 6), he writes. Estrangement

[13] Ibid. 532.
[14] Svetlana Boym, 'Poetics and Politics of Estrangement: Victor Shklovsky and Hannah Arendt', *Poetics Today* 26:4 (Winter 2005), 581–611, 606.

from such politically sponsored art is just another form of estrangement from the political order, a self-externalizing from the mass that wishes to co-opt one into itself. Describing his youthful 'escape' from high school, his first and possibly the definitive break from State control, Brodsky writes, 'The main thing, I suppose, was the change of exterior' (LTO, 11). The geological expeditions he would embark on in his late teens may have had the appeal of maximizing the dimensions of that exterior.

Personal essays make up the majority of Joseph Brodsky's prose, and consequently the corpus displays less analytical rigour than T. S. Eliot's writings, less focus on the literary than Seamus Heaney's, and less scholarly depth than Geoffrey Hill's. Eliotic 'impersonality' is not a quality which Brodsky displays, at least not in his prose. Nevertheless, despite his informal, narrative, sometimes confessional style, we do find in Brodsky lasting traces of high-modern poetics. He evokes Eliot's early idea of tradition—an 'unconscious community . . . between the true artists of any time' (SE, 24)—in his Nobel lecture, where he pays dues to the ghosts of great Russian- and English-language poets: 'In my better moments, I deem myself their sum total, though invariably inferior to any one of them individually' (GR, 45). Reflecting Eliot's requirement that artists 'shall cohere' to the order formed by the 'existing monuments' of literature (SW, 50), he later writes that 'the immediate consequence' of writing poetry is 'the sensation of immediately falling into dependence on it, on everything that has already been uttered, written, and accomplished in it' (GR, 57). Eliot's related ideas of 'duty' and 'integrity' are also picked up by Brodsky. Echoing Eliot's insistence that a poet's primary duty is to language, Brodsky writes, 'If a poet has any obligation toward society, it is to write well' (LTO, 359).

The primacy of the artist's relationship towards language is taken up repeatedly by Brodsky. Among other prominent roles in his essays, it forms a central theme of his address to the US Library of Congress. In his official capacity as its Poet Laureate Consultant in Poetry, Brodsky mused on the duties that the post might require. Claiming to speak 'in the spirit of a public servant' (GR, 200), Brodsky appears instead to absolve the poet of any obligation towards the public:

If one can speak of the social function of somebody who is essentially self-employed, then the social function of a poet is writing, which he does not by society's appointment but by his own volition. His only duty is to his language, that is, to write well. (GR, 205)

However, though the poet has no overtly social or political role, writing is necessarily a social act, dependent as it is on language, which is the basis of human interaction: 'By existing, by writing, especially by writing well, in the language of his society, a poet takes a large step toward it' (GR, 205). The main duty, Brodsky says, resides not with the poet, who writes out of natural proclivity, but with the public, to take the reciprocal step towards poetry, to read. As Brodsky says, 'It is society's job to meet [the poet] half way, that is, to open his book and read it' (GR, 205). In his Library of Congress address, Brodsky recasts the role of Poet Laureate from that of national bard—curator of what, as recent laureate Ted Kooser described it, constitutes 'a perennial expression of our emotional, spiritual and intellectual lives, as witnessed by the tens of thousands of poems written about the tragedy of September 11 that circulated on the Internet'[15]—to a sort of public promoter of literature, a manager and facilitator of the tricky business of getting people to meet poets halfway. The bulk of the speech is devoted to the details of his proposed national programme of subsidized publishing, in which 'Fifty million copies of an Anthology of American Poetry' would be sold at two dollars a copy to every American family. If his earnest defence of this scheme displays a tenuous grasp of economics and a naïvety regarding the priorities of American politics—not to mention American families—it also endearingly evidences Brodsky's conviction of poetry's place in the polis.

As I discussed earlier, Eliot expressed his belief in poetry as a necessary cultural guarantor in two main respects. The first defended poetry as an indicator and motivator of society's intellectual vigour: 'The people which ceases to produce literature ceases to move in thought and sensibility' (UPC, 15). Brodsky's insistence that people read their poets is similarly defended:

By failing to read or listen to poets, a society dooms itself to inferior modes of articulation—of the politician, or the salesman, or the charlatan—in short, to its own. It forfeits, in other words, its own evolutionary potential, for what distinguishes us from the rest of the animal kingdom is precisely the gift of speech. (GR, 205)

---

[15] US Newswire, 'Poetry Foundation, Library of Congress Co-sponsor Poet Laureate's "American Life in Poetry" Project Brings Poetry Back to Newspapers' (31 March 2005).

The second of Eliot's defences was much more immediate: with a pointed, if passing, reference to the Nazi occupation of Norway, he told a roomful of Norwegian refugees in 1943 that 'Unless [people] go on producing great authors, and especially great poets, their language will deteriorate, their culture will deteriorate and perhaps become absorbed in a stronger one' (OPP, 21). This too finds echo in Brodsky, though the Russian's historical frame of reference inclines him to locate danger from within:

society thinks of itself as having other options than reading verses, no matter how well written. Its failure to do so results in its sinking to that level of locution at which society falls easy prey to a demagogue or a tyrant. (LTO, 359)

Along with the basic didactic claim in poetry's favour, Brodsky is acknowledging the deceptive possibilities of language which Plato first warned against. The solution he advances, however, is a kind of inversion of Plato's: just as Robert Frost did,[16] Brodsky promotes the poet over the politician, arguing that the development of aesthetic judgement equips us against the demagogue's false rhetoric. A developed sense of taste puts one on guard against the 'refrains and the rhythmical incantations peculiar to any version of political demagogy' (GR, 49). In fact, this literary-critical capacity forms and sustains the general critical ability: 'The more one reads poetry, the less tolerant one becomes of any sort of verbosity, be it in political or philosophical discourse, in history, social studies, or the art of fiction' (GR, 100).

Like Eliot, Brodsky was a classicist in literature who nurtured a soft spot for the English Metaphysical poets. However, despite these and other affinities with Eliot's thought and practice, Brodsky's uncontested poetic model was W. H. Auden: Brodsky's paean to Auden, 'To Please a Shadow' (1983), is an elaboration of his frequently expressed admiration for that poet, an admiration which often swelled to adoration, infatuation, even idolization. In the story of Brodsky's gravitation towards that exemplar, however, Eliot plays an important guiding role in two respects. Brodsky tells how, during his arctic exile in Norinskaia, Arkhangel'sk, he was not intending to read Auden but another poet— the one who, in 1964, was the more likely to make acolytes of young

---

[16] Without education by poetry, Frost says, people 'don't know how to judge a political campaign...they don't know when they are being fooled by metaphor, an analogy, a parable'. See Robert Frost, *Collected Poems, Prose, and Plays* (New York: Library of America, 1995), 718–19.

readers. This of course was Eliot, 'who in those days reigned supreme in Eastern Europe. I was intending to read Eliot' (LTO, 361). Later Brodsky would reminisce, 'We all knew the name Eliot. For an Eastern European, Eliot is a kind of Anglo-Saxon brand name.... But it was very hard to get any stuff of his.'[17] It may be that in preparing to read Eliot in the original, Brodsky was clearing a receptive space for an English poetic exemplar—that, having been banned and branded by Soviet justice, he was turning to more welcoming literary contexts for inspiration. If Brodsky was indeed preparing the soil of his mind to accept an external mentor, it was Auden's seed—not Eliot's—that took root.

Though Brodsky took Auden as his ultimate and lifelong example, and though he constantly laboured to 'find myself in closer proximity to the man whom I considered the greatest mind of the twentieth century' (LTO, 357), it was Eliot who first led him in that direction, and it was he who provided the occasion for the first manifestation of this desire. Eliot died on 4 January 1965. Learning of this one week later, Brodsky immediately composed his elegy 'Verses on the Death of T. S. Eliot'.[18] By this time, he had been in Norinskaia almost nine months, and was suffering from the isolation and hard labour. In a letter to a friend, he wrote, 'It is simply physiologically unpleasant to write, to talk, to dip my pen in the ink-well etc.'[19] Nevertheless, the death of a great poet spurred Brodsky to begin his Audenesque apprenticeship by recreating—Brodsky has called it 'aping'[20]—Auden's elegy for Yeats.

Centred attention to the elegized is one thing Brodsky learned from his newfound mentor:

I frequently thought that the most interesting feature of the genre was the authors' unwitting attempts at self-portrayal with which nearly every poem 'in memoriam' is strewn—or soiled. (LTO, 361)

---

[17] Joseph Brodsky, interview with Sven Birkerts, 'The Art of Poetry XXVIII', *Paris Review* 83 (Spring 1982), 82–126, 90.

[18] George Kline reports that Brodsky wrote the poem within a twenty-four-hour period. See Brodsky, *Joseph Brodsky Selected Poems*, trans. George Kline (Harmondsworth: Penguin, 1973), 102n^1.

[19] Letter to Natalya Gorbanevskaya, quoted in Valentina Polukhina, *Joseph Brodsky a Poet for our Time* (Cambridge: Cambridge University Press, 1989), 24.

[20] Brodsky, 'The Art of Poetry XXVIII', 92.

By contrast,

The Auden poem had none of this; what's more, I soon realized that even its structure was designed to pay tribute to the dead poet, imitating in reverse order the great Irishman's own modes of stylistic development. (LTO, 361–2)

Given this ethic of imitation and tribute, it is somewhat incongruous that Brodsky's elegy takes Auden and not Eliot as its formal and thematic model.[21] The elegy is divided into three sections that closely follow 'In Memory of W. B. Yeats' in metre and rhyme scheme. The last section, in which Brodsky quickens into Auden's tetrameter quatrains (themselves modelled on Yeats's), is particularly imitative of the earlier poem:

> Hill and dale will honour him.
> Aeolus will guard his flame.
> Blades of grass his name will hold,
> just as Horace had foretold.   (JBSP, 101)

If the translation has trouble reproducing the natural pulse of the original, it does at least assiduously replicate its formal characteristics. Of Brodsky's faithful borrowings from Auden's original, the translator has retained exactly the trochaic tetrameter and approximated the rhyme scheme, but has had to forsake its intensifying repetition:

Будет помнить лес и дол.	*Budet pomnit' les i dol.*
Будет помнить сам Эол.	*Budet pomnit' sam Ėol.*
Будет помнить каждый злак,	*Budet pomnit' kazhdyĭ zlak,*
как хотел Гораций Флакк.	*kak khotel Goratsiĭ Flakk.*[22]

Far from the ruminative or punctuating reiteration which we associate with Eliot (e.g., 'Because I do not hope', 'HURRY UP PLEASE IT'S TIME'), the initial anaphora of Будет помнить ('*Budet pomnit'*'—'will remember') reproduces Auden's effect of accelerating his crisp short metre with repetition, especially of 'pardoned', 'pardon', 'pardons' in the excised third quatrain. Brodsky deploys other tricks found in Auden: the

---

[21] For a detailed formal comparison, see Polukhina, *Joseph Brodsky a Poet for our Time*, 81–8.

[22] Joseph Brodsky, *Остановка в Пустыне* (*Ostanovka v Pustyne*) (Ann Arbor: Ardis, 1978), 141.

unexpected vocative 'Thomas Stearns', recalling Auden's 'William Yeats', makes the subject more personally present by defamiliarizing the nom de plume. Similarly in the imagery Brodsky uses, Auden's original is recalled. From the opening 'He died at the start of the year, in January' (JBSP, 99), establishing a central death-as-winter motif which is also at the heart of the Auden poem, we follow the course plotted by 'In Memory of W. B. Yeats'. Brodsky testifies to the great loss the world has suffered, Nature's sympathetic mourning, and the immortality of the poetry that has been left in legacy. This poem could very well have been 'Elegy for a Great Poet, After Auden', were it not for references almost in passing to details of Eliot's biography and poetry.

If it is clear that Brodsky's elegy in the style of Auden fails Brodsky's own criterion of putting the elegized at the centre of the poem, we may go some way towards pardoning this fault with the observation that for one who once said, with all sincerity, that 'Auden, in my mind, in my heart, occupies far greater room than anything or anybody else on the earth',[23] first contact with his work must have been somewhat over-whelming. Normally a shrewd and perceptive reader of poetry, Brodsky never recognized (nor does he appear to see in retrospect) the ironic potential of Auden's lines about time worshipping language, forgiving Kipling and Claudel because they used it well. On reading them, he was left besotted, 'half-believing' the words:

Auden had indeed said that time (not *the* time) worships language, and the train of thought that statement set in motion in me is still trundling to this day. For 'worship' is an attitude of lesser towards greater. If time worships language, it means that language is greater, or older, than time, which is, in its turn, older and greater than space. (LTO, 363)

Brodsky was by that time already committed to some version of this metaphysical hierarchy, but to find confirmation of his ideas expressed poetically by Auden was an artistic and an ethical revelation: 'Then and there I was simply stunned' (LTO, 364). Though the Eliotic funda-mentals of 'integrity', 'duty', and poetic 'social function' are all present here, in Brodsky everything passes through the prism of his notion that aesthetic understanding is previous and superior to all other kinds of cognition. Poetry, as 'the supreme result of the entire language', is for

---

[23] Quoted in David Montenegro, *Points of Departure: International Writers on Writing and Politics* (Ann Arbor: University of Michigan Press, 1991), 133–48, 143.

Brodsky the ultimate aesthetic expression, and therefore also a key to ethical understanding.

THE STATE *v.* BRODSKY

The poem 'Plato Elaborated', which Brodsky wrote in 1977, begins by imagining an ideal city where a river would 'jut out from under a bridge like a hand from a sleeve, | and would flow toward the gulf, spreading its fingers | like Chopin, who never shook a fist at anyone as long as he lived' (CPE, 140). Plato's city, however, was never so welcoming to the artist, a fact the poem quickly incorporates. With a twinge of the 'grim and unhappy' concert hall that is the subject of the earlier poem 'A Halt in the Desert', Brodsky goes on to describe 'an Opera House, in which a slightly overripe | tenor would duly descant Mario's arias, keep- | ing the Tyrant amused' (CPE, 140). By the end of the poem, the imagined city has produced its inevitable conclusion:

> And when they would finally arrest me for espionage,
> for subversive activity, vagrancy, for *ménage*
> *à trois*, and the crowd, boiling around me, would bellow,
> poking me with their work-roughened forefingers, 'Outsider! We'll
>   settle your hash!'—   (CPE, 142)

The poem is effective as an 'elaboration' of Plato's antipathy towards art, and to the general tendency, following Plato, of civics to prefer the instruments of politics to the goods of cultural production. Plato was willing, albeit hypothetically, to readmit poetry to the just city should its practitioners and defenders prove its utility as well as its delightful-ness.[24] As is frequently the case with Plato, however, one gets the impression that his Socrates would make a less than impartial judge of such proof, that the terms of the debate have already been set in such a way as to favour Socrates's original position. But if this is acceptable, or at least tolerable, as a method for philosophical exposition, as a model for a real-life prosecution of a living, breathing poet—or of anyone—it is nothing short of grotesque. For the unsettling fact is that Brodsky's poem is also, in its final stanzas, a fairly accurate account of his trial, in which poets and defenders of poetry argued with tyrants over the utility

---

[24] See Plato, *Republic* [607d]–[608b].

of poetry, and which ended with the poet banished from the gates of the city.

Brodsky's conviction at the age of twenty-four on charges of social parasitism is astonishing in more ways than one. As an exposé of Soviet justice, the episode would be ridiculous if its consequences had not been so serious. The proceedings were the Kafkaesque cliché manifested. The judge, shouting down the defence, excluded all exculpatory evidence as 'irrelevant' while encouraging the testimonials of citizens with little or no relation to Brodsky: men who had read defamatory articles about him or knew of bad apples who had been reading his poetry. Most of the evidence was little more than opinion founded on rumour based on hearsay. The defendant was barely allowed to speak. The prosecutor, in contrast, talked on and on, sometimes barely cogent in his vituperation of the accused. When it was over, Brodsky received a sentence of five years' forced labour near the Arctic Circle. Those who testified in his defence were subsequently defamed and persecuted.

The episode can be interpreted in several ways. It was, politically speaking, a simplistic and fabulously inept piece of score-settling by Writers' Union bosses and local Party higher-ups whom Brodsky's verse had somehow rubbed the wrong way. The charge of social parasitism and the concomitant implication of anti-Sovietism are, on this reading, only an expedient excuse that turned out not so expedient after all. But, as Losev and others who have tried to make sense of the strange actions of the local KGB in this affair have observed, at the core of the persecution are the twin political crimes of idleness and non-conformism. On this level, the trial is a staging of Plato's charge against poetry—that it is an occupation without civic utility unless specifically authorized and co-opted by the State—a charge which is exaggerated in this context, where the accuser is vested in a totalizing ideology of economic necessity. Exaggerated, but played out in the utterly unembellished surroundings of the Dzerzhinsky District Court of Leningrad, with the soberest of consequences for the accused.

At least in the predictability of its outcome, Brodsky's trial resembled the secret processes that consigned Osip Mandel'shtam to the same five-year sentence in 1938.[25] That episode remains hidden from us, but in

---

[25] Mandel'shtam died during the first winter of his sentence. Several documents related to his arrests, including transcripts from his interrogations, have recently shed light on his experiences at the hands of NKVD operatives. See Chapter 9 of Vitaly Shentalinsky, *Arrested Voices: Resurrecting the Disappeared Writers of the Soviet Regime*, trans. John Crowfoot (New York: The Free Press, 1993).

considering the case of Brodsky it is worth keeping in mind two other memorable State proceedings against poets. In 1943 a Washington grand jury handed up an indictment on charges of treason against Ezra Pound, who had been living in Italy since 1924 and had since 1941 been broadcasting addresses on Italian state radio. When he was returned to America to face those charges, after being captured and caged in Pisa, a hearing to determine Pound's fitness to stand trial allowed itself to be convinced of his insanity. Pound was spared a potential guilty verdict and prison, at the cost of a thirteen-year incarceration at St Elizabeth's Hospital in Washington, known until 1916 as the Government Hospital for the Insane.[26] The complicity between judicial operatives and Pound's defenders in obtaining this result suggests a reluctance on the part of the State to prosecute one of its own poets for his speech. Pound was not the only player in that game to be spared a verdict—the excellently named Judge Bolitha Laws relieved himself and his court of that responsibility. Had he instead assumed it, dismissing out of hand the contention of insanity, as was his prerogative,[27] the trial of Ezra Pound might today be known, whatever its outcome, as a farcical playing out of Plato's suggestion in *Laws* that the poet's speech be put under strict watch of the good legislator.

The second informative example comes from the same country and decade, when the House Committee on Un-American Activities called Berthold Brecht as an 'unfriendly' witness in October of 1947. The thuggishness of those proceedings resembles what we know about Brodsky's trial. But that committee took no action against Brecht over his poems or plays (though it was interested in them, arguing nicely at times over points of translation), and those directors, screenwriters, and actors whom it did censure were convicted of declining to answer questions to a House committee, not of producing propagandistic materials. The results may have been bad for those refuseniks, but the formal means by which they were obtained were different from what Brodsky experienced, and significantly so. American apparatuses of civil

---

[26] Conrad L. Rushing, since 2003 Presiding Justice of the California Sixth District Court of Appeal, has argued that Pound and his supporters made a bad bargain, that on the evidence and according to precedent the poet would likely have been acquitted—or if found guilty, would probably have received no jail time. See Rushing, '"Mere Words": The Trial of Ezra Pound', *Critical Inquiry* 14:1 (Autumn 1987), 111–33.

[27] Rushing, '"Mere Words"', 122.

power, it seems, unlike those of the Soviet Union,[28] would not, or could not, bring a poet and his poems to trial.

We have a nearly complete version of Brodsky's two hearings thanks to Frida Vigdorova, a former schoolteacher turned journalist.[29] Officially a part of the Soviet propaganda machine, but acting privately and, secretly, against the interests of the State, Vigdorova quietly took down a transcript of the trial before she was finally noticed by the judge and ordered to stop. The reporter soon circulated her notes in *samizdat*, which quickly found its way out of the country. Within a month and a half, the Russian-language Paris weekly *Russkaia Mysl'* published a short summary of the proceedings. By the end of 1964, an abridged version of Vigdorova's record was available in German, Polish, and English translation.[30] The complete text, which included more witness statements and a summary of the trial's conclusion, was published in Russian, in New York, the following year.[31] Never before had the insides of the Soviet justice system been exposed to such widespread international scrutiny. In addition to causing embarrassment by winding their clandestine way into Western publications, the notes also served as the basis for organizing internal pressure on the government to return Brodsky from his exile. After eighteen months of his sentence, the pleas of Anna

---

[28] Brodsky's is only one example—and a mild one—of Soviet state persecution of authors. Shentalinsky's chapter on Mandel'shtam, to take one short episode, is littered with footnotes to the names of his literary friends and associates: 'arrested twice', 'died in camps', 'shot.' See Shentalinsky, *Arrested Voices*, 168–96. Shentalinsky's 'Biographical Notes of Principal Figures', a list of authors, poets, and playwrights who fell victim to Stalin's purges, is 18 pages long and names 136 people.

[29] The veracity of Vigdorova's account has recently been challenged by IUriĭ Begunov, whose account of the same proceedings depicts Brodsky as combative and unreasonable. Though his book *Правда о суде над Иосифом Бродским (Pravda o sude nad Iosifom Brodskim—The Truth about the Trial of Joseph Brodsky*, St Petersburg: Izdatel' stvo imeni A.S. Severina/Sojuz pistaelej Rossii, 1996), has been more or less discredited, the existence of his account cannot simply be ignored. See David MacFadyen's discussion in *Joseph Brodsky and the Baroque* (Liverpool: Liverpool University Press, 1998), 195–7.

[30] A short summary of Vigdorova's notes was first published in Russian in *Русская Мысль (Russkaia Mysl'*, 5 May 1964); in German in the Hamburg weekly *Die Zeit* (2 July 1964); in Polish in *Kultura* (July–August 1964), 3–28; and in English in the American bi-weekly *The New Leader* (31 August 1964). In the autumn, Stephen Spender's magazine *Encounter* 23:3 (September 1964), 84–91, reprinted the *New Leader* translation in England. All versions appeared anonymously.

[31] In *Воздушные пути: альманах (Vozdushnye puti: al'manakh*) 4 (1965), 279–303.

Akhmatova, Dmitrii Shostakovich, and others finally secured Brodsky's release. He returned to Leningrad an international literary celebrity.

Vigdorova's transcript survives in its most complete translated form as an appendix to *Notes of a Non-Conspirator*, a compilation of notes and reminiscences by the Russian exile Efim Etkind, who took the stand in Brodsky's defence in 1964.[32] His actions in Brodsky's cause resulted in some personal inconvenience. When it was decided to expel him from Russia ten years later, Etkind's 'political short-sightedness, lack of vigilance, and ideological illiteracy'[33] in the Brodsky affair were cited by Party officials. Etkind was expelled from the Union of Writers, stripped of his title as Professor, and finally was issued a visa to Israel with instructions to leave the country post-haste. It was a fate Brodsky had lived only two years previously.

Etkind first encountered Brodsky in the early sixties at a series of workshops called 'For the First Time in Russian', which Etkind organized and where Brodsky sometimes read his translations. Etkind's memory of Brodsky in *Notes* addresses the central charge levied against him during his trial: that his refusal to adopt a useful trade made him a 'social parasite':

I already knew that Brodsky was not simply an exceptionally gifted poet, but also an unusually hard-working person: in order to translate Gałczyński he had studied Polish, and in order to read in the original and translate John Donne and his other beloved metaphysical poets he had learnt English.[34]

The charge of social parasitism stemmed from the so-called 'Decree of the 4th of May',[35] issued against those who refused to do 'honest work' and who therefore subtracted from the communal good and hampered society's ongoing struggle towards communism. Etkind's description of Brodsky as a 'hard-working person' is meant as a direct refutation of this charge. But in attempting to defend Brodsky by claiming that his intellectual and creative work was of comparable difficulty and required

---

[32] Efim Etkind, *Notes of a Non-Conspirator*, trans. Peter France (Oxford: Oxford University Press, 1978). Etkind also includes the court record in his memoir *Brodski, ou, Le procès d'un poète* (Paris: Librairie Générale Française, 1988), which adds his own reminiscences of the trial in French.

[33] Etkind, *Notes*, 106. The quotation is from 'special reports' drawn up on Etkind and the other defence witnesses.

[34] Ibid. 89.

[35] The decree was originally issued on 4 May 1961 but was confirmed and extended by the Supreme Court in March 1963. It was originally intended for vagrants, prostitutes, gamblers, and other undesirables.

similar diligence to so-called 'useful work', Etkind accepts the premise of the accusation and enters into its logic. Instead of rejecting the accusers' contention out of hand, he presents evidence to dispute their conclusions, ultimately consigning himself to a losing position. Accepting the terms and definitions of his accusers is a trap that Brodsky avoided when making his own defence.

Instead, being unable to debate the merits of his accusers' position, the accused could only propose another mode of valuation, one which took poetry on its own terms. The exchanges during the trial, if they show anything, show how incompatible the two positions are:

JUDGE: What is your profession?
BRODSKY: Writing poetry. Translation. I think...
JUDGE: We don't want your thoughts. Stand up properly! Don't lean against the walls! [...] Do you have any regular work?
BRODSKY: I thought that was regular work.
JUDGE: Answer more precisely!
BRODSKY: I wrote poems. I thought they would be published. I thought...
JUDGE: We are not interested in your thoughts. Answer me, why didn't you work?
BRODSKY: I did work. I wrote poetry.
JUDGE: That doesn't interest us.
(94–5), [279][36]

With the interlocutors fighting for semantic control over 'work', the lack of agreed meaning produces an absurd exchange. Brodksy's utter deficit of political power in the face of his accuser is partially compensated by his power to make language work for him, or at least his refusal to allow it to work for the state. Unlike Etkind, he does not attempt to validate his poetic activity by the standards of the polity. He can only repeat what he considers a fair answer to the questions posed; his questioners can only keep asking them. It is a scene that is re-enacted throughout the trial, as in this exchange, provoked by the defending counsel's line of questioning:

COUNSEL: Had you any relations with the translators' section of the Writers' Union?
BRODSKY: Yes, I took part in the regular poetry readings called 'For the First Time in Russian' and read translations from the Polish.

---

[36] Here and in the passages that follow I quote France's English translation, published with Etkind's *Notes*, with references to the original Russian as published in *Воздушные пути: альманах* in square brackets. In the transcript, ellipses indicate a pause and not elided source material unless enclosed in square brackets.

JUDGE (TO COUNSEL): You should ask him about useful work, not about public appearances.

COUNSEL: His translations *are* his useful work.

JUDGE: Brodsky, it would be better if you explained to the court why you did not work during the intervals between jobs.

BRODSKY: I did work. I wrote poetry.

JUDGE: But that didn't have to stop you working.

BRODSKY: But I did work. I wrote poetry.

(248), [284]

As clumsy or transparent as the government's campaign against Brodsky may appear, by limiting the discourse to economic productivity the judge and prosecutor succeed in framing an easily winnable case. When the witnesses for the defence attempt to assess and quantify the amount of 'work' that has gone into Brodsky's translations, they are ridiculed by the judge and heckled by the audience. Etkind notes that in order to underscore the triviality of poetic enterprise, for the second hearing a large number of labourers were trucked in to fill the chamber. As the judge and prosecutor continued to portray Brodsky as a layabout, these 'shouted and cheered for the prosecution and showered the defence with taunts' (98). Vigdorova records some of these: 'Intellectuals, they're on their backs', 'I'm also going to get a prose translation and write poems!' (103).

Though Brodsky stayed aloof during most of his trial, in his infrequent responses to his accusers we can see the germs of the poetic theory that he would later develop in his prose essays. The following passage is the most frequently quoted portion of the trial. More than any poetry he had written at the time, it is responsible for Brodsky's early reputation at home and abroad. Brodsky has just enumerated some of the manual jobs he has held when the judge presses the matter, repeating, 'But what is your specialist qualification?'

BRODSKY: Poet. Poet-translator.

JUDGE: And who declared you to be a poet? Who put you on the list of poets?

BRODSKY: No one. (*Spontaneously.*) And who put me on the list of human beings?

JUDGE: And did you study for this?

BRODSKY: For what?

JUDGE: For being a poet. You didn't try to take a course in higher education where they train . . . teach . . .

BRODSKY: I didn't think it came from education.

JUDGE: How does one become a poet, then?

BRODSKY: I think it comes . . . (*embarrassed*) . . . from God . . .

(95), [280]

Brodsky's retorts are remarkable for more than just their audacity. They evidence innate and near total disregard for the institutions of the State. Education, Justice, Culture—all rigorously administered branches of the Revolution—are simply ignored by the young poet, whose conviction of his own worth and the worth of his vocation is apparently unassailable. In a state where permission to publish required membership in the local Union of Writers, Brodsky instead frequented writers' gatherings when they interested him or when he had something to read. He took no notice of capital-'C' Culture, defined and regulated by Moscow, choosing instead to immerse himself in the cultures of English, Polish, Serbian, and Spanish poetry.

Brodsky dramatizes the difference between Soviet-decreed big-'C' Culture and traditionally constituted small-'c' culture in his 1966 poem 'A Halt in the Desert'. Its subject is the erection of the October Concert Hall in Leningrad in the early 1960s, a time when 'Palaces of Culture' were altering city centres all over the Soviet bloc. These typically gargantuan agglutinations of concrete were often commissioned and paid for directly by Moscow, as 'gifts' from the Soviet empire to its satellite states. In this case, the new Monument to Culture comes at the expense of an ancient cultural monument:

> So few Greeks live in Leningrad today
> that we have razed a Greek church, to make space
> for a new concert hall, built in today's
> grim and unhappy style.   (JBSP, 131)

Classical inheritance and religious observance are important cultural signifiers for Brodsky. His lament for their passing insists that their relevance extends beyond the 'few Greeks' still living in Leningrad, that the passing-on of culture is not only an ethnic or national concern. When Brodsky admits that a place of music is 'not so grim a thing', and asks, 'And who's to blame | if virtuosity has more appeal | than the worn banners of an ancient faith?', we hear the hollow echo of justificatory self-delusion. This response ultimately fails to satisfy: instead of rationalization, Brodsky chooses passive acceptance of the usurpation of culture by Culture. The church 'succumbs' in the face of overwhelming mechanical force:

> A huge power shovel clanked up to the church,
> an iron ball dangling from its boom, and soon
> the walls began to give way peaceably.

> Not to give way would be ridiculous
> for a mere wall in face of such a foe.   (JBSP, 131)

It is not hard to recognize in this yielding Brodsky's own peaceable surrender to the political machinery of the State. But, notwithstanding the manifest objective power of the State, the poem establishes a timescale in which its clout is only fleeting. The title of the poem immediately establishes it as a painful moment of pause within a larger progress. The time of cultural travesty Brodsky observes is analogized as the Jews' stop in the wilderness, turning the poem's glance backwards, past the Egyptian captivity to a cultural Eden (represented by the Greek church), while at the same time looking forwards to a Promised Land in which culture will be recovered. The lingering presence of the destroyed church in the snouts of neighbourhood dogs is evidence that the church and the culture it represents persist beneath the surface of official reality: 'Dog-dreams have cancelled out reality', Brodsky writes. And, more than dog-dreams, there are human memories and passed-down cultural possessions:

> And, if I were to speak in earnest of
> the 'relay race of human history',
> I'd swear by nothing but this relay race—
> this race of all the generations who
> have sniffed, and who will sniff, the ancient smells.   (JBSP, 132)

The poem ends by linking preserved memory to a possible future: 'Does a new epoch wait | for us? And, if it does, what duty do we owe?' Victories of Culture over culture, unavoidable as they may be, are but temporary conditions to be endured; they are merely artefacts of social organization, of politics—of institutions with little or no permanent relevance.

It would be a mistake, however, to consider Brodsky's audacious insouciance for institutions, whether in his public life or in his private writing, as a challenge to communism per se. In one of Brodsky's rare unsolicited contributions to his proceedings, he counters that interpretation with vehemence:

NIKHOLAEV: [...] Brodsky's verses are disgusting and anti-Soviet.
BRODSKY: Give the names of my anti-Soviet poems. Quote just one line from them.

(255–6), [293]

Neither is it the case that Brodsky wrote pro-Soviet poems. What irks him is the accusation that he would write anything so base as a polemical poem, not because it would reveal his politics, but because it would impugn his poetry. Poetry is already for Brodsky, even at this early age, antecedent and superior to social organization. There is nothing in the transcript of Brodsky's trial to suggest that he harboured any political preference, only a preference for poetry over politics.

This is far from saying that Brodsky is an aestheticist whose interest in art is only for art's sake. To the contrary, Brodsky's elevation of poetry over the institutions of man allows him to make the highest of social claims for it. When the judge rephrases the issue of 'useful work' as one of patriotic duty, Brodsky makes his boldest statement of the proceedings:

JUDGE: And what have you done that is of value to the fatherland?
BRODSKY: I have written poems. That is my work. I am convinced . . . I believe that what I have written will be of service to people not only now but in generations to come.
VOICE FROM THE HALL: Go on! You're kidding yourself.
ANOTHER VOICE: He's a poet. He's bound to think that way.
JUDGE: So you think that your so-called poetry is of service to the people?
BRODSKY: Why do you say 'so-called poetry'?
JUDGE: We call your poetry 'so-called' because we have no other conception of it.
(247–8), [283]

The inadvertently telling final comment by the judge underlines the imbalance in the exchange—once again we find Brodsky inhabiting a higher plane of discourse than his interlocutor. The judge's question, which opens the possibility of his verse having some propaganda value, is recast by Brodsky, who deftly replaces the politically charged term *rodina* (родина—translated 'fatherland' above, actually 'motherland') with the neutral *liudi* (люди—'people', 'men').[37] Brodsky's *credo*—'I am convinced . . . I believe'—further distances him from mere patriotism by encompassing future generations of people as potential beneficiaries. Here, as in Brodsky's future writings, the timelessness of literature stands in stark contrast to the temporality—and the temporariness—of political organization. People live and die, arrange themselves socially in various ways, but their language almost always survives them, just as it preceded them. This concept forms the basis for Brodsky's idea of the social function of poetry:

---

[37] Brodsky also avoids using *narod* (народ—'the people', 'nation').

poetry as older and therefore of greater endurance and larger significance, than politics.

THE POET *v.* SOCIETY

We might venture that the imperturbable individualism that Brodsky displayed throughout his life, and which is so clearly evidenced in the transcript of his trial, forms the psychological basis for his poetics. As he told the graduating class of Williams College in 1984, individualism is not just the free expression of the self—it requires constant self-scrutiny and adjustment. It is, at its base, the conscientious taking of an ethical stance:

> the surest defense against Evil is extreme individualism, originality of thinking, whimsicality, even—if you will—eccentricity. That is, something that can't be feigned, faked, imitated; something even a seasoned impostor couldn't be happy with. Something, in other words, that can't be shared, like your own skin: not even by a minority. Evil is a sucker for solidity. It always goes for big numbers. (LTO, 385)

At the heart of this notion of individualism are the related Brodskian virtues of creativity, veracity, and privacy. Originality and whimsicality are trustworthy because they 'cannot be faked'—they are inimitable— and because they 'cannot be shared'—they are properly yours and only yours. These are, uncoincidentally, the qualities which Brodsky finds epitomized in poetry. For the author of the poem, but also for reader, the poem 'hoists a question mark over the individual' (GR, 82), calling into question his very individuality, forcing him to re-examine his conscience in this light. This view of poetry as extreme individuator is the foundation of Brodsky's defence of poetry, and explains for him the antipathy he has experienced between state and poet.

In 'The Social Function of Poetry' Eliot argued that by resuscitating and refining those linguistic elements common to people of variously constituted social groups, poetry could safeguard local culture while facilitating intercultural communication. Thus cultural relations within and among nations could play a role parallel to existing economic and political relations in bettering the local and the common goods. The Brodskian view shares Eliot's basic trust in culture as a timeless source and resource, but Brodsky's project is far from Eliot's. He is not, at least in his early career, concerned with issues of international reconciliation, nor does he show any interest in the idea of an 'international fraternity of men of letters'. Neither is he content for culture to enjoy equal status with economics and politics. Instead, Brodsky completely destabilizes Eliot's balancing act by subjugating the latter two categories, as modes of mere social organization, to poetry. Whereas Eliot accreted the social utility of poetry from reader to community to nation to world, Brodsky devolves the authority of poetry directly from the cultural wellspring to the individual.

Brodsky speaks repeatedly of poetry as something that 'cannot be shared'. The problem with politics, from Brodsky's individualistic point of view, is that it depends on a consensus—a shared view—be it large or small, free or forced. In every kind of political organization, from totalitarianism to democracy, the individual is necessarily subsumed by the collective. Poetry's individuating counter-effect is that it elicits the 'instinctive desire' on the part of 'every social order—be it a democracy, autocracy, theocracy, ideocracy, or bureaucracy—to compromise or belittle the authority of poetry' (GR, 81–2). In his Nobel acceptance speech, Brodsky connects 'solidity' and 'big numbers'—the Evil against which he warned in his Williams address—to political organization, personified by 'champions of the common good, masters of the masses, heralds of historical necessity' (GR, 46). Poetic art is here again depicted as a thorn in their side:

For there where art has stepped, where a poem has been read, they discover, in place of the anticipated consent and unanimity, indifference and polyphony. (GR, 46–7)

Brodsky's final oppositions are revelatory, and slightly surprising. Politics is associated with anticipation (i.e. predictability), consent, and unanimity; poetry with discovery (i.e. surprise), indifference, and polyphony. While the first and last pairs are certainly antonymous, consent/indifference are not necessarily contrary, unless indifference is taken to imply dissent. This assumption is characteristic of forms of government in which totalitarianism is justified by the constant forced consent of the citizenry. In such a system, indifference is a marker of heterodoxy, and is therefore as dangerous as an avowed political position. That poetry is an agent of political indifference, and that this is one of its most valuable functions in the lives of men, is a stance only Brodsky could take with any semblance of credibility. His early writing activity as well as his comportment throughout his trial and after testify to the power of that indifference, and the moral authority it earned him.

Related to and following from the individuating/totalizing opposition that Brodsky maintains between poetry and politics are the binary pairs of private/public, veracity/falsehood, heterogeneity/homogeneity, and indifference/consent. A final opposition is temporal: poetry is associated with *timelessness, infinity, present and future,* and *permanence,* while the state is *time-bound, finite, past-tense,* and *temporary.* We have seen how, in 'A Halt in the Desert', Brodsky employs several of these oppositions, setting the condemned Greek church against a Party-sponsored Culture Palace. There, the ancient and destroyed church is kept in the poetical present through the memories of dogs (those loyal beasts) and men, and so stands in contrast to the forgettable presence of the October Concert Hall. That emblem of Culture is rendered past tense before its time, as it were, by the poem, while the true culture of tradition is kept present and constitutes the implied future. Art, in this case represented by Hellenic culture, is the alpha and omega of human existence, the Eden which will be recovered in the Promised Land. Politics, and history its mother, are the quotidian fiddle that comes between: 'When it comes to collapsing time, our trade, I'm afraid, beats history, and smells, rather sharply, of geography' (GR, 441), Brodsky writes. Poetry is not a record of human events; it is the ground upon which those events are played out.

If poetry's individuating effect places it on a superior ethical plane to politics, its timelessness confirms its rights over politics. 'Time worships language' was the line of Auden's that so struck Brodsky during his northern exile. This 'attitude of lesser towards greater' is reciprocated with disdain bordering on contempt:

The revulsion, irony, or indifference often expressed by literature towards the state is essentially a reaction of the permanent—better yet, the infinite—against the temporary, against the finite. (GR, 47)

The authority that this categorical precedence confers on the creator of literature—and Brodsky is thinking of creators of poetry in particular (GR, 46)—is nothing short of total. To put it in Eliotic terms, the poet's 'duty to language' constitutes the highest kind of service, permitting him to scorn, if necessary, even the most ardently enforced social obligations. In attributing this far-reaching authority to the poet, Brodsky comes close to defining a concomitant 'duty to people'. The conflict between poetry and politics arises because poetry is always acting against the imposition of history on the present. But in defending the present, poetry opens up the possibility of a future:

> The philosophy of the state, its ethics—not to mention its aesthetics—are always 'yesterday'. Language and literature are always 'today', and often—particularly in the case where a political system is orthodox—they may even constitute 'tomorrow'. (GR, 48)

Brodsky is talking about an imagined tomorrow, what Seamus Heaney calls a 'glimpsed alternative, a revelation of potential' (RP, 4). Brodsky's idea of the eternal opposition of politics and poetry functions in an ethical crux: he insists that poets preserve their poetry against the politics that seeks to impose past upon present, that they keep poetry, including past poetry, in the realm of the present and future. In so doing, poetry will necessarily enter into conflict with the State, precisely because it resists the State's tendency towards the past tense. As Brodsky warns, 'a man whose profession is grammar is the last one who can afford to forget this' (GR, 47–8).

It is evident that the moral primacy and authority that Brodsky ascribes to poetry result in a purely confrontational—even retributive—approach to any relationship between it and politics. Eliot hoped culture could work in tandem with social institutions for the betterment of people and peoples. As I argue in the next chapter, after a period of cultural protectionism, Heaney becomes committed to a reconciliatory poetics which likens art to 'the writing in the sand in the face of which accusers and accused are left speechless and renewed' (GT, 107). Whether Brodsky would consider the 'accusers'—in his dramatis personae represented by the ideologues, Party officials, and petty functionaries of the State system—potential beneficiaries of poetry is not clear. Brodsky's sociopoetics is not at all reconciliatory. It assumes ineluctable conflict between poet and State, and seeks only to describe that conflict and defend poetry's part in it, as he does in 'To a Tyrant', a poem written in the first month of his last year in Russia. The tyrant is first remembered as a petty functionary:

> Arresting these café habitués—
> he started snuffing out world culture somewhat later—
> seemed sweet revenge (on Time, that is, not them)   (CPE, 55)

Clearly time is on world culture's side in this poem, not least because they share a common enemy: 'And Time has had to stomach that revenge', Brodsky continues. 'Time', here, is Brodsky's appropriated version of Auden's 'Time', Auden's 'Time that is intolerant' ghosting 'Time, that is, not them'. In this poem Time may be more tolerant than in Auden's—it will 'stomach', will *have* to stomach, the assault of a politician, not only on 'café habitués', but eventually also on the culture that has taken so much time to accrue. But to stomach is also to rise above, and the implication is that Time can take its time to digest and expel this temporary aberration from its long story. Even if it is considered successful by short-term instrumentalist criteria, the tyrant's revenge may not turn out as sweet as it once seemed.

In his essay on Osip Mandel´shtam (1977), whose persecution has moved many poets, Russian and Western, to meditate on the writing of poetry under oppressive regimes, Brodsky interprets Mandel´shtam's fate as another manifestation of the predestined clash between poet and State:

> With a poet, one's ethical posture, indeed one's very temperament, is determined and shaped by one's aesthetics. This is what accounts for poets finding themselves invariably at odds with the social reality. (LTO, 139)

Heaney too has deliberated on the tragedy of Mandel´shtam's persecution. Because his ambition was only 'to allow poems to form in language inside him', Heaney says, his 'responsibility was to sound rather than to the state, to language rather than to five-year plans, to etymology rather than to economics. . . . He therefore stands for the efficacy of song itself, an emblem of the poet as potent sound-wave' (GT, xix–xx). For Brodsky the issue is not one of efficacy or potency, it is one of superiority and endurance. Being shipped to the gulag is no sign of strength or influence, as Brodsky knows from experience. Brodsky avoids Heaney's romantic image of poet under government duress while retaining the audacity of the claim for poetry. The state's treatment of Mandel´shtam was not a reaction of the weak to the strong; rather it was the reaction of the inferior to the superior, of the temporary to the eternal:

> For lyricism is the ethics of language and the superiority of this lyricism to anything that could be achieved within human interplays of whatever denomination, is what makes for a work of art and lets it survive. That is why the iron broom, whose purpose was the spiritual castration of the entire populace, couldn't have missed him. (LTO, 137)

Though the 'iron broom' is a potent and effective way of dealing with poets, it is no match for poetry itself. The 'ethics of language' will always outlast and in the long run outperform the will of power, since power waxes and wanes, whereas language endures:

He worked in Russian poetry for thirty years, and what he did will last as long as the Russian language exists. It will certainly outlast the present and any subsequent regime in that country, because of both its lyricism and its profundity. (LTO, 138)

It is not so much a vindication of the poet as it is a confirmation of poetry itself. By allowing himself to be a tool of language the poet chooses the way of permanence. As Brodsky insists, 'art is never owned—neither by its patrons nor even by the artists themselves. It has its own self-generating dynamics, its own logic, its own pedigree and its own future.'[38] This autonomy guarantees its survival, and through it, the endurance of poets and artists.

Brodsky's poetics, since it orders poetry before and above social organization, baulks at placing any specific social burden on the poet. Instead the onus is placed on society to read its poets and thereby advance itself. In the manner of Eliot, Brodsky triangulates the poet's duty to society via his duty to language, to 'write well' (LTO, 359; GR, 205), and thereby appears to excuse him from direct consideration of his social impact. But for someone who writes, 'I am quite positive that a man who reads poetry is harder to prevail upon than one who doesn't' (GR, 61), it is hard to maintain authorial remove. When envisaging the poet's relationship with an individual reader as opposed to a readership or a society, Brodsky is willing to take on a measure of responsibility. In a formulation reminiscent of Heaney's invocation of 'the rhythmic contract of metre and iambic pentameter' which 'implies audience',[39] Brodsky writes:

Art basically is an operation within a certain contract, and you have to abide by all the clauses of the contract. You write poetry, to begin with, in order to influence minds, to influence hearts, to *move* hearts, to move people.[40]

In this uncharacteristically pragmatic assertion, Brodsky seems to have exceeded the Horatian aims of poetic writing to include Cicero's third

[38] Joseph Brodsky, 'Why Milan Kundera is Wrong about Dostoyevsky', *The New York Times* (17 February 1985), BR31.
[39] Seamus Heaney, interview with James Randall, *Ploughshares* 5:3 (1979), 7–22, 16.
[40] Quoted in Montenegro, *Points of Departure*, 140; original emphasis.

goal of oratory, 'to move'.[41] The difference is that Brodsky is not concerned with influencing minds in the direction of a particular proposition or argument, but in the direction of poetry itself and the aesthetic mode of valuation it requires. Just as in a legal contract two parties are bound by their word, in the lyrical contract readers' minds and hearts are moved closer to the poet's—and through him, closer to art and to all the ethical felicities which Brodsky associates with it. To achieve the kind of 'movement' he describes, Brodsky continues, 'you have to produce something that has an appearance of inevitability and that is memorable, so that it will stick in the mind of the reader'.[42] For all its rejection of social orders, Brodsky's poetics is in fact a social theory of poetry: it describes how, through the writing and reading of poetry, members of societies can maintain their individuality within social systems that seek always to compromise it. In other words, Brodsky offers literary experience and the attendant development of aesthetic judgement as an internal check, enabling individuals to function autonomously within the social framework.

For all that, Brodsky's dogged self-distancing from politics could not make him an autonomous, apolitical figure. As Mikhail Gorbachev was winding down the Soviet empire and liberalizing Russian society, the Swedish Academy for the Prize in Literature passed over contenders Octavio Paz, V. S. Naipaul, and Mario Vargas Llosa to select Brodsky, instantly prompting comparisons with previous Kremlin bugbears Alexander Solzhenitsyn (winner in 1970) and Boris Pasternak (in 1958),[43] and continuing the Academy's Reagan-era penchant for 'dissident' poets from the Eastern bloc.[44] Their decision was felt in Moscow, where the Soviet Foreign Ministry spokesman commented wryly that 'the tastes of the Nobel committee are somewhat strange sometimes...

---

[41] Cf. Cicero, *De Oratore* II.xxviii.121: 'quibus ex locis ad eas tres res, quae ad fidem faciendam solae valent, ducatur oratio, ut et concilientur animi et doceantur et moveantur' ('Dealing with those commonplaces from which may be drawn a speech such as to attain those three things which alone can carry conviction; I mean the winning over, the instructing and the stirring of men's minds'). The translation is from the Loeb Classical Library text, trans. E. W. Sutton (London: William Heinemann, 1959), 285.

[42] Quoted in Montenegro, *Points of Departure*, 140.

[43] See Tony Barber, 'Brodsky Prize Recalls Past Sensitive Awards to Soviet Writers', *Reuters News* (22 October 1987), and David Remnick, 'Soviet Exile Wins Nobel for Literature', *Washington Post* (23 October 1987), A1.

[44] In addition to Brodsky in 1987, the Academy honoured Czesław Miłosz in 1980 and Jaroslav Seifert in 1984.

sometimes there is a political aftertaste'.[45] In a moment widely felt as an instance of poetic justice—a verdict on Brodsky that was completely the reverse of the one he had heard two decades previously in Leningrad— still Brodsky avoided being co-opted into a game of political spin. Instead of indulging the sense of justice that his friends and admirers felt on his behalf, Brodsky used the occasion to deny the instrumental political value of literature, to deny even the value of the politically instrumental, while repeating and reinforcing his ethical claim for literature. While acknowledging all sorts of personal or public psychological motivations for writing a poem, at the Nobel podium Brodsky described poetry not as reflecting a relation between poet and state or poet and people, but as instigating a relation between poet and language which is really a 'flight' from the social relation, a movement towards the private, the unique, the artistic, and the ethical.

THE POEM AND THE PERSON, FACE TO FACE

How does poetry move people? How does it promote individuality, and through this, autonomy? In what way does it give birth to ethics? In this final section I want to reconstruct a Brodskian answer to these questions by interrogating his famous maxim, 'aesthetics is the mother of ethics' via a second recurrent figure in his prose. This is the image of the human face, a figure which for Brodsky can encompass both the aesthetic and the ethical value of literary art. These two figures—art as mother, art as face—are related but separate metaphors that extend the aesthetic into the ethical. To understand their relation to each other is to understand Brodsky's idea of how poetry works on the individual, how it helps one to realize one's own individuality.

An idiosyncrasy of Brodsky's theory of poetry's effects on readers is that it appears to be derived from his broader social theory, and not, as one might expect, vice versa. So, often we find statements about the function of literature coloured by typically Brodskian negative associations of the State with the time-bound, the historical, and the public:

One of literature's merits is precisely that it helps a person to make the time of his existence more specific, to distinguish himself from the crowd of his

---

[45] Quoted in 'Soviet-Born Poet Awarded Nobel Prize for Literature', *Toronto Star* (23 October 1987), A3.

predecessors as well as his like numbers, to avoid tautology—that is, the fate otherwise known by the honorific term, 'victim of history'. (GR, 48)

'Tautology' is the logico-linguistic manifestation of 'historical necessity', that concept which the State invariably invokes *post facto* on its own behalf. The tyranny that 'necessity' imposes on the individual can be and is resisted in art, since 'aesthetic necessity', according to Brodsky, is 'a contradiction in terms'.[46] Because aesthetics is 'a linear phenomenon', he writes, 'it has no retroactive power over its progress.'[47] The experience of reading poetry is, because of this, a way for the reader to place himself outside the deterministic ontology of his social system. To 'make the time of his existence more specific' is to extricate the reader from history itself, to restore him to his individuality and autonomy.

The individual's existence outside a historically determined universe is more free, more aware, and more amenable to an ethical understanding. Recasting his maxim, 'aesthetics is the mother of ethics', Brodsky writes, 'the categories of "good" and "bad" are, first and foremost, aesthetic ones, at least etymologically preceding the categories of "good" and "evil"' (GR, 49).[48] The more one experiences aesthetically, the closer one is to making sense of one's own ethics: this is because art exists 'by continually creating a new aesthetic reality' and because 'every new aesthetic reality makes man's ethical reality more precise' (GR, 48, 49). Brodsky is talking about taste, the developed faculty of aesthetic judgement, which is refined with the accumulation of aesthetic experience. He pushes the subsuming of the ethical categories good/evil by the aesthetic categories good/bad when he identifies taste as an essential contributor to the moral sense:

evil, especially political evil, is always a bad stylist. The more substantial an individual's aesthetic experience is, the sounder his taste, the sharper his moral focus, the freer—though not necessarily the happier—he is. (GR, 49–50)

The immanence of the faculty of taste guarantees its veracity. Because it is felt immediately, privately, and undeniably by the subject, it cannot be subverted by argument or suppressed by the collective will: 'Aesthetic choice is a highly individual matter, and aesthetic experience is always a

---

[46] Brodsky, 'Kundera', BR31.
[47] Ibid.
[48] It is not clear what Brodsky means by 'etymologically' here, as he is comparing *khorosho* (хорошо—'good') and *plokho* (плохо—'bad') with non-cognates *dobra* (добра—'good') and *zla* (зла—'evil').

private one. Every new aesthetic reality makes one's experience even more private' (GR, 49).

For Brodsky, aesthetic experience creates and conditions the judging self. It is chronologically as well as categorically previous. To illustrate his point that the categories of 'good' and 'bad' are 'first and foremost aesthetic ones', Brodsky invokes the image of 'The tender babe who cries and rejects the stranger or who, on the contrary, reaches out to him' as exemplifying the original and instinctive aesthetic imperative, calling the baby's rejection an 'aesthetic choice, not a moral one' (GR, 49). Beginning at this moment, and continuing throughout the life of the self, aesthetic encounter returns the self to itself, affirming and confirming its individuality:

Being the most ancient as well as the most literal form of private enterprise, [art] fosters in a man, knowingly or unwittingly, a sense of his uniqueness, of individuality, of separateness—thus turning him from a social animal into an autonomous 'I'. (GR, 46)

'Separateness' here is the key feature of the autonomous self. The self's separateness may at first be realized as a separateness from the artwork itself, as a recognition of the artwork's uniqueness that provokes a corresponding recognition of one's own uniqueness. Though the art-work is not 'unknowable', it resists attempts to reduce its difference, and the revelation of that difference dislocates the self from totality, drawing a line around the separateness of the self. The constitution of the self is, in this sense, essentially relational (though not exactly the product of a relationship), depending on aesthetic encounter with a separate, differ-ent, unique other.

I closed the last section with Brodsky's declaration that the poet writes primarily in order to influence as well as to instruct and delight. Even in this atypically prescriptive declaration, Brodsky avoids specify-ing a particular destination towards which audiences should move, saying only that they should be moved towards literature and the literary per se. In fact, 'should' is a rare word in the Brodskian vocabulary, and this points to a salient feature of his poetics: that it is not, in fact, an aesthetic theory at all, in the sense that Horace intended for his *Ars Poetica*—not a set of principles or maxims to guide and inform creation. Brodsky's poetics might more accurately be called a proto-ethics, or a meta-ethics, a proposed context in which one's judging self is formed and operates. His repeated assertion that aesthetics is 'the mother' of ethics expresses this relationship well: for Brodsky, the aesthetic sense gives birth to the ethical sense; it creates the environment in which ethics comes to exist and in which it is nourished. It is in this sense that an aesthetically individuated reader can be said to act ethically or unethically—without aesthetic experience he acts only as a cog in the vast self-perpetuating social engine, an ethical automaton.

If there is a conflict between art and politics, it is because politics always seeks to incorporate the individual into the collective, to deny him the creativity, the veracity, and the privacy that are the signs of his individuality, whereas art always seeks to promote these. This distinction may be sharpest when it comes to Soviet politics, but it also applies to other forms of social organization, indeed to social organization in general. In an interview not published in English, Brodsky predicts a bureaucratic future where the self and other collapse into an undifferentiated mass, into an all-encompassing social 'process'. Of his own analysis, he says,

This certainly irritates (rubs the wrong way) all those who speak of socialism per se, of the human face of socialism, etc. I find it hard to imagine any future 'ism' having a very impersonal and bureaucratic face.[49]

'The human face of socialism' is a commonplace intended to emphasize the theoretical humanitarianism of socialism, its avowed concern for the less and least fortunate in society, its inherent values taken separately from whatever atrocities can be pinned on Stalin or Mao. But for Brodsky, who contradicts the cliché just by literalizing it, there is nothing 'human' about state bureaucracy. The image that this particular bureaucracy could and did deploy to represent its beneficence was similarly devoid of anything suggesting a real human being: the Soviet portraits of Lenin that 'plagued almost every textbook, every class wall, postage stamps, money' were 'utterly lacking in character', with 'nothing specific in that face' (LTO, 5–6).

When human faces appear in Brodsky's poetry, often they are faces imprisoned in a social order that seeks to erase their individuality. In 'Nature Morte' (1971), one of the last poems Brodsky would write in

[49] 'Cela prend certainement à rebrousse-poil tous ceux qui parlent du socialisme en soi, du socialisme à visage humain, etc. J'imagine mal pour l'avenir un quelconque « isme » ayant un visage humain. Il aura un visage très impersonnel et bureaucratique.' Joseph Brodsky, 'Joseph Brodsky: poésie et dissidence', *L'Infini* 21 (Spring 1988), 54–9, 55.

the Soviet Union, he contrasts people and things, finally preferring things:

> People are not my thing.
>
> .   .   .   .
>
> Grafted to life's great tree,
> each face is firmly stuck
> and cannot be torn free.
>
> Something the mind abhors
> shows in each face and form.   (JBSP, 161)

What the mind abhors is the fiction of collective flourishing; it abhors the slavery of group thought, which is 'Something like flattery | of persons quite unknown', as Brodsky says. In a later poem entitled 'An Admonition' (1986), Brodsky gives advice to the lone visitor to the East: 'Try not to stand out—either in profile or | full face; simply don't wash your face at times' (CPE, 357). The conceit of the poem is a list of prudent advice given to a traveller in a strange land, but the real stranger is the addressee; in the country where he finds himself, everything and everyone is conspiring to kill his strangeness, to 'blend your flesh with the earth'. The stratagem for survival is to hide what is different, what is unique, about his face.

Brodsky thinks about the state and the effects of State culture in terms of inhuman, characterless, unspecific faces. Art, on the other hand, is often imagined in terms of genuine, individuated faces. If aesthetic experience is the source of individuation, its emblem is the human face: unique, untransferable, and irreproducible. For instance, Brodsky is attracted to Dante's idea that 'the notion of beauty was contingent on the beholder's ability to discern in the human face's oval just seven letters comprising the term "Homo Dei"' (GR, 89).[50] The conceit would have the face as both a picture and a grammar, an arrangement of letters and words into meaning. In this arrangement the

---

[50] Brodsky gets the orthography wrong in his reference to Dante's invocation in *Purgatorio*, Canto XXIII, of the medieval idea that God had 'signed' the human face with the (six) letters O, M, O, D, E, I ('man of God'). The face could thus be represented pictorially with the Os as eyes, M as eyebrows and nose, D as ears, and horizontal E and I as nostrils and mouth, as so:

Dante's passage is ambiguous as to whether he himself (or even his narrator) subscribes to this belief, as Brodsky strongly implies.

aesthetic recognition of beauty is joined with the ethical recognition of shared humanity. Brodsky makes a similar alignment in his Nobel acceptance speech, where he recognizes the Dantesque picto-grammatical face, with the help of art, even inside the 'big numbers' for which Evil is such a sucker:

> into the little zeros with which the champions of the common good and the rulers of the masses tend to operate, art introduces a 'period, period, comma, and a minus,' transforming each zero into a tiny human, albeit not always pretty, face. (GR, 47)

The 'little zeros' are in the first place markers of magnitude—the hundreds, thousands, and millions, etc., that give weight to official numbers. But for the individual subsumed into them they also represent his nilness, the erasure of his individuality. The action of art in Brodsky's figuration—here again a cross between drawing and writing, centred in the facial oval—is a restoration of individuality, of humanity, a filling in of blanks with eyes (period, period), nose (comma), and mouth (minus).[51] From this artistic palimpsest of the grammatical over the numerical can come the image of a face, a sign of human individuality and proof of the existence of individuated selves within the mass of millions. Conversely, the changefulness of the human face is representative of possibilities of linguistic expression: the poet, Brodsky writes, 'discerns in that changing oval far more than the seven letters of *Homo Dei*; he discerns the entire alphabet, in all its combinations, i.e. the language' (GR, 93–4).

In an early post-exile poem (1976), Brodsky reverses the relation, discerning a Dantean face in letters, even as he puts them to paper:

> Men's lives turn into scratches of pen on paper, into the stitching of letters,
> their tiny wedges and hooks; and—since it is slippery work—
> into commas and colons. Only consider
> how often, meaning to write the letter 'M' in some word,
> the pen will have stumbled and fashioned two eyebrows instead.
> That is, ink on the page is more honest than blood.[52]

---

[51] For instance:

[52] Joseph Brodsky, 'December in Florence', trans. George Kline and Maurice English, *Shearsman* 7 (1982), 19–21. I have quoted from this translation because the one by Brodsky included in CPE is, especially in this stanza, nearly unreadable. See CPE, 130–2.

In Dante's story, emaciated faces on purgatory mountain reveal under their tautening skin the hidden 'M' God put there when He signed Creation. Here the poet is writing his own self into the work, seeing for an instant his own face on the page, as if looking into a mirror. 'Read the work' was Brodsky's admonishment when it came to Solzhenitsyn's life story. He would later write, 'A poet's biography is in his vowels and sibilants, in his meters, rhymes, and metaphors' (GR, 164). The image of the face moves metaphorically between the two planes on which the writer exists: he is both a human being with a human face and a led life, and also a corpus into which he has written his life and signed his grammatical 'face'.

The trope that would conceive of literature in terms of the face and vice versa is developed in Brodsky's Nobel lecture, where he quotes from Evgeniĭ Baratynskiĭ's 1829 poem 'Муза' (*Muza*—'[The] Muse'), in which the power of poetry is conveyed by the muse's 'лица необщим выраженьем' (*litsa neobshchim vyrazhen'em*): by her original, uncommon, or singular facial expression. Jill Higgs renders this phrase as 'rare expression'.[53] Barry Rubin, who translates Brodsky's Nobel address into English, chooses 'uncommon visage', which is the title Brodsky gives to the reprinted translation in his 1996 collection of essays. Brodsky writes:

The great Baratynsky, speaking of his Muse, characterized her as possessing an 'uncommon visage'. It's in acquiring this 'uncommon visage' that the meaning of human existence seems to lie, since for this uncommonness we are, as it were, prepared genetically. (GR, 47)

If the human being considered by himself is genetically prepared for originality and singularity, for rareness of expression or uncommonness of countenance, there is still work to be done in nurturing this predisposition into fulfilment. This involves self-extraction from the social fabric and is achieved mainly through literary experience. 'At the speed of the turning page', Brodsky writes, reading generates a 'movement', which is nothing like a political movement or even a literary movement, but is instead an individual's 'flight from the common denominator':

This flight is the flight in the direction of 'uncommon visage', in the direction of the numerator, in the direction of autonomy, in the direction of privacy. (GR, 51–2)

---

[53] Evgeniĭ Abramovich Baratynskiĭ, *Selected Poems of Yevgeny Abramovitch Baratynsky*, trans. Jill Higgs (Spalding: Hub Editions, 2004), 115.

In other words, via literature the individual can escape the collective in the direction of his own individuality. Here, as everywhere in Brodsky, escape and estrangement from the political are helped and hastened by encounter and engagement with the aesthetic. The 'uncommon visage' beckons the individual out of the mass, helping him towards the autonomy and privacy of which it is itself a symbol, and for which he is already 'prepared genetically'. Thus the face, in its physical uniqueness as much as in its expressive changefulness—which is to say, in its uncommonness—is a sign of the individuality and the humanity of human persons, and is simultaneously symbolic of the originality, difference, polyphony, and veracity of art. 'Acquiring' it may mean developing one's own rareness of expression, but to do so involves first seeking out and encountering the uncommon visage of literature.

The encounter with literature is repeatedly figured by Brodsky as an encounter of faces. It is a face-watching or an eye-gazing, a meeting of souls and minds, the pondering of a photograph of a lost and somehow loved person. Brodsky describes the poem as address, a vocative which engages the reader head-to-head:

Lots of things can be shared... but not a poem by, say, Rainer Maria Rilke. A work of art, of literature especially, and a poem in particular, addresses a man *tête-à-tête*, entering with him into direct—free of any go-betweens—relations. (GR, 46)

Paul Celan famously compared the poem to a handshake.[54] The goodwill that the figure of the handshake connotes—the open, proffered hand, the facing of one to another, the mutual reception—all of these are bound up in the positive association between truth and poem that Celan makes. Brodsky's figure of the *tête-à-tête* reproduces these associations even more affectingly: it is a facing towards one another, a proximity of faces which reveals the one to the other. As in Celan's handshaking, in Brodsky's face meeting the moment of aesthetic encounter gives rise to the ethical revelation of another's humanity.

One can usefully extend Brodsky's metaphor of aesthetics giving birth to ethics, by thinking of the face-to-face as the moment of conception of ethics. This extension is already implicit in much of

---

[54] In a letter to Hans Bender dated 18 May 1960, Celan writes, 'Nur wahre Hände schreiben wahre Gedichte. Ich sehe keinen prinzipiellen Unterschied zwischen Händedruck und Gedicht.' ('Only true hands write true poems. I see no difference in principle between a handshake and a poem.') Paul Celan, *Collected Prose*, trans. Rosmarie Waldrop (Manchester: Carcanet, 1986), 28.

Brodsky's prose, for there is something very intimate, something both immanent and imminent—indeed something pregnant—in the way he treats faces. He dwells on them, especially when they are those of friends or of artists he admires. He writes that 'I fell in love with a photograph of Samuel Beckett long before I'd read a line of his' (LTO, 22). He lingers even more intently on the faces in a photograph of his poet-friends Spender and Auden: 'Stephen is much taller than any of us, and there is an almost detectable tenderness in his profile as he faces Wystan, who, hands in his pockets, is immensely cheered. Their eyes meet; at this juncture, they have known each other for forty years, and they are happy in each other's company' (GR, 465–6). Reminiscing about a lunch, he is again drawn to Spender's face: 'Isaiah Berlin is there, and also my wife, who cannot take her young eyes off Stephen's face' (GR, 478). When asked in an interview what he most misses about Russia, Brodsky replies, 'Several faces, and an element of unpredictability in human relations.'[55] In another interview, he meditates again on the face of his revered and beloved friend: 'When I look at [Auden], it is like seeing a landscape. But when he raises his eyebrows, I see what I always saw in the photographs of Auden as an unwrinkled young man: that strange nose, so formal, but a bit surprised, as in his poetry.'[56] This close focus on features, which is at once a reading-into and a drawing-out-of, is typical of Brodsky's attention to faces, as is his return at the end of his description to Auden's verse. Faces are more than representative, for Brodsky; they are revelatory. In the case of Auden, his face seems to personify his writing. The appearance of the face can be intimate, but it can also intimate in the way that art intimates.

In his conversations with Solomon Volkov, Brodsky is drawn into an extended description of the face of the man whom he had called 'the greatest mind of the 20th Century' (LTO, 358) and for whom he felt 'sentiments...of the intensity which should be reserved...for the figures of the Creed'.[57] Volkov prompts him:

VOLKOV: ...Could you describe Auden's face to me?

BRODSKY: It's often compared to a map. In fact, it did resemble a map, with the eyes in the middle. That's how creased it was, with wrinkles fanning out

[55] Brodsky, interview with Noel Russell, *Literary Review* (January 1986), 10–12, 10.
[56] Levy, 'Think it Over Brodsky', 8.
[57] Brodsky, interview with Russell, 12.

in all directions. Auden's face reminded me of the surface of a lizard or a tortoise.

VOLKOV: Stravinsky complained that to see how Auden actually looked, you would have to iron out his face. Henry Moore went into raptures over the 'monumental ruggedness of his face, its deep furrows like plow marks crossing a field'. Auden himself jokingly compared his face to a wedding cake after a rain.

BRODSKY: It was a striking face. If I could choose a face for myself, I'd choose either Auden's or Beckett's. More likely Auden's.

VOLKOV: When Auden got to talking, did his face move? Did it come alive?

BRODSKY: Yes, it was very expressive.[58]

Volkov and Brodsky are having fun with a mini-tradition of physiognomic joking about Auden's features. Brodsky starts it, but when Volkov begins to list off famous quips (not mentioning David Hockney's unmentionable one),[59] Brodsky seems less willing to play along, becoming suddenly sincere. Brodsky's initial face-as-map image—a hybrid of the commonplace 'his face was an open book' and Brodsky's previous 'like seeing a landscape' simile—is much more in accord with how he feels about the human face. In Brodsky's image Auden's wrinkles spread out concentrically from the eyes, which, as the givers and receivers of gaze, constitute the meeting point of observer and observed, as in Brodsky's description of the Auden-Spender photograph. Through his figuration, Auden's most recognizable facial feature—his deep furrows—can be seen to direct our eyes from his face's periphery towards its centre, finally to the eyes which confront us with a reciprocal gaze. The *bons mots* of Stravinsky, Moore, and Auden himself lack this element of encountering, as much in their concept as in their rhetorical neatness.

Volkov asks if Auden's face 'came alive' when he started talking, which allows Brodsky to continue downplaying 'monumental' comparisons. The contrast between a monument and a 'very expressive' face is one to which Brodsky later returns in some detail: recalling a boyhood experience of casting shadows on a Roman marble, he writes, 'At once her facial expression changed. I moved my hand a bit to the side: it changed again' (GR, 275). Brodsky refers to the sculpture as a *fanciulla*, a maiden or young girl,[60]

---

[58] Volkov, *Conversations*, 125.

[59] Alan Bennett attributes this remark to Hockney: 'I kept thinking, if his face looks like this, what must his balls look like?' See Bennett, *Writing Home* (London: Faber and Faber, 1994), 515.

[60] Also, an artwork depicting a young girl. A *fanciulla* is a marriageable but unmarried girl, and in this liminal condition she is often represented in art as either sexually inviting,

suggesting if only briefly an erotic dimension to the story. He is Pygmalion bringing Galatea to life, but the animating gesture, which metaphorizes both erotic and imaginative creation, is squarely focused on the face: 'I began moving both my arms rather frantically, casting each time a different shadow upon her features: the face came to life' (GR, 275). The association between procreation and art-creation is part and parcel of the concept of the muse,[61] and it is at the heart of the Pygmalion myth. In Brodsky's appropriation of this myth we see an example of the 'uncommon visage' that he associates with his muse. The ever-changing facial expression is like the 'very expressive' face of the poet, which is like his verse. As if commenting on his earlier invocation, via Dante, of the poet discerning the entire alphabet in a changing face, or again on his description of Auden's nose as possessing similar qualities to his poetry, Brodsky says of his *fanciulla*, 'there are ways of turning viewing into reading' (GR, 275).

In a late essay, one of his very last, Brodsky tries, but ultimately fails, to turn a reading into a viewing, and here too, coincidentally, a poet's nose figures centrally. Even if he gives Heaney the impression of being already in an 'intimate, face-to-face relationship with the masters',[62] in a paean to his favourite Roman poets (Horace, Propertius, Virgil), Brodsky professes his longing for a real-life face-to-face meeting. In 'A Letter to Horace', he enters into a kind of direct address:

Ah, what I wouldn't give to know what the four of you looked like! To put a face to the lyric, not to mention the epic. (GR, 432)

The register is more conversational than it is epistolary—Brodsky wants the relation between him and his imagined (albeit historical) interlocutor

---

as in Giovanni Boldini's *Fanciulla sdraiata*, or ambiguously as both childish and seductive, as in Francesco Gioli's *Fanciulla in riva al mare*.

[61] In the extended or allusive sense of the word: see OED3, 'muse, *n.*[1]' 2a: 'The inspiring goddess of a particular poet; (hence)... the character of a particular poet's style'; and 2c: 'A person (often a female lover) or thing regarded as the source of an artist's inspiration.' In his treatment of Brodsky's 1983 poem 'Galatea Encore', Leon Burnett observes that 'Galatea may be regarded as an incarnation of the creative principle in art, which male poets have traditionally associated with the Muse of composition.' The poem, Burnett argues, may be read 'as a meta-commentary on writing poetry in English, that is to say, on a literary activity that goes beyond "the process of composition" to encompass what Brodsky referred to at the start of his 1987 Nobel Lecture as "the creative process itself"'. See Burnett, 'Galatea Encore', in Lev Losev and Valentina Polukhina (eds), *Joseph Brodsky: The Art of the Poem* (New York: Palgrave, 1999), 150–76, 155.

[62] Heaney, 'Brodsky's Nobel', BR1.

to be informal and intimate, despite his temporal remoteness. But the one-on-one tone, set against this remoteness, only highlights the un-availability of the poets' faces. Though Brodsky is writing to Horace, it is the face of Publius Ovidius Naso—Ovid, nicknamed 'The Nose'—that most frustrates his imagination:

No, I never could conjure Naso's face. Sometimes I see him played by James Mason—a hazel eye soggy with grief and mischief; at other times, though, it's Paul Newman's winter-gray stare. (GR, 433)

Brodsky calls Ovid by his lesser known cognomen, employing the same defamiliarization he had practised in his early elegy for Eliot. 'Naso' names a man; 'Ovid', like 'W. B. Yeats' and 'T. S. Eliot', names a literary corpus. Imagining the man's face only produces ersatz like-nesses—stock images borrowed from the popular imagination. That the face of an actor may come to represent iconically some particular human characteristic (Mason equals expressive emotion, Newman taci-turn toughness) is not in itself surprising or disappointing: dramatic roles are by their nature simplifications of human personality. But this simplified face, the face of fixed significance, is in the end of no significance compared with the 'very expressive' face, the changing face, which can only be discerned in the poetry. 'Naso was a very protean fellow, with Janus no doubt presiding over his lares' (GR, 433), Brodsky writes, but for all that he 'never assumed anyone else's shape' (GR, 458). No number of stock images can encompass the variety and uniqueness present in the work. No imagined face will do justice to it, but no imagining is necessary because of the presence of that work:

I can't conjure up your faces, [Naso's] especially; not even in a dream. Funny, isn't it, not to have any idea how those whom you think you know most intimately looked? For nothing is more revealing than one's use of iambs and trochees. (GR, 434)

The truest representation of Naso the man is, finally, Ovid the corpus. His poetry intimates and is intimate; it is 'revealing' of the other. And even as Brodsky finds it impossible to conjure up a visage, a visage is unveiled in the form of iambs and trochees. Again using the less publicly recognizable, and so more intimate address, Brodsky tells Horace, 'So stay faceless, Flaccus, stay unconjured. This way you may last for two millennia more' (GR, 441). The potential for direct relations, for the revelation that the face comes to symbolize for Brodsky, is already fully present in the poetry. Brodsky only demands—and it is a great de-mand—that the reader engage head-to-head, or face-to-face, with that potentiality.

Two main objections might now be registered against Brodsky's 'meta-ethics', as I have attempted to describe it. The first of these would note that in promoting the ethical value of aesthetic experience, Brodsky disregards the other, much more usual sense of the phrase 'aesthetic value', that is, the relative success, assessed on aesthetic grounds, of a work of art. We know, or think we know, that there are many more bad poets than good ones. How does bad poetry figure, if at all, in the shaping of the judging self? Brodsky himself seems to have this problem in mind when he expresses the evidently untenable position that he would forgive a good poet for his bad deeds, but not necessarily vice versa.[63] If this exaggeration is meant to highlight Brodsky's prefer-ence for cultural possessions over civic institutions, it succeeds at being true to the spirit of his poetics, but it also points to an important gap there: if the private, individual self has his autonomy, and so his ethical judgement, fostered and nurtured by aesthetic experience, what fosters and nurtures his aesthetic judgement?

The answer to this first objection is in some ways a concession, with an elaboration that may only be partially satisfactory. It is true that almost nowhere in Brodsky's many essays about the value of poetry does he address the seemingly relevant (though not easy) question of poetic content, nor is he likely to give illustrative examples of either 'good' or 'bad' technique, imagery, or subject matter. It is not that such judging is impossible; it is presumed to happen as a matter of course. Rather, the 'good' or 'bad' of art appears not relevant to the essential moment of encounter, not an important factor in the forming and fostering of the separate and autonomous 'I'. Whatever the content of a poem, its effect is the same: Brodsky writes that the authority of poetry 'hoists a question mark over the individual himself, over his achievements and mental security, over his very significance' (GR, 82). This disruption, dislocation, or interruption of the self is central to Brodsky's aesthetics, and to the ethics it engenders. Volkov has observed that, 'to an extent I've never observed in anyone else', Brodsky's 'mind was essentially

---

[63] In a seeming echo of Auden's line about Time forgiving everyone who lives by language, Brodsky says, 'I would say that even if I know a person is dreadful I would be the first to find justifications for that dreadfulness if the writing was good.' See Brodsky, 'The Art of Poetry XXVIII', 116.

dialogic... with everything existing in flux, subject to open-ended questioning by a free mind. [He] thrived on paradox, ambiguity, and contrariness.'[64] For Brodsky, wherever poetry is being experienced, the reading self is being called into question, called to account, and through this interrogation or interpellation, may be reconfirmed as an individual.

The second objection is more fundamental. It can be stated like this: Isn't Brodsky's autonomous 'I' an unabashedly egotistical self, concerned only with itself, detached from and insouciant of the others who make up the world? In other words, isn't Brodsky's 'I' a totalizing 'I', attempting to incorporate existence into itself just as ravenously as the State attempts to incorporate existence? Hasn't Brodsky only countered one totalization with a competing totalization? If so, all this talk of ethics is at best a category confusion. At worst it is a self-justificatory, self-promoting sham, played at the cost of sincere, perhaps even constructive deliberations over what ethical responsibility towards others might mean.

In this respect calling Brodsky's defence of poetry a 'meta-ethics' is an important precision. In almost all of his writings on poetics, it is language and the forms it takes in literature that incite duties of responsibility, not other people. In other words, Brodsky's ethics is devotedly focused on the other; only the other in this case is language. And here a feature of the first objection returns to inform an answer to the second. Brodsky is reluctant to give instances of ethical verse, speaking mostly synoptically or in generalities, because quotation immediately brings the poetry into prose. If exploited as mere illustration of a proposition, a line of poetry loses the very thing which makes it revelatory in the poem. Brodsky resists any such conscription of poetry into prose, preferring formulations which distance the genre as much as possible from other forms of language. This flight from other varieties of language—from counterfeit, or petrified, or clichéd language—is actually a return to the origin of language:

Ideally, however, [poetry] is language negating its own mass and the laws of gravity; it is language's striving upward—or sideways—to that beginning where the Word was. In any case, it is movement of language into pre- (supra-) genre realms, that is, into the spheres from which it sprang. (LTO, 186)

If the 'mass' of language exerts a constant downwards, ground-wards force, a grounding or tethering of language to the great mass of all that

---

[64] Volkov, *Conversations*, xi.

has already been said—in other words if language exhibits a tendency towards cliché—then poetry represents the countertendency towards newness which is also a return in the direction of the originary, originating Word. In the beginning was the Word, but Brodsky's Word is not with God, nor is it God Himself, nor even is it only chronologically a beginning. Brodsky's description of poetry as 'striving' towards, and 'moving into' pre-original and originary spaces is both imperative and unachievable. For Brodsky, linguistic stagnation—and its consequence, cultural stagnation—is the danger which ethical language must continually counteract. So Brodsky describes poetry as linguistic self-negation, as disruption through language of what has already been said and done in language. For Brodsky's poet, achieving this means extreme individuation and innovation:

To avoid cliché, our poet continually has to get where nobody has ever been before—mentally, psychologically, or lexically. Once he gets there, he discovers that indeed there's nobody about, save perhaps the word's original meaning or that initial discernible sound. (GR, 85)

The space where no one has ever been, where only the new or the initial exists—the truly 'original' space in both the past and future senses of the word—this is the locus of poetic invention. Brodsky believes in the originariness of poetic language: if the poet can 'get to' the originary and empty space 'where nobody has ever been before', and bring back from there a poem, then that poem will be completely other, irreducibly separate. And, in achieving this separateness, it can open the possibility of true encounter, of direct relations, of *tête-à-tête*. This is what Brodsky demands of poets; this is why he demands that readers read. 'Writing poetry is a man's tête-à-tête with his language, not with his beloved, peers, neighbors, or compatriots',[65] Brodsky once told an audience in Albuquerque, New Mexico, who had come to hear him talk about the poet's obligations to society. He ended his presentation by quoting the final lines of 'Uncommon Visage'—'One who finds himself in this sort of dependency on language is, I guess, what they call a poet' (GR, 58)—then adding, for measure: 'The rest is society.'

*

[65] Draft of 'Does the Poet Have an Obligation to Society?', Joseph Brodsky Papers, Beinecke Rare Book and Manuscript Library, Yale University.

The two objections cited above are more closely connected than they may seem at first. On the question of poetic content, above I observed that Brodsky is loath to cite specific examples of 'good' or 'bad' poetry, in either senses of those words. As is often the case with Brodsky, however, there are illuminating exceptions. Auden's verse is one. Another is Rilke's: on at least one occasion, Brodsky does offer a quotation to illustrate what pure exposure to poetry may be like. The lines are from 'Archaic Torso of Apollo':

> . . . this torso shouts at you with its every muscle:
> 'Do change your life!'   (LTO, 273)[66]

Rilke's imperative—*Du mußt dein Leben ändern*—is both originary and revelatory; for Brodsky it is emblematic of poetry's special ability to offer 'a route of departure from the known, captive self' (LTO, 273). That offering, Brodsky writes, places the reader in a position of imminent response-ability: 'if there is a chance for men to become anything but victims or villains of their time, it lies in their prompt response' to Rilke's command (LTO, 273).

Because poetry is, according to Brodsky, the ultimate individuator, aesthetic experience of poetry gives rise to something ethical. It makes us individually response-able and responsible, separated from the coercion of the collective but also from the moral anonymity it confers. By 'holding a question mark' over the individual, by constantly interrupting our notions of our selves, by forcing re-evaluation—in Brodsky's terms by 'helping a person to make the time of his existence more specific', by making 'man's ethical reality more precise' (GR, 48–9)— poetry allows for the emergence of ethics. This is why the Brodskian 'I' cannot be an egotistical, totalizing I. The I's encounter with poetry does not seek to impose itself on poetry, but rather exposes itself to poetry, asking poetry to impose itself on the I. And if this sounds too much like abstruse theorizing and too little like known experience, perhaps it is appropriate to end with an account of the effect of Brodsky's first public reading in the West:

---

[66] It is not clear what version or translation Brodsky is quoting from, or whether indeed he has misquoted from memory. The original German lines are 'denn da ist keine Stelle, | die dich nicht sieht. Du mußt dein Leben ändern', which J. B. Leishman, in vol. 2 of Rilke's *Selected Works* (London: Hogarth, 1960), renders: 'for there's no place therein | that does not see you. You must change your living.' (143). Don Paterson does better in his version from *Landing Light*: 'for there is nowhere to hide, nothing here | that does not see you. *Now change your life*' (London: Faber and Faber, 2003), 61.

When he ended, his audience was as stunned as the poet on the stage was now silent. . . . It was as if the air had been drained of sound. And the appropriate response would have been that—a soundlessness, in which you would hear only your own breathing, be aware only of your own physicality, of your isolated self.[67]

[67] Daniel Weissbort, *From Russian with Love: Joseph Brodsky in English* (London: Anvil, 2004), 10.

3

Seamus Heaney: Beyond the 'Dialect of the Tribe'

I mean, I admire aesthetes and find them very stimulating, but I always have the nagging feeling that they really ought to be thinking about commitment, the public world of politics. Then when I come across what I think are essentially philistine committed writers and critics, I move in the other direction and think of the pure delight of art.

Tom Paulin, interview with John Haffenden, 1979

You will not be astonished to hear that I believe it is inevitable that any serious poetry written at the present time will be inextricably caught up in politics. I do not mean that it has to be a naive vehicle for the transmission of political opinions and sentiments.

Geoffrey Hill, Collège de France, 2008

When Seamus Heaney chose to 'credit poetry' in his Nobel lecture (1995), it was to Yeats's example that he turned, recalling the address his predecessor gave to the Swedish Academy in 1923. Noting that Ireland had then just emerged from civil war, Heaney found nothing in Yeats's subject matter—'The Irish Dramatic Movement'—to suggest that he was ignoring the times' emergencies. Though Yeats 'barely alluded' to the two wars Ireland had recently suffered, according to Heaney he was telling 'the world that the local work of poets and dramatists had been as important to the transformation of his native place and times as the ambushes of guerrilla armies' (CR, 41). That Heaney, in his greatest moment of public approval and recognition, reads Yeats's lecture as apologia reflects his own persisting engagement with what Eliot called the 'use of poetry', what Heaney calls its 'present use' (RP, 1). The relation between the social and artistic, between the ethical and the aesthetic, is a subject to which Heaney regularly returns in his critical prose and which exerts a constant pressure on his poetry.

That Heaney invokes Yeats in *Crediting Poetry* is to be expected, given their corresponding statures—as early as 1975 Robert Lowell was calling Heaney 'the best Irish poet since Yeats'.[1] For effectiveness of example, however, Heaney could have turned to Eliot's late socio-literary criticism. He might have drawn similar inspiration from Eliot's address on the occasion of the fall of Rome, or more generally from his insistence during the War on the power of poetry to resist oppression while also assisting the peaceful cooperation among people. Though Heaney has not published on Eliot's late prose, he acquired the early prose in enough depth to appeal to it repeatedly in lectures throughout the 1970s, and certainly he is aware, as early as 1986, of one of Eliot's more personal reactions to the War. 'The Government of the Tongue', one of four T. S. Eliot Memorial Lectures delivered at Eliot College, University of Kent, is an early extended reflection on the place of poetry. In the concluding paragraphs he quotes Eliot's gloomy letter to E. Martin Browne, in which Eliot writes that it is difficult, in wartime, to believe that 'fiddling with words and rhythms is justified activity' (GT, 107). Eliot might have been thinking of a stance Marianne Moore once took on poetry: 'I, too, dislike it: there are things that are important beyond all this fiddle',[2] and may have been, as she was, playing on the double sense of 'fiddling': both making music (OED2, *v.* 1a) and performing useless or trifling actions (OED2, *v.* 3a). Whatever the case, the anxiety that Eliot expresses to his friend stems from the duty every social creature feels to help—to be of use—during an emergency. It is not a neurotic anxiety so much as a Neronic one: even for the poet, whose trade is making music, it is an affront to fiddle while the city is burning.

Heaney has described a time in early 1968 during which he was not exactly fiddling, but when he *was* engaged in music-making as part of a travelling programme of poetry and song, called 'Room to Rhyme', which also included fellow poet Michael Longley and the singer David Hammond. Heaney associates this tour with a 'change for the better' (SS, 118) at that time in the social and political atmosphere of Ulster. It was not to be a lasting one. The autumn of the same year saw civil rights marches countered with police violence, an escalation which hastened the transformation of Northern Ireland into a war zone. In

[1] Robert Lowell, 'Books of the Year', *The Observer* (December 1975).
[2] Marianne Moore, *Complete Poems* (New York: Penguin, 1994), 266.

The Government of the Tongue (1989), Heaney relates an anecdote about another poetry and music collaboration with Hammond, this one to take place in the midst of that war zone, in Belfast, 1972. It was aborted when, on the way to the recording studio, 'a number of explosions occurred in the city and the air was full of the sirens of ambulances and fire engines' (GT, xi). There would be no recording: 'What David Hammond and I were experiencing, at a most immediate and obvious level, was a feeling that song constituted a betrayal of suffering' (GT, xii).

Heaney spends much of the rest of the book negotiating a way through this seeming crisis by drawing on the examples of other poets. On the one hand he admires Wilfred Owen and Sorley MacLean for their impulse to 'elevate truth over beauty' (GT, xviii). On the other he feels a kinship with Mandel´shtam, who 'had no immediate social aim'. Because his ambition was only 'to allow poems to form in language inside him', his 'responsibility was to sound rather than to the state, to language rather than to five-year plans, to etymology rather than to economics' (GT, xix). Heaney seizes on the fact that Mandel´shtam fell out of favour with the Kremlin—not because he was anti-communist but because 'he would not change his tune'—as evidence that a poet can pursue art disinterestedly and with complete Eliotic integrity and still perform a moral good, an example 'of the way purely artistic utterance can put a crack into the officially moulded shape of truth in a totalitarian society' (GT, xx). Having taken note of the anti-poetic poetry of Owen, Heaney ends by accepting Mandel´shtam's example as proof that 'humanity is served by the purely poetic fidelity of the poet to all words in their pristine being' (GT, xx). Heaney is especially drawn to the ethics of Mandel´shtam's position, couching it in terms of duty ('fidelity' to words) and integrity ('*purely* poetic', 'their *pristine* being'). This is typical of the way in which Heaney overcomes the song/suffering division. Returning to that trope, he asks retrospectively, 'Did we not see that song and poetry added to the volume of good in the world?' (GT, xix).

For Heaney, Eliot's self-doubt encapsulates 'the great paradox of poetry and of the imaginative arts in general', that poetry is at once powerful and powerless:

Faced with the brutality of the historical onslaught, [poetry is] practically useless. . . . In one sense the efficacy of poetry is nil—no lyric has ever stopped a tank. In another sense, it is unlimited. It is like the writing in the sand in the face of which accusers and accused are left speechless and renewed. (GT, 107)

The 'writing in the sand' is from the New Testament story in which Jesus challenges the sinless among the gathered crowd to cast the first stone at a condemned adulteress (John 8:3–11). Jesus's absolving words are bracketed by two mysterious acts of stooping down to write in the sand with his finger. This writing, for Heaney, is symbolic of poetry:

It does not say to the accusing crowd or to the helpless accused, 'Now a solution will take place', it does not propose to be instrumental or effective. Instead, in the rift between what is going to happen and whatever we would wish to happen, poetry holds attention for a space, functions not as a distraction but as pure concentration, a focus where our power to concentrate is concentrated back on ourselves. (GT, 108)

Heaney's answer to Eliot's crisis is not unlike Eliot's own, depending as it does on his trust in the oblique power of poetry. Poetry need not engage directly with the troubles of the time. It need not enter into the logic of those troubles, nor need it address their root causes nor even propose a way around them. It does not propose, precisely because all propositions are eventually gainsaid by counter-propositions, just as all offences are eventually avenged by counter-offences. Instead, like the words of Jesus, poetry comes at the minds of its readers from an unexpected angle, and for a moment dislocates the cycle of offence and retribution. If Eliot posits an indirect duty of poets towards people, achieved through a devotion to language, Heaney too imagines a mutually reinforcing triangular relationship among poets, poems, and people. He is similarly committed to a form of poetic 'integrity', and aware that the preservation of that integrity is essential to the other, indirect uses poetry may have.

REDRESSES

'The Redress of Poetry' (1989), one of Heaney's lectures as Professor of Poetry at Oxford and the title of the collecting volume (1995), constitutes the most concise expression of this indirect power of poetry. The essay begins by locating itself within a long apologetic tradition:

Professors of poetry, apologists for it, practitioners of it, from Sir Philip Sidney to Wallace Stevens, all sooner or later are tempted to show how poetry's existence as a form of art relates to our existence as citizens of society—how it is 'of present use'. (RP, 1)

Heaney searches recent literary history for examples of poets who were 'of present use' in their time. Wilfred Owen, Irina Ratushinskaia, Václav Havel, Czesław Miłosz, Osip Mandel´shtam, W. B. Yeats, and others are read approvingly in terms of their social impact. Their poetry can 'hold its own and balance out against the historical situation' because it represents 'a glimpsed alternative, a revelation of potential that is denied or constantly threatened by circumstances' (RP, 3–4). Heaney values the role these poets play in allowing repressed voices to speak. He professes his sympathy for ' "silence-breaking" writing of all kinds' (RP, 5) and in the modern context acknowledges that 'poetry is understandably pressed to give voice to much that has hitherto been denied expression in the ethnic, social, sexual and political life' (RP, 5). This is not quite pandering, but it is clearly a concession. 'Understandably' tries to mitigate that which it cannot condone outright; 'pressed' insists on the unnatural posture of the act.

Given its power 'as an agent for proclaiming and correcting injustices' (RP, 5) Heaney finds it natural that some 'will want poetry to be more than [just] an imagined response to conditions in the world' (RP, 2). Activists of various persuasions 'will urgently want to know why it should not be an applied art, harnessed to movements which attempt to alleviate those conditions by direct action' (RP, 2). Heaney's answer to this, that 'Poetry cannot afford to lose its fundamentally self-delighting inventiveness, its joy in being a process of language as well as a representation of things in the world' (RP, 5), comes from an instinct for what Eliot called 'poetic integrity'. Heaney writes,

But in discharging this [social] function, poets are in danger of slighting another imperative, namely, to redress poetry *as* poetry, to set it up as its own category, an eminence established and a pressure exercised by distinctly linguistic means. (RP, 5–6)

The point is essentially the same as Eliot made in the 1928 preface to *The Sacred Wood*, that 'when we are considering poetry we must consider it primarily as poetry and not another thing' (SW, *viii*). What makes the poem a poem is its 'process of language', and the poet's allegiance should cleave to that.

The title word 'redress'—as Heaney constructs and deconstructs it— contains within it both poetic imperatives. The phrase 'The Redress of Poetry' takes advantage of the natural ambiguity of the English genitive: 'poetry' is notionally both active subject—poetry redresses—and passive object—poetry is redressed. Poetry has a power to redress social ills, but the poet's job is to redress poetry itself, to restore, re-establish, and safeguard its linguistic excellence. Yet in discharging one function the poet ends by serving the other. Commenting on this duality in the final essay of the collection, 'The Frontiers of Writing' (1993), Heaney writes, 'To effect the redress of poetry, it is not necessary for the poet to be aiming deliberately at social or political change' (RP, 191–2). The civic intent of the poet can be subsidiary to his linguistic designs. What Heaney requires of the poet is deliberate attention to the poem's linguistic achievement and to its imaginative innovation. Heaney concludes, 'To redress poetry in this sense is to know it and celebrate it for its forcibleness as itself' (RP, 192).

Heaney's insistence that the poet's intent be focused on the poem itself and not on its ancillary uses is taken a step further in 'Extending the Alphabet' (1991), his Oxford lecture on Christopher Marlowe. Here Heaney observes that the content of a poem also takes a back seat to the sounds it makes:

it is obvious that poetry's answer to the world is not given only in terms of the content of its statements. It is given perhaps even more emphatically in terms of metre and syntax, of tone and musical trueness. (RP, 25)

The auditory qualities of the poem that Heaney picks out—its metre, syntax, tone, and musicality—are what distinguish poetry from prose, the elements Eliot identified as making the 'music of poetry' in his 1942 essay. Intellectual inventiveness, imagination, the ability to see the world in a different way are certainly some attributes of good poetry, but what the poet says is in the end less crucial than the way in which he says it.

In *The Redress of Poetry*, Heaney considers what happens when poems interact with the 'real' world of society and politics. But the language he uses to describe poetry consciously and forcefully demarcates it from that world and any other. Poetry, '*as* poetry', in its '*own* category'— which is '*distinctly* linguistic'—is '*self*-delighting', possessing a 'forcibleness as *itself*'. It is elsewhere 'an upright, resistant, and self-bracing entity within the general flux and flex of language' (RP, 15). There may be a hint of a reaction here to contemporary trends in literary theory,[3]

---

[3] For more by Heaney on trends in modern criticism, see, for instance, 'On His Work in the English Tongue' (EL, 61–4); 'On Poetry and Professing: II' (FK, 71); *Seamus Heaney in Conversation with Karl Miller* (London: Between the Lines, 2000), 46; Heaney's interview with John Breslin in *The Critic* 46:2 (Winter 1991), 35; and *Stepping Stones*, 104. Helen Vendler's claim, in *Soul Says: On Recent Poetry* (Cambridge, MA: Harvard University Press, 1995), that 'Knowingly or not, Heaney . . . breaks definitively with most of the literary theory that is interested in the social function of literature' (196) is over-strong, though the implication that Heaney has resisted the political inflection of the Theory movements is no doubt correct.

but more importantly this insistence establishes the basis of integrity for poetic 'present use'. Poetry must be preserved itself on its own terms before it can be of true use to anyone or anything. Heaney says that poetry 'separates itself off from the rest of language and says, "Treat me as separated off"'.[4] Once this basis of independence is established, commerce between poetry and the 'real' world can be profitable. 'Frontiers of Writing' ends by affirming that 'within our individual selves we can reconcile two orders of knowledge which we might call the practical and the poetic' and, what is more, that 'each form of knowledge redresses the other and that the frontier between them is there for the crossing' (RP, 203). Even in this reconciliatory summation, Heaney's language emphasizes the essential integrity of poetry. Knowledge of the world and knowledge of art are different orders of knowledge altogether. Though things may pass between them, the separating frontier remains.

If Heaney is no anti-aesthetic Wilfrid Owen, neither is he always a completely disinterested Osip Mandel'shtam. In 1966, when 'most poets in Ireland were straining to celebrate the anniversary of the 1916 Easter Rising' (P, 56), Heaney answers with 'Requiem for the Croppies':

> Terraced thousands died, shaking scythes at cannon.
> The hillside blushed, soaked in our broken wave.
> They buried us without shroud or coffin
> And in August the barley grew up out of the grave.   (DD, 24)

This is a political poem in the sense that it gives a voice to an oppressed and silenced group. It is unmistakably on one 'side' of a past conflict which informs the present one. In mythologizing the massacre of the rebel Nationalists of 1798 the poem contributes to the cultural arsenal of the Catholic and the nationalist. It is, however, still song: a little song, a sonnet of suffering sung in fourteen rhyming lines of loose iambic pentameter. It can be read, too, as an allegory for the crisis of Art and Life that Heaney mulls over in his prose. Like the poem that figures them, the croppies when faced with the reality of the situation are in one sense ineffectual. Their scythe-shaking and cattle-stampeding are no match for the onslaught of history. But in another sense they do achieve something. In the regenerative image that concludes the poem we read

---

[4] Seamus Heaney and Robert Hass, *Sounding Lines: The Art of Translating Poetry* (Berkeley: Townsend Center, 1999), 30.

hope and redemption, the possibility of an eventual solution. Like Yeats, whose poem commemorating the Rising hoped that 'England may keep faith',[5] Heaney ends his song of suffering with a glimpse of possibility.

This hope is vindicated, if only partially and temporarily. In a 1994 piece on the occasion of the IRA ceasefire, Heaney remembers that period of détente in the late 1960s during which he, Longley, and Hammond toured 'all over' the North: 'The fact that I felt free to read a poem about the 1798 rebels to a rather staid audience of middle-class unionists was one such small symptom of a new tolerance' (FK, 46). Heaney doesn't say whether they *liked* 'Requiem for the Croppies', but the choice to read it is significant on its own account. 'I'd guess there was nobody who didn't feel a frisson of transgression at the fact of a so-to-speak rebel poem surfacing in an official context,' Heaney writes, 'even though that particular context permitted it' (SS, 118). On a certain reading, the poem can even be taken to imply that the symbolic harvest of barley may be reaped for the general benefit of both sides of the political divide. But as détente turns to disaster in Northern Ireland, Heaney feels less at ease with 'Requiem for the Croppies' as a public articulation of belonging. The perceived threat is not, as one might expect, from the incitement of 'middle-class unionists' against Catholics, but rather from the ultraviolent contingents of the nationalist cause, and their claim on Catholic nationalist identity. There was 'dismaying hardness and ruthlessness in the violence all round, and at that stage a reading aloud of the poem would have been taken as overt support for the Provisionals' campaign', Heaney says, 'So that's when I stopped' (SS, 118–19).

Heaney's reticence to perform a serviceable poem in public, for fear of endorsing, against his conscience, violence being carried out in his name, does not dampen the creative impulse to make poetry from experience. As the Troubles worsen in the early 1970s, Heaney writes several poems which thematically underwrite the cause of nationalism in the North. 'Craig's Dragoons' (1972), a piece of light verse written in the tradition of the rebel anthem, begins with a call to action:

Come all ye Ulster loyalists and in full chorus join,
Think on the deeds of Craig's Dragoons who strike below the groin.   (SS, 111)

Another poem, 'Intimidation' (1971), responds to Twelfth of July bonfires and marches commemorating the Battle of the Boyne:

> Ghetto rats! Are they the ones
> To do the smoking out?
> They'll come streaming past
> To taste their ashes yet.[6]

Though Heaney has acknowledged that 'Requiem for the Croppies' would fairly in some contexts be interpreted as a nationalist polemic (FK, 46), there is no context in which these two early poems could *not* be read in that way. It says something, however, that the first was never published and the second never collected. Though these poems do address relevant socio-ethical topics, the principle of poetic integrity excludes them from a permanent place in the corpus. Their unpolished technique compounds the bluntness of their thesis: forced metrics and stock imagery underline the fact that these poems come at the problem too directly and from an identifiably politicized point of view. They are, as Heaney remembers 'Craig's Dragoons', 'Head-on stuff', to be re- velled in perhaps for their 'swagger', but ultimately 'too coarse, linguis- tically and politically' (SS, 111). They can be dismissed in the same spirit of easy partisanship in which they were written.

Despite the eventual exclusion of 'Intimidation', its first stanza at least foreshadows the technique of Heaney's more successful poems of the period:

> Their bonfire scorched his gable.
> He comes home to kick through
> A tumulus of ash,
> A hot stour in the moonlight.[7]

Michael Molino has noted that Heaney passes up the Irish word 'cairn' in favour of the Latinate 'tumulus', which orthographically and pho- netically suggests 'tumult' or 'tumultuous'[8] (all three are cognates of *tumere*—'to swell'). In addition to 'cairn' there is an available Germanic

---

[6] Seamus Heaney, 'Intimidation', *Malahat Review* 17 (1971), 34.
[7] Ibid.
[8] Michael R. Molino, *Questioning Tradition, Language, and Myth: The Poetry of Seamus Heaney* (Washington, DC: Catholic University of America Press, 1994), 60. Molino's treatment of 'Intimidation' is similar to mine but he makes more of Spenser's strong association with 'stour'. His argument would be further strengthened by an account of the Scots definition of 'stour'—which I take to be the primary denotation here—and of Burns's association with that word.

alternative—'barrow'—which might suggest 'sorrow' in the same rhyming way as 'tumulus' suggests 'tumultuous'.[9] But the use of 'stour' confirms the choice of 'tumulus'. The primary meaning of the word is likely the Scots, as used by Burns,[10] meaning a windstorm of dust or any fine particle (OED2, *n.*[1] II.5). However, 'stour' can also mean a battle or conflict, or more generally, as Spenser uses it, a 'time of turmoil or stress' (OED2, *n.*[1] I.1–3). Heaney constructs a double synonymy with 'tumulus' and 'stour', each referring to 'ash' (heaped or swirling) but evoking 'trouble'. Here the full range of denotative, connotative, and auditory qualities of words—qualities which evoke regional (place-specific) and obsolete (time-specific) meanings—is probed for all possible connections, with some being retrieved and redressed for the present time and place.

SOUNDINGS

From the beginning of Heaney's publishing career, probing is a recurring productive metaphor for the poetic act. 'Digging' (1964) is a paradigmatic 'first' poem mainly because it so assuredly announces this trope. Heaney's resolve in that poem to dig with his pen is the first of many such excavations: from the outset there is a world of meaning below the surface which the poet must labour to access. Sounding—figuratively, in the sense of probing, the gauging of a depth (OED2, *vbl. n.*[2] 1a)—is both theme and practice in the early poetry. In the 1976 essay 'Englands of the Mind' he puts the practice of poetic digging into the Eliotic framework of the 'auditory imagination', establishing a basis for his later invocation of 'echo soundings' (SI, 94), to play on the word's other sense of 'utterance' (OED2, *vbl. n.*[1] 2a). Here one must quote Heaney's appeal to Eliot at length:

---

[9] The word 'barrow' is in fact being employed by Heaney at the time, notably in 'Nocturne', published on the very next page of the *Malahat Review*, where he writes of 'drifted barrow, sunk glacial rock' (35), and in the earlier poem 'In Gallarus Oratory': 'Founded there like heroes in a barrow' (DD, 22).

[10] Burns uses the word, for example, in 'To John Maxwell': 'Rake them, like Sodom and Gomorrah, | In brunstane [brimstone] stoure.' See Robert Burns, *The Canongate Burns: The Complete Poems and Songs of Robert Burns*, ed. Andrew Noble and Patrick Scott (Edinburgh: Canongate, 2003), 762. Heaney reuses 'stour' in this sense, in a later poem called 'The Real Names': 'The hard sticks | He dumped down at the opening of the scene | Raised a stour off the boards' (EL, 45).

One of the most precise and suggestive of T. S. Eliot's critical formulations was his notion of what he called 'the auditory imagination', the 'feeling for syllable and rhythm, penetrating far below the conscious levels of thought and feeling, invigorating every word; sinking to the most primitive and forgotten, returning to the origin and bringing something back', fusing 'the most ancient and the most civilized mentality'. I presume Eliot was thinking here about the cultural depth-charges latent in certain words and rhythms, that binding secret between words in poetry that delights not just the ear but the whole backward and abysm of mind and body; thinking of the energies beating in and between words that the poet brings into half-deliberate play; thinking of the relationship between the word as pure vocable, as articulate noise, and the word as etymological occurrence, a symptom of human history, memory and attachments. (P, 150)

There are deliberate or half-deliberate energies beating even within this passage—Heaney deftly submarines a Shakespearean archaism behind the cultural depth-charges he says Eliot is evoking. Maintaining the use of 'backward' as a noun gives the secret away, even if the subject 'of mind and body' modifies (while also incorporating) Prospero's reference to memory, that 'backward and abysm of time'.[11] This embodiment of time and memory reflects one important difference between Heaney's and Eliot's ways of thinking about the auditory imagination. Whereas Eliot is less concerned with the facts of the 'primitive' and 'forgotten' culture than its affective evocation, Heaney draws a direct link between word sounds and human history. The 'attachments' that Heaney's 'articulate noise' evokes are attachments of race, religion, and politics. Like Eliot's syllable and rhythm, they both divide and unite groups of readers—and wider groups of people—based as they are on the culturally unique rhythms, sounds, and secondary meanings of words.

Heaney's own 'auditory imagination' is as strong a mover of his critical prose as it is of his poetry. Explaining his feelings on the opening lines of 'The Hollow Men', Heaney describes loving 'the pitch of their music, their nerve-end tremulousness, their treble in the helix of the ear', even if his 'ear was never pulled outside in by what it heard' (FK, 28–9) in Eliot. A 1997 piece on the poetry of Robert Burns is typical of the way in which Heaney listens to texts. His diction tends always towards aural, even musical, metaphor: Burns 'orchestrates' the 'rhythm and melody' of the poem; he 'strikes a note', achieving 'earworthiness',

---

[11] William Shakespeare, *The Tempest*, 1.2.50.

'aural trustworthiness', and a 'nugget of harmony'.[12] The juxtaposition of value terms like 'worthy' and 'trustworthy' with 'ear' and 'aural' and the double valence of 'harmony' are typical of the associations Heaney makes between the sound of Burns's verse and its evocation of secondary meanings. Heaney takes up more than a page to sound out the first syllable of 'To a Mouse':

Even before a metre or a melody could be established, the word 'wee' put its stressed foot down and in one pre-emptive vocative strike took over the emotional and cultural ground, dispossessing the rights of written standard English and offering asylum to all vernacular comers. (FK, 347)

The choice and placing of this syllable, 'wee' though it is, is significant: it establishes the 'aural trustworthiness' (FK, 349) of the poem, locating it firmly in the language of place. 'Wee' reclaims poetic idiom from standard English to the Scots vernacular from the beginning, and in the final stanza's 'But Och! I backward cast my e'e', Heaney hears the confirmation of that reclamation: 'it is a matter of the profoundest phonetic satisfaction that the exclamation "Och" should be at the centre of this semi-visionary final stanza' (FK, 350). The pleasing of Heaney's auditory sense is accompanied by the satisfaction of his ideas about what poetry should do. 'Och' is 'a common, almost pre-linguistic particle' (FK, 350), belonging to the 'abysm of mind', at once 'pure vocable', 'articulate noise' and also a 'symptom . . . of memory and attachments' to a certain way of speaking and living. For Heaney, it is a way back to and authorization for what he would later call 'the "hidden Scotland" at the back of my own ear'.[13] As 'a kind of *nunc dimittis* positioned near the end' (FK, 350), it opens the way to a new poetic language, which though rooted in the distant past nonetheless bodes a renewal of future speech.

Eliot's description of the 'auditory imagination', though it certainly takes account of regional and national differences in dialect—and depends on them for its vigour—does not seem aware or interested in any tension among them. Very unpostmodernly, naïvely perhaps even for his time, Eliot imagined that the many strains of English could coexist benignly in the poet's imagination, eventually combining happily on the page to improve English-speaking culture. Heaney's English

---

[12] 'Nugget of harmony' is a phrase Heaney borrows from Nadezhda Mandel´shtam.
[13] Seamus Heaney, *The Testament of Cresseid and Seven Fables* (London: Faber and Faber, 2009), xiii.

imaginings are much more afflicted—for him, the English language is on one hand a means and symbol of Irish subjugation, and on the other his own means of expressive liberation. Through the many phases of this productive conflict, Heaney's take on Eliot's 'auditory imagination' is a constant compass. From his earliest to his latest collection Heaney fathoms the English language for its 'cultural depth-charges', setting them off to explosive effect.

One of Heaney's earliest and most often treated probings of the 'abysm of mind and body' occurs in his meditations on the names of a few localities in the immediate environs of his childhood homes: Toome, Broagh, Anahorish, Derrygarve, and Castledawson.[14] These are poems of aural, phonological, and semantic 'redress', in the sense of setting straight, or restoring to a preferred anterior condition, which gives strength to Eliot's assertion that a 'people may have its language taken away from it, suppressed . . . and it will reappear in poetry, which is the vehicle of feeling' (OPP, 19). They are soundings—probing cultural history and gauging it—as well as soundings of old sounds, old ways of speech. So they demonstrate Heaney's adaptation and enactment of the Eliotic auditory imagination, as he turns to etymology and phonology, not just as tools of poetic praxis but also as important poetic subjects.

In 'A New Song', Heaney probes 'Derrygarve', an anglicization of *doire garbh*, the 'rough oak (grove)'. In the poem, hearing the name sends Heaney into linguistic rumination:

> And Derrygarve, I thought, was just:
> Vanished music, twilit water—
> A smooth libation of the past   (WO, 23)

Like 'Anahorish', which gives voice to a 'forgotten Gaelic music in the throat' (P, 36), this poem grows up from deep in the buried past. The name is 'lost', a 'vanished music', a 'smooth libation of the past', but the sound of it nevertheless triggers memories of the place's topography, its denizen wildlife and evocative intangibles. The name is not merely correct or appropriate, it is 'just', suggesting there are such ethical things as 'just' and 'unjust' names. And just as justice is often concerned with

---

[14] These names, and more that are familiar from the poetry, appear in 'Map 3 – South County Derry (detail)', in the opening pages of *Stepping Stones*, which shows an area of approximately 10 km × 14 km (SS, xxiii).

retribution for past injustice, the final stanzas develop the rhyme on 'just' and 'past' with retributive re-naming:

> But now our river tongues must rise
> From licking deep in native haunts
> To flood, with vowelling embrace,
> Demesnes staked out in consonants.
>
> And Castledawson we'll enlist
> And Upperlands, each planted bawn—
> Like bleaching-greens resumed by grass—
> A vocable, as rath and bullaun.   (WO, 23)

An Irish-language dictionary will say that a 'rath' is a circular earthen-ring fort, deriving from the obsolete term *ráth*, meaning a fortress or dwelling place, which is to say that it is the Irish counterpart to Elizabethan Hiberno-English 'bawn'.[15] Its homonym *rath* means 'good luck' and is used as a blessing.[16] A 'bullaun' is a kind of megalith with a deep circular depression (the cup or 'bowl', whence *bollán* and eventually 'bullaun') and is associated with ancient churches and mon-asteries.[17] Semantically speaking, then, ancient Irish constructions and marking stones come back to replace the newer English ones. More important, however, is the linguistic process of reclamation. 'Rath' and 'bullaun' function primarily beyond their semantic fields, as 'voc-ables'—the term Heaney uses in his discussion of the 'auditory imagi-nation'. In imagining the resurpation of the Irish countryside as an auditory one, Heaney enacts his Eliotically derived notion of sound and syllable as both 'pure vocable' and 'symptom of human history' (P, 150). The long and dense English place names 'Castledawson' and 'Upperlands', thick with plosives and stops, are opposed and eventually overcome by the flowing Gaelic sounds. Here, as in so many Heaney poems of the period, pre-British Ireland is imagined as emerging from

[15] From Irish *bábhún*, but nonetheless associated with the planter faction. This association is reinforced in a literary sense by the word's appearance in Spenser. Heaney's preferred etymology traces 'bawn' to Middle Irish *bó-dhún*, which more clearly suggests 'cattle-fort'.

[16] See 'rath', 'ráth', in *Dictionary of Hiberno-English*, ed. Terence Patrick Dolan (Dublin: Gill and MacMillan, 1998); and 'rath', in *Concise Ulster Dictionary*, ed. C. I. Macafee (Oxford: Oxford University Press, 1996), which includes an instructive illus-tration. The earth mound and depression depicted here closely resembles a bullaun, though on a much larger scale.

[17] An illustrated atlas of Irish bullaun stones is available online at http://www.megalithomania.com/show/type/bullaun+stones, accessed 31 May 2010.

its earthy burying place—the grass seeds sprouting green from the ground, the buried dwelling place and ensconced ceremonial stone suddenly called to purpose. Linguistically, tongues are said to 'rise | From licking deep in native haunts'. 'Rath' and 'bullaun' are similarly raised out of the forgotten depths of language and put to use.

Unlike the other place-name poems in *Wintering Out*, 'Broagh' does not place the poet on one side of a Catholic-Protestant, nationalist-unionist, vowel-consonant divide. The dialect words in this poem— 'rigs', 'docken', 'pad', 'boortrees'—are not drawn from Gaelic etymology but this time from Ulster Scots, reaching back to dialects of the Lowlands, Borders, and northern England.[18] An outsider puzzled by these terms may find them readily enough in the OED. He may learn from a dialect dictionary that the name 'boortree' is connected with a kind of toy gun which is made from the wood of the tree[19]—and perhaps go on to relate this to the 'blades' of rhubarb in the poem. He may also find that while dock is commonly thought of as an antidote to the sting of nettles, and may therefore have a soothing or curative connotation, a 'docken-trampler' is a derogatory epithet among Ulster Loyalists for a Twelfth of July marcher who walks just outside the ranks, threatening tribal cohesion.[20] These multifarious connotations, lost on the casual reader and requiring a trip to the library for the dedicated one, would be immediately obvious and available to most readers from Heaney's area. If 'A New Song' uses the sounds of language to oppose nationalist to unionist and Catholic to Protestant, 'Broagh' uses it to draw them together in a different kind of exclusive community—the local community. Neil Corcoran is one of many critics to take note of this deliberate redrawing of dividing lines in 'Broagh': 'Its point is that conflicted histories have resulted in a community whose individual members,

---

[18] Here I quibble with O'Donoghue's assertion, in *Seamus Heaney and the Language of Poetry* (London: Harvester Wheatsheaf, 1994), following Tom Paulin, that the unfamiliar words represent 'the full Northern Irish linguistic complex' (63) and specifically that 'boortrees' represents the Irish factor. The OED confirms Scottish and northern English dialectical usage for each of these words. Certainly the title word is from the Irish *brúach*, and most readers, including Heaney himself, have observed that 'docken' is etymologically an antiquated English plural form. However, the linguistic heartland of the poem is the Borders of Scotland and surrounding areas.

[19] The *Concise Ulster Dictionary* suggests that the Scots and N. Irish name 'boortree', once 'bourtree' or 'boretree', may come from the practice of boring the elder's branches to make these popguns.

[20] See 'dock, docken', 'boortree' in *Concise Ulster Dictionary*, and 'dock-leaf' in *Dictionary of Hiberno-English*.

whatever their political or religious affinity, now all speak the same language, whether derived from Irish or English or Scots roots.'[21]

The dialectical choices made in 'Broagh' are the results of a new exclusive inclusivity, but the emblem of it is the name of the place itself, its constituent phonemes italicized to emphasize their uniqueness. The 'black' *O* requires two stanzas of description—one visual, the other auditory—to convey. Comparatively, the *gh* receives little in the way of epithet: 'that last | *gh* the strangers found | difficult to manage' (WO, 17). The single important fact about the *gh* is its unpronounceability outside the community. Elsewhere Heaney has called the *gh* in Broagh a 'sound native to Ireland, common to Unionist and Nationalist, but unavailable to an English person'.[22] Considering it a 'native' sound suggests that *gh*—like 'native' flora and fauna—is a token of the region, just as the region can be represented by the phoneme. It also accords 'native' status—in the sense of a native people—to those who can produce the sound naturally, obviating one distinction between the 'original' inhabitants and colonist, planter, or settler. We observe in 'Broagh' a double linguistic reconciliation. If the *gh* is 'native', certainly the Scots terms of the first stanzas are 'introduced'—Corcoran deploys the suggestive term 'planted'.[23] Nevertheless, both linguistic strata are fluently present in the local dialect, just as introduced plant or animal species, if it does not eliminate them and is not eliminated by them, will eventually arrive at a stable state among the native ones.

Drawing attention to a local cultural and linguistic consonance instead of the sectarian dissonances within that unity does tell an under-told truth about the intimacies that attend certain kinds of social enmity. But even this gesture is not without its own socio-political pitfalls. Heaney recalls being educated in 'political spin' after the publication of *Wintering Out* by the Northern Irish Parliament's Minister for Community Relations, who remarked on Heaney's poems much in the same vein as Corcoran, Paulin, O'Donoghue, and I have remarked on 'Broagh':

The man was saying something perfectly true, namely that much of my work was immediately accessible to everybody in Northern Ireland, whatever their religious or political affiliations.   (SS, 128)

[21] Neil Corcoran, *Seamus Heaney: A Critical Study* (London: Faber and Faber, 1998), 47.

[22] Seamus Heaney, *Among Schoolchildren* (John Malone Memorial Committee, 1983), 9.

[23] Corcoran, *Seamus Heaney*, 47.

For this official, Heaney's poems 'proved how much common ground we shared and so on—perfectly harmless decent-speak on the part of a minister'. Decent perhaps, but the sound of a government representative reading 'some kind of endorsement of the Northern status quo' (SS, 128) into Heaney's work rings the warning bell just as loudly as the prospect of nationalist paramilitaries claiming Heaney for themselves. It is often the case that politics will polarize people and their ideas, just as it is often the case, as Brodsky knew, that prominent people of careful and independent thought will eventually find themselves co-opted by one political faction or another. Heaney has as much as any artist been pushed and pulled in opposing directions, which is both the effect and the cause of a faults-on-both-sides stance in much of his poetry that deals thematically with the Troubles of Northern Ireland. What remains constant in Heaney's early poetry, across the shifting points of view and the various apportioning of loss and blame, is a resistance to the 'harnessing' of poetry—as Heaney later called it—to the instrumentalism that requests of poetry that it be an 'applied art'.

This defence of poetic integrity is nothing like a commitment to impartiality, or magnanimity, or even good faith. What is most significant about 'Broagh' is not that it gives voice to a kind of belonging that runs parallel to sectarian belonging, but that it must overtly exclude—literally everyone outside the region, but implicitly the English specifically—in order to establish new lines of inclusiveness. This is a sometimes surprising characteristic of Heaney's increasing hostility in the early 1970s, as the Troubles intensify, towards the sounds of the English language and the traditions of English literature. 'Traditions' is one of several poems in which Heaney aligns what is native in the Irish tradition with guttural, vowel, and female, and what has been introduced by English conquest with alliterative, consonantal, and 'imperially | Male' (N, 49), as another poem straightforwardly puts it. 'Traditions' begins:

> Our guttural muse
> was bulled long ago
> by the alliterative tradition,
> her uvula grows
>
> vestigial, forgotten
> like the coccyx   (WO, 21)

Conquest as rape is a well-worn trope—Heaney invokes it even more directly in 'Ocean's Love to Ireland' (N, 46) and 'Act of Union' (N, 49).

What has happened in 'Traditions' is not quite rape, but it is not quite love, either: the coupling is not generative but degenerative, withering the phonological articulators out of the mouth of Ireland. The poem develops the tropes of 'Anahorish', 'Toome', 'A New Song', and 'Broagh' in an altogether expected direction.

How surprising, then, to find in 'Bone Dreams', a long and slender poem in *North*, the 'alliterative tradition' presented not as aural vestige of imperial England, but as an antidote to the English tradition. Heaney would later tell Frank Kinahan that at the time he felt that the 'music, the melodious grace of the English line, was some kind of affront, that it needed to be wrecked'.[24] In a predatory twist on the 'auditory imagination', Heaney here rejects euphony not just to convey a mood, but because of the cultural associations that attach to that way of making music. Here the Anglo-Saxon alliterative mode is rediscovered at the bottom of accumulated philological strata:

> I push back,
> through dictions,
> Elizabethan canopies
> Norman devices,
>
> the erotic mayflowers
> of Provence
> and the ivied latins
> of churchmen
>
> to the scop's
> twang, the iron
> flash of consonants
> cleaving the line.   (N, 28)

In 'Toome', Heaney had written, 'I push into a souterrain | prospecting' past the accumulated artefacts of history until he came to pure silt and bogwater. In 'Bone Dreams' the journey is an auditory one to the centre of the language, in which Heaney peels back layers of addition and innovation to arrive at a core of linguistic sound. The last two lines quoted resemble an Anglo-Saxon line, separated by a line break instead of a caesura: 'flash of consonants | cleaving the line' is a fair approximation of the Old English alliterative mode. Heaney will again take on the role of the scop, in *The Haw Lantern* (1987), *Electric Light* (2001), and,

---

[24] Seamus Heaney, interview with Frank Kinahan, *Critical Inquiry* 8 (1982), 405–14, 412.

most thoroughly, in his translation of *Beowulf* (1999). In *North*, however, returning to an 'original' English is seen as another way of divesting oneself of the oppressive 'English line', as if the history of England and its colonies could itself be rolled back to pre-colonial times. 'I push back' is not mere exploration; it is retaliation, the response to being 'pushed around'.

It is a found bone fragment that sets 'Bone Dreams' going, provoking the literary memory of 'bone-house'/*'ban-hus'* and through this an etymological link to the Anglo-Saxon language. But instead of serving as a bridge between traditions, in the confrontational context of *North* this link to Old English becomes a weapon turned against modern English. Heaney writes, of the piece of bone:

> I touch it again
> I wind it in
>
> the sling of my mind
> to pitch it at England   (N, 27)

The David and Goliath trope is yet another way of re-imagining the possibility of efficacious poetry on the acoustic plane. Here Heaney turns the auditory core of English against England. Like biblical David, his posture is defensive, protective of his people against a more powerful aggressor. Heaney accomplishes this in ways that are consistent both with his version of poetic integrity, in which poetry asks to be treated as 'separated off' from the rest of human discourse, and with his adaptation of Eliot's auditory imagination, in which the poet exploits the relationship between a word 'as articulate noise, and the word as etymological occurrence, a symptom of human history, memory and attachments' (P, 150). But if Eliot sought to balance the local, tribal roots of poetry with a programme of collaborative intercultural exchange, Heaney's early adaptations of Eliot ignore completely this second balancing element. This changes gradually, partially in response to the slow healing of Northern Irish society, partially as a result of Heaney's self-extrication from those immediate surroundings, followed by an immersion in an international community of higher learning.

CROSSINGS

Any Heaney primer will mention his early assaults on the long 'English line'. One very schematic way to document this metrical contraction and subsequent relengthening is to calculate the average (mean) number of syllables per line for each of his collections. These are, ordered chronologically: DN, 9.0; DD, 8.0; WO, 6.5; N, 6.8 (N-I, 6.0; N-II, 9.3); FW, 8.6; SI, 8.5; HL, 10.0; ST, 10.3; SL, 9.8; EL, 10.0; DC, 8.9.[25] Not only are most poems broader after Part I of *North*, the skinny poem disappears as a relied-upon metrical containment until *District and Circle* (2006), where it comes back divested of its angst. In *Field Work* (1979), only 'Casualty' echoes both the metrical and the ethical unease of the previous collection. Commenting somewhat more qualitatively on this change, Heaney expresses it as a return to the natural sounds and rhythms of English poetry:

I suppose, then, that the shift from *North* to *Field Work* is a shift in trust: a learning to trust melody, to trust art as reality, to trust artfulness as an affirmation and not to go into the self-punishment so much.[26]

This 'trust' in art and in artfulness signals not only a change in attitude towards the poetic tradition, but towards the reader as well. Whereas poems in *Wintering Out* and *North* purposely exclude groups of readers in order to give voice to others, now Heaney is explicit about mending the breach he has created:

in the new book *Field Work*, I very deliberately set out to lengthen the line again because the narrow line was becoming habit. The shortness of a line constricts, in a sense, the breadth of your movement.... the rhythmic contract of metre and iambic pentameter and long line implies audience.[27]

Heaney's new attitude towards English metres is couched in a new and positive attitude towards readers. This change in alignment nevertheless retains Heaney's early emphasis on the ethical charge of poetic form: metre here is not simply an artistic choice taken to evoke one mood or another, nor is it only a matter of the poet's reaction to poetry that has gone before. It is, as Heaney now figures it, like a 'contract' between him

---

[25] Prose poems are not factored. Values for *North* parts I and II are given to illustrate the formal division of that collection. One can also show the progression by calculating the median line-length in syllables: DN, 10; DD, 8; WO, 6; N, 6 (N-I, 6; N-II, 10); FW, 9; SI, 9; HL, 10; ST, 10; SL, 10; EL, 11; DC, 10. (The median represents the value that lies in the middle of the sample, meaning that, for example, at most half the lines of *North* are shorter than six syllables and at most half are longer.) The syllable length of a line is of course only correlated with its metrical length, for which we have no good algorithms.

[26] Seamus Heaney, interview with Kinahan, 412.

[27] Seamus Heaney, interview with James Randall, *Ploughshares* 5.3 (1979), 7–22, 16.

and the reader, with all the goodwill and good faith this implies, or requires. Heaney's metrical contract, like Paul Celan's handshake, Joseph Brodsky's *tête-à-tête*, and Geoffrey Hill's 'bond', is a figure which implicates the writing of poetry with the undertaking of obligation, of responsibility. This new covenant, instead of isolating groups of readers to resist the dominance of English culture, now 'implies'—we might say 'implicates'—audience, bringing readers together under an umbrella of inclusiveness.

The physical and emotional centre of *Field Work* is a ten-poem sequence entitled 'Glanmore Sonnets', which reflects on the poet's recent move from the North to the Irish Republic. As the title announces, Heaney employs the classic fourteen-line English form: most of these poems loosely follow the model of four pentameter quatrains with a final rhyming couplet. Here we find lines that Heaney had written in 1974,[28] five years before their eventual publication, which when they occurred to him caused some surprise:

> This evening the cuckoo and the corncrake
> (So much, too much) consorted at twilight.
> It was all crepuscular and iambic.   (FW, 35)

The lines may not be all that iambic, let alone pentametric—and prosodically speaking neither term describes the calls of the cuckoo or corncrake—but Heaney recalls thinking, 'What the hell is all this iambic pentameter doing in my life?' (SS, 162). In the social and political conditions that surrounded the publication of *North*, the sonnet's 'sweetness disabled it somehow'.[29]

The poem, if it is primarily about the domestic implications of Heaney's change of place ('I won't relapse | From this strange loneliness I've brought us into'), is also about the accompanying change of artistic environment. The third line's 'It was all crepuscular and iambic' describes, according to Heaney, 'the too literary nature of the reality of Wicklow that evening' (SS, 162–3). In Heaney's new setting it is the setting itself that suggests a more musical verse. It may have been only a premonition in 1974, but by the time *Field Work* is published, five years later, Heaney can publicly own up to a melodiousness that had once been 'disabling':

> Outside a rustling and twig-combing breeze
> Refreshes and relents. Is cadences.   (FW, 35)

---

[28] See Heaney, interview with Kinahan, 412; and SS, 162–3.
[29] Heaney, interview with Kinahan, 412.

In the final phrase, which connects the rhythm of the wind to the iambs of the introductory birds' song, 'Is'—awkward as it seems—supplies the short syllable needed to make a perfect iambic pentameter, an almost 'too literary' line. 'Refreshes' and 'relents', like the falling and rising beats of the line, convey a new ambience of calm and comfort.

Though some poems in *Field Work* retain an echo of threat or dolour appropriate to the continuing situation in the North, as a whole the book expresses a new confidence in its ability to be both beautiful and hopeful in the face of that situation. Heaney, ready now to 'trust melody [and] artfulness', is making room in this collection for a poetry which sees beyond the historical moment. This change in posture is addressed discursively in the poems themselves. In 'Oysters' he writes of a 'clear light, like poetry or freedom | coming in from the sea' (FW, 11). Heaney's contemplation of 'The Harvest Bow' ends by invoking Coventry Patmore's dictum: '*The end of art is peace* | Could be the motto of this frail device' (FW, 58). In 'Song', Heaney again considers the relation of literature to life:

> There are the mud-flowers of dialect
> And the immortelles of perfect pitch
> And that moment when the bird sings very close
> To the music of what happens.   (FW, 56)

In bounding the auditory range of the literary between the poles of 'dialect' and 'perfect pitch', Heaney demarcates a new poetic scope for himself. In the mud-flower patch (where long he dwelt) is direct, concrete, and local poetry; among the immortelles flourishes the 'universal' transcendent poetry of erudite tradition. Played somewhere on that scale is the 'moment' of the poem, a counterpoint of dialect and perfect pitch which is also a relevant 'music of what happens'. So, when considering what his response might be to the dirty protests at Long Kesh, Heaney undertakes his first literary translation. Passing from mythic to canonical, from allusion to translation, his rendition of Dante's *Inferno*, Cantos XXXII and XXXIII, is the ambitious first appropriation of a foreign literary tradition.

Heaney's poetic interest in Dante is at least partially responsible for his critical interest in Eliot, and it is after *Field Work*, as Heaney engages ever more deeply with the Italian poet, that he begins to comment freely on Eliot's verse.[30] For instance, the suggestively entitled 'Envies and

---

[30] This is not the case with Eliot's prose, which is central to the younger Heaney's criticism (cf. 'Englands of the Mind', from 1976). For an elegant and persuasive account

Identifications: Dante and the Modern Poet' (1985), though it finally prefers Mandel'shtam's example to Eliot's, is illuminating in its appraisal of 'Little Gidding':

> That poetry...is at a third remove from the local historical moment and is suspended in the ether of a contemplative mind. The language conducts us away from the contingent. It is not mimetic of the cold morning cityscape but of the calescent imagination.[31]

The 'universality' of Eliot's later verse—a quality Eliot had admired in Dante—is what strikes Heaney most, because it 'seeks for things which "men of various races and lands could think together"'.[32] No goal could seem more foreign to a poet whose language has been consciously, often programmatically, even grammatically, local, whose poetry built barriers out of sounds which 'strangers found hard to manage'. One main objective of 'Envies and Identifications' is to re-read Dante, against the Eliotic interpretation, as a poet of local flavour (as per Mandel'shtam). Notwithstanding this critical instinct, Heaney's frontal engagement with Eliot's removed, contemplative, and un-contingent verse coincides with an emerging process of disentanglement from the nets of language which his early poetry and prose have set. Heaney's mid-career is characterized by the repeated crossing of the barriers he had erected in his earlier poetry.

In the long poem 'Station Island' (SI, 61–94), Heaney arrogates the tradition of the *Commedia* and its imitators to interrogate real-life personages of Ireland who have previously found their way into his poetry in some form or another. The poem ends with the ghost of Joyce imparting a kind of valediction. He begins by chastising the poet:

> ...The English language
> belongs to us. You are raking at dead fires,
>
> a waste of time for somebody of your age.
> That subject people stuff is a cod's game,
> Infantile, like your[33] peasant pilgrimage.

and ends in permission and exhortation:

---

of Eliot's formative influence on Heaney, see the third chapter of Michael Cavanagh, *Professing Poetry: Seamus Heaney's Poetics* (Washington, DC: Catholic University of America Press, 2009), 74–108.

[31] Heaney, 'Envies and Identifications', 8.
[32] Ibid. 9. Heaney is quoting Eliot's 1929 essay 'Dante' (SE, 239).
[33] The version reprinted in *Opened Ground* has 'this' for 'your'.

> When they make the circle wide, it's time to swim
> out on your own and fill the element
> with signatures on your own frequency,
> echo soundings, searches, probes, allurements.   (SI, 93–4)

Corcoran thinks Heaney's terza rima technique in this poem is inferior to Eliot's in 'Little Gidding' II and Yeats's in 'Cuchulain Comforted', a judgement contested by O'Donoghue,[34] and by Michael Cavanagh, who has taken the fullest measure of the connections between Heaney's Eliot and Heaney's Dante.[35] Heaney himself has written about the relationship between 'Little Gidding' and 'Station Island',[36] but insists that it is on the whole limited to its form, a contention Cavanagh spends a good deal of time interrogating. Heaney's appropriation of Dantesque themes and conventions resembles Eliot's in at least one other significant respect. Eliot's shade, we remember, urges the poet to 'purify the dialect of the tribe' (CP, 204), a function which is assigned to him as a liberation from worn and constrictive precedent: 'My thought and theory... | These things have served their purpose: let them be' (CP, 204). With the same sense of release, Heaney's ghost tells him 'Let go, let fly, forget | You've listened long enough. Now strike your note' (SI, 93). Similarly, Eliot's 'The day was breaking. In the disfigured street | He left me, with a kind of valediction, | And faded on the blowing of the horn' (CP, 205) finds an echo in 'The shower broke... the tarmac | fumed and sizzled. As he moved off quickly' (SI, 94). Both break the dream state of the poet, leaving him to reckon with the advice he has been given. As Heaney says of Eliot's ending, these lines 'toll us back to ourselves'.[37] The 'us' here is not so much the 'us' of audience, but 'us' the poets—the Virgils, Dantes, Yeatses, Eliots, and Heaneys who must contend with the advice of shades.

In 'Little Gidding' the ghost of Virgil predicts another voice for 'next year's words', but urges both 'aftersight and foresight' in purifying the 'dialect of the tribe'. In 'Station Island', the apparition frees Heaney from tribal responsibility—'Your obligation | is not discharged by any common rite. | What you do you must do on your own' (SI, 92)—but at the same time makes what is basically a tribal claim on the English language itself: that it belongs to 'us', the Irish, as much as to any other.

---

[34] See Corcoran, *Seamus Heaney*, 124–5, O'Donoghue, *Seamus Heaney and the Language of Poetry*, 99, and Corcoran's rejoinder, Corcoran, *Seamus Heaney*, 124.
[35] Cavanagh, *Professing Poetry*, 164.
[36] Heaney, 'Envies and Identifications', 18.   [37] Ibid. 8.

Heaney may absolve himself of the duty to act in accordance with sectarian imperative—of participating in the 'common rite'—but he is no more able to imagine language in anything but tribal terms. The shade urges Heaney to 'fill the element' with 'signatures on your own frequency', but even these are not created *ex nihilo* by the creative genius of the poet. Instead they are 'echo soundings, searches, probes, allurements', each of which implies an object to be sounded, searched, probed, or allured. In setting out to write 'his own' poetry, Heaney has not only freed himself from the 'cod's game' of linguistic antagonism, he has also taken possession of a language and tradition which he can now safely and publicly call his own.

This announcement of linguistic emancipation coincides with a more tempered view of the demands of the moment. Again taking his cue from Dante, Heaney writes:

Dante could place himself in a historical world yet submit that world to scrutiny from a perspective beyond history,... he could accommodate the political and the transcendent.[38]

Cavanagh has taken note of the bridging, connective 'and' that tends to appear between opposing propositions when Heaney writes about Dante.[39] 'Accommodation', the making of room, is another, compatible way of characterizing the change that 'Station Island', Heaney's Dantesque experiment, announces. 'Room to Rhyme' was the name of the music and poetry tour that Heaney undertook in 1968 when he felt—too briefly, as it turned out—that the socio-political situation in the North was in a condition to accommodate. Heaney has spoken of poetry as dwelling simultaneously in the parish and the universe,[40] and though the conceit is adapted from Joyce's *Portrait of the Artist as a Young Man*, clearly Dante is the poet who most represents this dual citizenship. In 1989 Heaney writes, 'In Ireland we grew up as rural Catholics with little shrines at the crossroads. . . . Then I read Dante and I found in a great work of world literature that that little shrine in a corner had this cosmic significance.'[41] Like the institution of the universal, holy, catholic, and apostolic Church, which locates 'your puny

[38] Cavanagh, *Professing Poetry*, 18.
[39] Ibid. 149.
[40] Seamus Heaney, quoted in Richard Covington, 'A Scruffy Fighting Place', *Salon. com* (1996); http://archive.salon.com/weekly/heaney2.html, accessed 31 May 2010.
[41] Quoted in Carla de Petris, 'Heaney and Dante', in Robert F. Garrat (ed.), *Critical Essays on Seamus Heaney* (London: Prentice Hall, 1995), 161–71, 161.

south Derry being within the great echoing acoustic of a universe of light and dark' (SS, 471), the *Commedia* was a place in which Heaney's local 'Irish Catholic subculture', long demeaned as the superstitious rituals of an uneducated rural class, 'received high cultural ratification' (SS, 472). The worldly and the other-worldly, the local and the cosmic—these are the opposites which Heaney now begins to accommodate in his poetry.

If 'Station Island' articulates an imperative of release from the strictures of tribal language, for extension of poetic scope, *Seeing Things* (1991) represents the emphatic pursuit of these goals. O'Donoghue has observed, in line with others, that the transparency implied in the title is a motif for the entire collection, which is themed on crossings 'between this world and the next, between youth and age, between the terrestrial and the extra-terrestrial'.[42] The last book Heaney would publish before receiving his Nobel prize, it is also about seeing beyond the horizon of local context. In 'Envies and Identifications' Heaney asserts in a deferential but ultimately disapproving way that 'Eliot's achievement in his Dantean stanzas is to create . . . an illusion of oracular authority by the hypnotic deployment of perfected Latinate words'.[43] In 'Seeing Things' (ST, 16–18) he employs this very technique himself:

> *Claritas.* The dry-eyed Latin word
> Is perfect for the carved stone of the water   (ST, 17)

The clarity of *claritas*—a word which evokes both the seeable and the see-throughable—embodies the visionary perception of the poem:

> And yet in that utter visibility,
> The stone's alive with what's invisible:
> Waterweed, stirred sand-grains hurrying off,
> The shadowy, unshadowed stream itself.   (ST, 17)

The 'carved stone' is a bas-relief on a cathedral wall depicting the baptism of Christ. The bare simplicity of the carving, its 'utter visibility' so visible that it becomes suddenly transparent, allows the poet to see through to the unrepresented invisibilities, from the infinitesimal individual grains of sand to the infinite 'hieroglyph for life itself' (ST, 17). Heaney's deployment of the 'perfect' Latin word *claritas* aurally encapsulates the vision of clarity he describes in the poem.

---

[42] O'Donoghue, *Seamus Heaney and the Language of Poetry*, 120.
[43] Heaney, 'Envies and Identifications', 9.

The three parts of 'Seeing Things' are each about knowledge arrived at while making some kind of water crossing—a Dantean trope, itself borrowed from Virgil and ultimately deriving from Greek myths about the underworld. The influence of this tradition, with the *Commedia* as a proximate source, pervades *Seeing Things* almost as much as *Station Island*, from the uncasually borrowed line, 'Poet, you were *nel mezzo del cammin*' in 'The Schoolbag' (ST, 30) to Heaney's translation of Canto III, which he entitles 'The Crossing' (ST, 111–13). This poem, which closes the collection, balances the prefatory 'The Golden Bough' (ST, 1–3), a translation of the *Aeneid*, Book VI, which is also set in the moment preceding a journey to the underworld. The Classical prologue is quickly brought up-to-date in the second poem (the first 'original' one, and so the beginning of the collection proper), which from the start sets up a continuity of tradition, establishing Heaney as successor, the latest of a lineage. Just as the shade of Virgil appeared to Dante, Larkin appears to Heaney, and in his advice implies a connecting 'appearance' of Dante to Larkin:

> The Journey Back
> Larkin's shade surprised me. He quoted Dante:
>
> . . . . .
>
> I alone was girding myself to face
> The ordeal of my journey and my duty   (ST, 7)

The juxtaposition of 'journey' and 'duty' echoes the warning and advice of the Sybil of Cumae in 'The Golden Bough', who tells Aeneas to search for the sacred branch which gives permission to 'go down to earth's hidden places':

> Therefore look up and search deep and when you have found it
> Take hold of it boldly and duly. If fate has called you,
> The bough will come away easily, of its own accord.   (ST, 3)

In both of these 'first' poems, there is a dual sense of entitlement and obligation—a permission which when granted cannot then be refused—which is bestowed on the poet, and which Heaney claims as his in this collection. In so doing he grants himself safe passage across mythical, literary, and linguistic thresholds, to the 'earth's hidden places' but also to places outside the local or familiar. This is not more vertical bog delving, but an expansion on the horizontal plane of literature.

Dantean crossings to the previously unseen or unknown are made repeatedly in *Seeing Things*. In some cases, this involves a second look at the previously observed, a re-visioning of past subjects. So we get 'Glanmore Revisited' (ST, 31–7), a series of seven sonnets which gloss the focal 'Glanmore Sonnets' (FW, 33–42) of *Field Work*. These sonnets—this time, appropriate to the collection's Italian influence, in octave/sestet form—take full advantage of the new poetic range which the original sequence hoped for. This is reflected in the spatial imagination of the poems. In the first Glanmore set, the area just outside the cottage is a zone of uncertainty observed from the safety of the indoors. Both dangerous and exciting, it is a reflection of Heaney's deracination from his home in the North and its domestic and professional implications. A black rat spotted through a window in Sonnet IX is seen as an ill omen, leading Heaney to second-guess: 'What is my apology for poetry?' (FW, 41). In Sonnet VIII he wonders 'what would I meet, blood-boltered, on the road? | How deep in the woodpile sat the toad?' (FW, 40). But the unfamiliar outdoor setting also represents a new potential for his poetry. Sonnet III, in which Heaney hears the refreshing iambic calls of the cuckoo and corncrake, is representative of this potential: '(I've seen them too from the window of the house, | Like connoisseurs, inquisitive of air)' (FW, 35). Heaney too is sniffing the air, testing himself and his new environment.

In 'Glanmore Revisited', the promise of the 'Glanmore Sonnets' has been achieved and surpassed. Sonnet 7—entitled 'The Skylight'—sees the protective barrier of the house penetrated, destroying the 'claustrophobic, nest-up-in-the-roof | Effect' which had previously comforted Heaney:

> But when the slates came off, extravagant
> Sky entered and held surprise wide open.
> For days I felt like an inhabitant
> Of that house where the man sick of palsy
> Was lowered through the roof, had his sins forgiven,
> Was healed, took up his bed and walked away.   (ST, 37)

Exposure to the unknown, 'extravagant' expanse is finally not threatening but redeeming. The dusty confines of the Glanmore cottage garret are broken through to reveal another level of possibility, the infinite potential of open sky. Later Heaney returns to this image, seeing in the ruin of a house, 'Unroofed scope. Knowledge-freshening wind' (ST, 55). The unroofing dramatized in 'The Skylight' is a reflection of what

Corcoran has called an 'opulent...lexicon of luminosity' in *Seeing Things*.[44] The trope of redeeming light (heavenly light—'Sky-light'— is also implied in the title) employed here is particularly associated with the Eliotic Dante—Corcoran points to Eliot's description of the 'masterly use of that imagery of *light* which is the form of certain types of mystical experience' (SE, 267) as evidence of this mediated inheritance.[45] Heaney is becoming more and more comfortable operating in the visionary transcendent poetic style which Dante represents and which Eliot also adopted.

Encouraging extravagances of this kind is both modus operandi and autoglossic theme in *Seeing Things*. The second half of the book consists of forty-eight poems in an invented form which Heaney calls 'Squarings'. Consisting of four tetrameter tercets, they form a sort of square on the page.[46] Heaney has been formally innovative before, but never so ambitiously. These squarings are no adapted sonnets or cut-up quatrains, but a new and highly stylized form which recalls others—Dantean terza rima, chiefly, but also the sonnet and the broad stanzas of Yeats— without imitating them.[47] The freedom to innovate in such a way—to perform yet more poetic crossings—is evoked in 'Crossings, xxviii':

> Running and readying and letting go
> Into a sheerness that was its own reward:
> A farewell to surefootedness, a pitch
>
> Beyond our usual hold upon ourselves.   (ST, 86)

This conceit for poetry—a child's day spent sliding on an icy hill—is all exhilaration and devil-may-care, a confident and purposeful launch 'Beyond our usual hold upon ourselves'. 'Sheerness' and 'pitch', referring to the steepness of the incline, also connote the 'utterness' and

---

[44] Corcoran, *Seamus Heaney*, 174.

[45] Ibid.

[46] Heaney's metrics are loose in this form: in many poems the lines extend to pentameter, and (more rarely) shrink to trimeter, but four beats per line seems to be the default rule. Visually the square is achieved with help from the blank lines separating the stanzas: the poem is made up of a title and 16 lines (four tercets plus four interspaced blank lines), each line comprising four beats. Considered metrically as a group, an even grander sort of square emerges: 4 (stanzas) × 3 (lines per stanza) × 4 (beats per line) = 48 (beats per poem). All together they form a square measuring 48 beats per poem × 48 poems. And, just as an individual poem has four stanzas of twelve beats, the 'Squarings' sequence is divided into four sections of twelve poems each.

[47] The essential feature of terza rima being the weaved rhyme over a long set—often pages' worth—of tercets. Heaney's 'Squarings' are far too short to achieve such an effect. In fact they could be considered a 'cross' between a sonnet and a terza rima.

'musical note' of poetry. When Heaney wrote about 'immortelles of perfect pitch' (FW, 56) to evoke the 'ideal melodies'[48] that certain types of poetry aspire to, he was taking his first tentative steps out of the safe and homey mud-patch. Now he revels in the 'pitch | Beyond', the 'sheerness' or utterness which he associates with free and untethered poetic motion. This joy in 'letting go', in experiencing uncontrolled fall, betokens a trust in his own instinct to go beyond the established local parameters of his verse and the comforts they afford, a trust that expansive, allusive poetry can reach for perfect pitch while remaining observant of the social and ethical demands that had previously called that mode into question. The 'free passage and return' (ST, 86) from local to cosmic, from mud-flower to immortelle, from centre to circumference of poetic scope, is a liberty which Heaney is now confident in taking. 'Everything flows' (ST, 85), begins another poem in 'Crossings'. Picking up on this perhaps, Henry Hart has described Heaney's 'Squarings' sequence as proceeding in 'a flow of often unconnected associations',[49] implying at the same time connection and disconnection. The potential of poetic association opened up by Heaney's newfound 'free passage' will be fully realized only in Heaney's subsequent collections. Having successfully crossed many of the boundaries he had himself drawn—boundaries of poetic style and substance which were also social and ethical boundaries—in his late career Heaney will be concerned with bringing things together in poetry, including people, not setting them apart.

CONNECTIONS

Heaney's auditory and visionary breaking out, the 'letting go' of his established poetic strictures, is pursued in *The Spirit Level* (1996) and in his most recent collections, *Electric Light* (2001) and *District and Circle* (2006). In these books there is a palpable sense of poetry which travels long distances, bridging great divides. Heaney has, by now, lived and taught in California and Massachusetts as well as Oxford, Dublin, and

---

[48] This is the phrase Heaney uses in 'Envies and Identifications', 9, to describe 'our perennial expectations of art', that it offer 'a purely delineated realm of wisdom and beauty'.

[49] Henry Hart, 'What is Heaney Seeing in Seeing Things?', *Colby Quarterly* 30:1 (March 1994), 33–42, 35.

Belfast. He has 'been to Stockholm', and trotted the globe to read or lecture. This experience lends an ever more important international, urbane flavour to Heaney's late poetry. Heaney has written about other places before, but almost always allegorically, as stand-ins for a Northern Ireland beset by social difficulties common to other societies in different times. In *The Spirit Level*, 'The Flight Path' takes him 'Across and across and across' (SL, 24), jetting in a few short stanzas between Wicklow and Manhattan, Boston and California. In 'Tollund' (SL, 69) Heaney journeys to fulfil the prediction and promise he made a quarter of a century earlier, in 'The Tollund Man': 'Some day I will travel to Aarhus | To see his peat-brown head' (WO, 36). We can suppose that Heaney did in fact pay a visit to the Tollund man in Silkeborg Museum before driving the 10 km to Tollund Moss,[50] but the bog-body does not enter into the eventual poem. Instead Heaney writes about the place itself:

> It could have been a still out of the bright
> 'Townland of Peace', that poem of dream farms
> Outside all contention. The scarecrow's arms
> Stood open opposite the satellite
>
> Dish in the paddock, where a standing stone
> Had been resituated and landscaped
> With tourist signs in *futhark* runic script
> In Danish and in English. Things had moved on.   (SL, 69)

As a re-writing of 'The Tollund Man', 'Tollund' is a statement that everything has changed. Gone is the close-up voyeur who notices the 'mild pods of his eyelids' and spots 'winter seeds | caked in his stomach' (WO, 36); gone is the desperate imagination which sees the bog suck up its tribute; gone too is the confining dimeter and trimeter form that made 'The Tollund Man' so stilted and pained. Now the landscape calls to mind the cohabitation envisioned in John Hewitt's poem, and everything opens into space and modernity: scarecrow and paddock, which could be elements of Heaney's rural/tribal myth-making, instead frame a satellite dish, immediately locating them and their observer as a point on a mapped and orbited globe. The dish itself is a visible token of

[50] In *Stepping Stones*, Heaney describes seeing the Tollund Man for the first time in 1973 (SS, 163), and later the 'extraordinary' coincidence of finding himself again in Denmark for a reading on the weekend in the late summer of 1994 after the IRA announced its ceasefire, when an impromptu visit to the archaeological site was arranged (SS, 350–1).

the modern age, but it also represents a spot seen from the heavens—one of millions receiving messages bounced from space. The relevant dimensions of the place, which were once confined to a few metres of peat, are now exploded to include an awareness of the rest of the world, local place as part of the planet, parish as part of the universe. Reinforcing this sense of opening and contact is the standing stone, also suggestive of Heaney's past poetic totems, which has become a multilingual signpost, guiding travellers from around the world. Tollund is now just another stop on a flight plan. It can be visited and then left. Things have moved on, mercifully, from the prehistory of bog-dwellers, leaving evidence to be viewed and contemplated, but not relived.

'Tollund' is dated 'September 1994', pointing to the ceasefire announced by the IRA on 31 August of that year (as part of the Good Friday Agreement), and establishing a subtext for the poem. When the IRA renounced violence, Heaney wrote in the Dublin *Sunday Tribune*:

a blind seemed to rise somewhere at the back of my mind and the light came flooding in. . . . The cessation of violence is an opportunity to open a space—and not just in the political arena but in the first level of each person's consciousness—a space where hope can grow. (FK, 44–7)

This triptych of light, space, and hope—the Eliotic-Dantean elements which first found purchase in *Seeing Things*—has now replaced the alignment of mist, confinement, and desperation which had previously characterized Heaney's poetry. 'The Tollund Man' ended:

> Out there in Jutland
> In the old man-killing parishes
> I will feel lost,
> Unhappy and at home.   (WO, 37)

'Parishes' immediately brought the poem into the Northern Irish context, reinforcing the analogy between the modern sectarian violence of Ulster and the prehistoric tribal violence of Jutland. In 'Tollund', the relation between 'home' and the tribe is reversed:

> . . . it was user-friendly outback
> Where we stood footloose, at home beyond the tribe,
>
> More scouts than strangers, ghosts who'd walked abroad
> Unfazed by light, to make a new beginning
> And make a go of it, alive and sinning,
> Ourselves again, free-willed again, not bad.   (SL, 69)

Now home is 'beyond the tribe', not only in the geographic sense of being far from Ireland, but in the notional sense of having escaped the imperative of the 'common rite', of being allowed, finally, to see the landscape not as killing field but as 'friendly outback'. The final stanza is a poetic rendering of Heaney's account in the *Sunday Tribune*—the hope of 'a new beginning' emerges in an open and illuminated landscape of potential, which can now be scouted and discovered. In its closing line an Irish reader might recognize the audible signatures of Republican anthems: 'Ourselves again, free-willed again' playing on the Irish *sinn féin* ('we ourselves') as well as evoking the repetition of 'again' in the rebel song 'A Nation Once Again'. Heaney remarks that he liked 'the complicating echo' of those words (SS, 351). But in the echoing these sounds have gained new connotations appropriate to the shift in the political situation. The ideal of Republicanism, that of Catholic self-determination, can in this new and positive context be freed from the man-killing violence which had previously desecrated it. In this foot-loose, unfazed opening up of the poetic space, Heaney also sees the possibility of a return to the home parishes that will not be unhappy, not bad. The re-writing of 'The Tollund Man' is both re-vision and return, an enactment of Heaney's changed poetics.

In *The Spirit Level*, the re-writing of previous themes is not limited to re-visions through the lens of a new and promising political context. In 'M.' (for Mandel´shtam), Heaney renovates the image of diviner or *vates* which populated his first collections. A two-stanza poem, the first half establishes the conceit of a 'deaf phonetician', who can identify diphthong and vowel by sensing vibrations in the speaker's skull, a ken that goes beyond the natural senses. A symbol for the poet, he has a quasi-mystical 'hearing touch'—an auditory perception which works not directly from sounds but from their secondary reverberations. In the second half of the poem Heaney takes his place as *vates*, and the world replaces the human head:

> A globe stops spinning. I set my palm
> On a contour cold as permafrost
> And imagine axle-hum and the steadfast
> Russian of Osip Mandelstam.   (SL, 57)

Poetry is still a thing to be sensed below the surface, but the creative and fertile ground, once so tightly focused upon, is now seen from an infinitely more removed vantage point, a god's-eye-view which takes in not just the local earth, but Planet Earth. A globe spins on its axis, the imaginary line connecting its two unmoving, unspinning points, and that connection is renovated here in 'axle-hum', a translinguistic pun on the Russian *os′* (ось—'axle', 'axis'), the same pun Mandel′shtam himself employed to link his first name to his persecutor's in the ill-fated ode to Stalin.[51] Part 'still point of the turning world', part crystal ball, in Heaney's hand the globe becomes a conduit to another place and another language, to another poetry.

Poetic conduits such as this form the backbone of Heaney's latest collections, *Electric Light* (2001) and *District and Circle* (2006), in which Heaney fully embraces the literary-allusive style foreshadowed in his poetry since the ghost of Joyce counselled 'echo soundings, searches, probes, allurements'. Part II of *Electric Light*, a collection of elegies, kens the genius of poets past. In eleven poems, the shades of fourteen poets are felt: from the English tradition, the Beowulf poet, Chaucer, Shakespeare, Ted Hughes, and G. M. Hopkins; from Scotland, Norman MacCaig, Iain Crichton Smith, Sorley MacLean, and George Mackay Brown; and from the East, Aleksandr Pushkin, Miłosz, Zbigniew Herbert, and Brodsky (by way of W. H. Auden). Heaney's tributes are partly elegiac and partly mimetic, as if he is picking up where others have left off. In a poem juxtaposing Ted Hughes and the Beowulf poet, Heaney inserts himself as a modern scop: 'And the poet draws from his word-hoard a weird tale | . . . which I reword here' (EL, 62) and as such establishes himself as heir to the Beowulf poet and to Hughes. In 'Electric Light' he is by turns Eliotic and Chauceresque: 'To Southwark too I came, | From tube-mouth into sunlight | Moyola-breath by Thames' "straunge stronde"'[52] (EL, 81), as if his own literary journey had begun amongst the pilgrims in Harry Bailey's tavern.

Heaney was a friend and great admirer of Joseph Brodsky. In 1987 he paid homage to the recent Nobel laureate in the *New York Times*, where he praised the integrity of his vocation, his rejection of easy political

---

[51] In Gregory Freidin's translation, the poet declares, 'I would speak about him who has shifted the world's axis'. See Freidin, *A Coat of Many Colors* (Berkeley: University of California Press, 1987), 258–60. For a discussion of this and another use of the same punning technique by Mandel′shtam, see Tony Brinkley and Raina Kostova, '"The Road to Stalin": Mandelstam's Ode to Stalin and "The Lines on the Unknown Soldier"', *Shofar: An Interdisciplinary Journal of Jewish Studies* 21:4 (2003), 32–62, 35–40.

[52] The syntax and cadence of 'To Southwark too I came' recalls Eliot's 'To Carthage then I came' (CP, 64) while the third line references the General Prologue of *The Canterbury Tales*: 'Thanne longen folk to goon on pilgrimages | And palmeres for to seken straunge strondes' (I.12–13).

partisanship, his faith in language and in literature.[53] Less than ten years later, he wrote that publication's obituary for Brodsky, where he said that 'every encounter with him constituted a renewal of belief in the possibilities of poetry'.[54] It is likely that meeting Brodsky in 1972 encouraged Heaney's burgeoning interest in Eastern bloc poetry: his first essay on an Eastern poet ('Faith, Hope and Poetry: Osip Mandelstam', 1974), boldly written and with a stridency more characteristic of late Brodsky than of early Heaney, appears in *Hibernia* two years later. It may also be, as Carmen Bugan has suggested, that Heaney's translation of *Buile Suibhne* (as *Sweeney Astray*, 1983) is motivated by the same growing sense of exile that makes Brodsky so personally attractive to him.[55] Whatever the case, Heaney's admiration for his friend exists primarily outside the aesthetic or technical. His 1987 *Times* piece hardly mentions the poet's verse, focusing instead on the qualities of his character, his philosophy of language and literature, his devotion to his work. For Heaney, Brodsky represents an ideal of poetic integrity and moral credibility. To read *Crediting Poetry* alongside Brodsky's own Nobel lecture is to realize how impressive an exemplar he was for Heaney.

Heaney's two latest collections each include a poem for Brodsky. In *Electric Light*, 'Audenesque' appropriates the form of 'In Memory of W. B. Yeats' to elegize him:

> Joseph, yes, you know the beat.
> Wystan Auden's metric feet
> Marched to it, unstressed and stressed,
> Laying William Yeats to rest.   (EL, 64)

Significantly, this is not the metre of the first two parts of Auden's poem, but that of the last part, much reduced by Auden but most prized by Brodsky, in which the poet insists on poetic continuation in the face of loss, imploring his elegized predecessor to give us the audience reason for joy. The coincidence that Brodsky died on the same date as Yeats ('Double-crossed and death-marched date | January twenty-eight') allows Heaney to construct a poem around four poets, himself a

---

[53] Seamus Heaney, 'Brodsky's Nobel: What the Applause Was About', *The New York Times* (8 November 1987), BR1.

[54] Seamus Heaney, 'The Singer of Tales: On Joseph Brodsky', *The New York Times* (3 March 1996), BR31.

[55] Carmen Bugan, 'Poetics of Exile: East European Poetry in Translation and Seamus Heaney's Ars Poetica', Dissertation, University of Oxford, 2004, 88 ff.

recognized orchestrating presence. There are biographical connections which also recommend Auden as a model to be followed. Brodsky often cited 'In Memory of W. B. Yeats' as the trigger of his poetic epiphany,[56] and that poem's 'Time... | Worships language' is representative of Brodsky's concept of language as thing harried and oppressed (by tyrants) or liberated and developed (by poets), what Heaney calls his 'peremptory trust | In words' (EL, 64), and elsewhere his 'total conviction about poetry as a force for good' (FK, 438). In the literary-allusive background lie Brodsky's two elegies for Auden and his other Auden-esque elegy, 'Verses on the Death of T. S. Eliot' (1965).

In Heaney's poem, links amongst the four mentioned poets are forged almost effortlessly, but connections that seem like found things are in fact more intricate than they appear. The two trochees 'Wystan Auden's' reproduce both the cadence and the first-name unfamiliarity of Auden's 'William Yeats (is)', and Brodsky's '*Tomas Sterns, (ne)*' (Томас Стернс, не—'Thomas Stearns, don't') in his elegy for Eliot. As eulogist and eulogized, Heaney is to Brodsky as Auden is to Yeats; as poets and poetic subjects, Heaney and Auden correspond to Brodsky and Yeats; as poetic forebears, Yeats is to Heaney as Auden is to Brodsky. A visual representation of these relationships would have arrows of influence pointing in different directions to and from each name. Breaching the separation of time, space, and language, Heaney's poem knits him into an international, intergenerational, even interlinguistic poetic grouping. This is accomplished by allusiveness and associativity: referring to Auden's poem, Heaney writes, 'Its measured ways I tread again' and 'repetition is the rule', and he does faithfully reproduce Auden's pulse and metre. He also weaves in words and images from the original: 'airport', 'ice', 'locked in frost', and 'worshipped language' make re-appearances in this re-written poem. There is also the sense, however, of 'justness' beyond mere appropriateness, that this is a poem which Auden *should* have written, or perhaps would have if he had lived another twenty-five years. 'In Memory of W. B. Yeats' raises the question of the redemptive power of poetry (in the long version Time 'pardons' Kipling and Claudel for their work in language), and it is fitting that 'Audenesque' should be written for someone who believed as completely in this power as Brodsky did. It is also a confirmation of Heaney's own belief in

---

[56] See Brodsky's account of this on pp. 61–2, 64 above.

poetry's effectiveness. 'Worshipped language' may not be enough to conquer death, but it does give poets a sort of life after death. Heaney's valedictory advice to his friend is a turn on Auden's aphorism: 'Do again what Auden said | Good poets do: bite, break their bread' (EL, 66).

'Breaking bread with the dead' would do as an alternate title for *Electric Light*, as would 'Finders Keepers', the title of Heaney's 2002 edition of selected prose. So would 'The Real Names'[57]—the title of a poem for Brian Friel about school theatre: through seventy-eight pages of poetry, in its titles, dedications, and poems, *Electric Light* drops ninety non-fictional proper names, fifty-six of which are delivered fully as both given and family name.[58] The avatars of Heaney's early poetry have given way to real people with real names—this poetry connects itself to literary and non-literary personages alike, and in doing so connects them to each other. It is a manifestation of Heaney's belief in literature as a shared cultural phenomenon: 'I believe in the handing-on of the possessions, from one generation to the next, and I believe in preserving the cultural memory.'[59] *Electric Light* pursues this goal, drawing from a complement of poets varied enough to include Virgil (in 'Bann Valley Eclogue') and German poet Hans Magnus Enzensberger (in 'Known World').

Several reviewers critiqued Heaney for the bookishness of *Electric Light*, arguing that the immediacy of his previous books had disappeared behind a veil of erudition.[60] There is certainly a sense of shored-up fragments conveyed by the associative range Heaney has permitted himself in *Electric Light*, one which allows him to see Hopkins's Felix Randal in the image of his dying father ('Seeing the Sick'; EL, 79) and to connect Patrick Kavanagh, biblical quotation, *Tess of the*

---

[57] Before writing what would become the title poem, Heaney considered 'The Real Names' as a title for the collection. See Seamus Heaney, 'Lux Perpetua: Seamus Heaney on the Making of his Recent Collection, *Electric Light*', *The Guardian* (16 June 2001), 9.

[58] Excluding names from myth, the Bible, and literature or where they are used metonymically, as 'A Botticelli' (EL, 30). Some names are used more than once, and where they appear in different poems, I have counted them again. 'The Real Names' accounts for twenty of the total.

[59] Seamus Heaney with Karl Miller, 46.

[60] For instance, Robert Potts, in *The Guardian* (7 April 2001), 8, calls Heaney's literary allusions 'emblems of instant authority' in which he seemed 'comfortably cosseted'. In *The New Statesman* (16 April 2001), 53, Adam Newey echoes the sentiment when he writes that in Heaney's 'nods to departed greats...one can almost hear the ripple of audience applause at the mention of each name'.

D'Urbervilles, and the story of Michael Collins in one allusive drift ('The Loose Box'; EL, 14–16). In 'Vitruviana', Heaney claims, with another nod to Eliot, 'On Sandymount Strand I can connect | Some bits and pieces' (EL, 53). This constant recourse to 'cultural memory', manifested in the individual accumulated memory of a man who has spent a lifetime in literature, has a definite preservative purpose. The 'handing-on of [cultural] possessions' is of vital importance:

> There's no religious pulpit for the young anymore, there's no belief in political leaders, there's no bond. Literature was one of the last elements in such a bond, and if you stop teaching literature . . . it's perilous, I think. Soviety, even.[61]

The recurrent principle of 'connection' in *Electric Light*, which links 'bits and pieces' of the cultural memory in the ranging mind of the poet, is implicated in this recourse to 'bond'—a shared experience of literature and the culture it represents—as an element of protection against totalitarianism. The influence of Brodsky can be felt in Heaney's opposition of 'literature' and 'Soviet', as can Eliot's idea that cultures which do not fortify themselves with literature 'will deteriorate and perhaps become absorbed in a stronger one' (OPP, 21). *Electric Light*, with its closely knitted fabric of literary allusion, is exemplary of Heaney's desire to preserve the shared literature of the past in his current poetry, to fortify the bond between readers and that culture.

Heaney is alert to the charge, also levied against Eliot's literary allusiveness (not to mention, for the moment, Geoffrey Hill's), that this poetry challenges the ability of the average reader to play along—that it participates in the kind of exclusivity that is often called 'elitism'. At this stage in his career, however, exclusiveness is no longer a poetic technique to be revelled in. Though literary allusiveness may be 'difficult to manage', unlike the unpronounceable phoneme or the subjugated *colonisé*, it does not have to be so for long. So while Heaney acknowledges that the 'risk was that the poem might then range too freely beyond the reader's ken', he concludes, 'still that seemed a risk worth taking'[62] The taking of this risk betokens a 'trust that the reader will go with'[63] the allusions that the poet deploys, that the learning displayed will not be a burden but an opportunity for the audience. This is dramatized in 'The Bookcase', for instance, which delights in voicing the proper names of poets, naming Hugh MacDiarmid, Elizabeth

---

[61] Seamus Heaney with Karl Miller, 46.
[62] Heaney, 'Lux Perpetua', 9.   [63] Ibid.

Bishop, Yeats, Hardy, Frost, Stevens, and Dylan (Thomas). These are poets under whom 'the bookcase held and never sagged' (EL, 51). The bookcase, as a symbol of a literary education, is in the end much less daunting than it first appeared:

> I imagine us bracing ourselves for the first big lift,
> Then staggering for balance, it has grown so light.   (EL, 52)

This is the most recent adaptation of a trope which can be traced to Heaney's early comparison of the pen and the spade. It is echoed in 'The Schoolbag'—'*Learning's easy carried!* The bag is light' (ST, 30)—and taken up again in Heaney's appropriation of Virgil's eclogues. There, in 'Glanmore Eclogue', his interlocutor tells him:

> Book-learning is the thing. You're a lucky man.
> No stock to feed, no milking times, no tillage
> Nor blisters on your hand nor weather-worries.   (EL, 36)

Heaney has referred to the pastoral—the eclogue in particular—as a poetic genre that 'involves a self-conscious literary performance', requiring 'at least a minimal awareness of tradition on the part of both the poet and the audience'.[64] In this passage he follows the eclogue's convention of an encounter in a pastoral setting, and in doing so recalls the many less than literate personages in Heaney's poetry (as well as his anecdotal prose) who approach him and his hyper-literary world with mitigated approval, a well-wishing curiosity tempered by an instinctive suspicion of the highfalutin. It is really a dialogue between two halves of himself, the 'lived, illiterate and unconscious' and the 'learned, literate and conscious' (P, 131) self, and as such it represents the beginning and the end of a lifelong journey into literature.

The 'trust' that mitigates the 'risk' Heaney takes in *Electric Light* is not so much that the reader will be as learned as him, but that he will 'go with' him on some part of this allusive journey, that there be a shared delight and pleasure in the re-enactment of literature. Fittingly, this is a process that Heaney describes in 'Learning from Eliot', in reference to his own reading experience of 'difficult' poetry:

Poetry that was initially beyond you, generating the need to understand and overcome its strangeness, becomes in the end a familiar path within you, a grain

---

[64] Seamus Heaney, 'Eclogues *in Extremis*: On the Staying Power of the Pastoral', *Proceedings of the Royal Irish Academy* 103C:1 (2003), 1–12, 1.

along which your imagination opens pleasurably backwards towards an origin and a seclusion. Your last state is therefore a thousand times better than your first, for the experience of poetry is one which truly deepens and fortifies itself with re-enactment. (FK, 28)

The slow incorporation of a work of poetry, the marking of a 'path within you' along which the mind can freely travel, is a way of reading which is reflected in Heaney's progressive adoption of translation and literary allusion within his poetry. If the poems in *Electric Light* move unencumbered from the Classical to the postmodern, it is an invitation to join Heaney in journeying 'pleasurably backwards', to share with him his own and our common experience of literature, and to learn from that experience. This literary journeying can have a specific social and personal ethical effect on the reader. Lecturing on Virgil's eclogues, Heaney connects literariness with a version of *alethia*, the uncovering of truth that Heidegger and others claim in favour of art:

The literary is one of the methods human beings have devised for getting at reality: if it is concerned with its own appearance, that is only because it wants to show up or get behind other appearances. Its diversions are not to be taken as deceptions but as roads less travelled by where the country we thought we knew is seen again in a new and revealing light.[65]

The inflection of 'country' is as much national as it is bucolic—in Virgil's pastorals Heaney highlights the historical-political setting to support his claim that they are 'capable of compelling a serious interest as well as giving a serious pleasure'.[66] That a performance of literariness can 'get behind' appearances, that it can uncover a truth, or an aspect of truth, as Virgil's does and as Heaney's aims to do, is one way in which it can achieve its ethics from within its integral literary sphere.

The revision of Heaney's early 'pushing back' mode into a 'pleasurably backwards' movement continues in *District and Circle* (2006). In his second collection Heaney had written, 'All I know is a door into the dark', imagining his poetic vocation as a path to the occulted insides of a blacksmith's forge, where the owner 'grunts and goes in, with a slam and flick | To beat real iron out, to work the bellows' (DD, 19). In the new book, Heaney re-visions this trope with the same expanding, expansive technique as 'Tollund' employs in revising 'The Tollund Man'. In 'Midnight Anvil', the occasion is a celebration of the new millennium

---

[65] Ibid. 4.   [66] Ibid. 5.

set in 'the same Devlin forge' as the earlier poem.[67] But despite the year's-end ritual described in the poem—twelve strokes of hammer on anvil—here too things have moved on. The blacksmith himself was a nebulous, archetypal 'he' in 'The Forge'. Now he is just 'Barney Devlin', translated from early-Heaney avatar into late-Heaney 'real name'. And, as in 'Tollund', satellites are broadcasting the event from the local into the universe:

> His nephew heard it
> In Edmonton, Alberta:
> The cellular phone
> Held high as a horse's ear   (DC, 26)

Against the old-world goings-on of a country forge at the turn of the millennium, one would be hard pressed to counterpoise a less mythic, less fabulous or occulted or numinous place—a more distant place, more even in associative resonance than in sheer *kilométrage* (6,192 km)—than Edmonton, Alberta. But for the third millennium, this linkage is entirely appropriate, situating the ritual event in the clear and accessible present, and confirming it there, where cultural, traditional, and family ties are sustained over great distances. This is not to renounce the tradition invoked by the act: it puts Heaney in mind of 'those waterburning | Medieval smiths',

> And Eoghan Rua
> Asking Séamus MacGearailt
> To forge him a spade   (DC, 26–7)

We are put in the presence of tradition here—a local tradition that associates artistic and artisanal 'making', the poetic craft and the handicraft. In linking bits of this tradition,[68] Heaney also calls up George Herbert (*church bels beyond the starres heard*), fifteenth-century Middle English lyric, and seventeenth-century Irish-language poet Eoghan Rua Ó Súilleabháin, echoing Heaney's own first poem, in which he resolved to use the pen as his forebears used the spade. But in this poem, we are brought into the presence of the tradition without being immersed for long in its attendant mythology. Heaney skips, quatrain by quatrain,

---

[67] Seamus Heaney, 'One Poet in Search of a Title', *Times Online* (25 March 2006); http://www.thetimes.co.uk/tto/arts/books/article2450529.ece, accessed 31 May 2010.

[68] An early title for the poem was 'Linked Verses'. See Seamus Heaney, 'Linked Verses', *AGNI* 57 (2003), 8.

from the Devlin forge to Edmonton, then quickly on to Herbert's 'Prayer' and the anonymous 'The Smiths', finally ending with Eoghan Rua, a brisk 'moving on', connecting 'bits and pieces' into a usefully pleasurable—but not a controlling, all-consuming—literary and cultural lineage.

District and Circle makes a final, perhaps an ultimate, step in the direction of reconciliation in the formal range that it employs. The collection contains twenty-one sonnets (including the five that make up 'District and Circle' and the six parts of 'The Tollund Man in Springtime'), ten long-metre poems in quatrains, five prose poems (the first published since *Stations*, in 1975), several hybrid and miscellaneous forms, and seven 'skinny poems' in trimeters and dimeters, more than in any collection since *North*, after which the form was intentionally abandoned in favour of the 'melodious grace' of the longer 'English line'.[69] In the intervening collections, where the thin form was revived it instantly recalled the ambient desolation of *North*. For example, 'Cassandra' in *The Spirit Level* is a brutally thin poem, in places compressing dimeter to monometer:

> her clipped, devast-
> ated, scabbed
> punk head,
> the char-eyed
>
> famine gawk —
> she looked
> camp-fucked
> and simple   (SL, 30–1)

But in *District and Circle*, the short line is sweetened and the theme lightened. It is not a vehicle of closed-in, claustrophobic anxiety, but of release and opening-out, as in the *nunc dimittis* ending of 'Nonce Words':

> And blessed myself
> in the name of the nonce,
> and happenstance,
> the *Who knows*
> and *What nexts*
> and *So be its.*   (DC, 45)

---

[69] Heaney, interview with Kinahan, 412.

Amen. Metre and theme confirm each other here, as they do in the early work, but in the opposing direction: the poem is not halting but forward-leading, the unstressed initial syllables running the lines onward towards glad assent to the unavoidable vicissitudes of any life. Here is an inevitability that is utterly at odds with the inevitability of going one day to Aarhus, of feeling 'lost | Unhappy and at home', the ineluctability of revenge, of 'memory incubating the spilled blood' ('North'; N, 20). Heaney has freed himself from these preoccupations enough to return to the form they spawned with renewed optimism and readiness.

The freeing of the short line from its metric and thematic 'difficulty' is dramatized on both planes in 'To Mick Joyce in Heaven', the first and longest thin poem in *District and Circle*. The poem opens with a man's transformation from army man to craftsman. The initial dactyls of the first lines are reminiscent of the halting early-Heaney kennings:

> Kit-bag to tool-bag,
> Warshirt to workshirt —
> Out of your element

But as Mick Joyce's transition progresses, the line-cleaving initial stresses quickly melt into line-bridging down-beats:

> A demobbed Achilles
> Who was never a killer,
> The strongest instead
> Of the world's stretcher-bearers,
> Turning your hand
> To the bricklaying trade.   (DC, 8)

The change of occupation turns out to be more congruous than initially intimated, the war-work having been heroic rescue, not heroic slaying. Similarly, Heaney's transition from a halting poetry of insular self-protection to one of unanxious inclusion has been easier than could have been expected in the 1970s. Having made two major rhythmic departures on socio-ethical grounds as much as on acoustic grounds, first from the 'English line' and then from the short line that was to stand against it, Heaney in the late stages of his career can incorporate both with alacrity—even with joy—and neither offend the demands of the historical moment nor the integrity of poetic craft.

TRANSLATIONS

Heaney's progression towards a far-ranging incorporative poetry is reflected in a fifteen-year effort to produce a new translation of the Anglo-Saxon epic *Beowulf,* which is finally published in 1999.[70] In 1984 Heaney was appointed Boylston Professor of Rhetoric and Oratory at Harvard University, which for more than ten years required him to spend six months per year in Cambridge, Massachusetts. He reports that this semi-annual hiatus from Ireland was accompanied by a sort of auditory homesickness. Surrounded by the 'unmoored speech of contemporary American poetry' (B, xxii), Heaney was searching for a guarantee of aural integrity, a tether to his linguistic centre. So, at the same time that the *Beowulf* translation is an extension of his incorporative poetic project, it is also an auditory 'return to the sources':

Saying yes to the *Beowulf* commission would be (I argued with myself) a kind of aural antidote, a way of ensuring that my linguistic anchor would stay lodged on the Anglo-Saxon sea floor. (B, xxii)

Despite this attitude of at-home comfort with the acoustics of Old English poetry, most of Heaney's 'About this Translation' section is spent establishing translator's rights within a political and historical context that would make a vexed pair of an Old English text and a Northern Irish interpreter. Chris Jones is correct in observing that 'Heaney has set his own critical agenda in this respect',[71] with perhaps more flair for postcolonial controversy than the task itself may warrant.[72] But if it is true that Heaney has trumped up charges against himself in order successfully to fend them off, it is just as true that this is of a piece with his early ambivalent attitude towards the 'alliterative tradition'. That the ambivalence is worked out here in discursive prose

---

[70] In his conversation with Robert Hass, 5, Heaney remembers translating 150 lines of *Beowulf* as early as 1984–5, his first academic year at Harvard, and a similar account appears in his *Seamus Heaney in Conversation with Karl Miller,* 40. *The Haw Lantern* (1987) publishes twenty-six translated lines under the title 'A Ship of Death'.

[71] Chris Jones, *Strange Likeness: The Use of Old English in Twentieth Century Poetry* (Oxford: Oxford University Press, 2006), 229.

[72] Jones argues persuasively that, not only are the advertised Hibernicisms in Heaney's *Beowulf* fewer and less significant than Heaney makes out, but in any event the controversy is mainly invented, since *Beowulf* has 'never been a document used to ramify the authority of a metropolitan English identity or to legitimize a dominant English tradition' (230).

may expose it to a different kind of scrutiny—and justly so—but it also confirms how, for Heaney (if not for Jones or others), acoustics that reverberate with English associations can only be approached once their specific socio-ethical ramifications have been established and interrogated.

Heaney is echoing the shade in 'Station Island' when he states, 'I consider *Beowulf* to be part of my voice-right' (B, xxiii). Yet to claim this in his own voice requires additional data rooted from the depths of the auditory imagination. Whereas in earlier life Heaney dug up sounds and associations to delineate his poetry from the English tradition, what he requires here is a linguistic bridge to link him with it, a 'region where one's language would not be simply a badge of ethnicity or a matter of cultural preference or an official imposition, but an entry into a further language' (B, xxv). This region is eventually discovered within the phonetic bounds of one Old English word. In a Stephen Dedalus moment, Heaney recalls finding in *Beowulf* the word *polian*—'endure'—which he had heard from his aunt as a child in Northern Ireland. He writes:

And now suddenly here was 'thole' in the official textual world, mediated through the apparatus of a scholarly edition, a little bleeper to remind me that my aunt's language was not just a self-enclosed family possession but an historical heritage. (B, xxv)

Between the very Irish use of 'thole' and the very English use of *polian*, Heaney narrates a kind of philological travelogue, envisioning 'the journey *polian* had made north into Scotland and then across into Ulster with the planters, and then across from the planters to the locals who originally spoke Irish, and then farther across again when the Scots Irish emigrated to the American South in the eighteenth century' (B, xxv). This linguistic voyage links the people that mark its path. Like the diverse local factions that manage to pronounce *Broagh* with the proper *O* and *gh*, here people from distant places and times are united in a linguistic community. Crucially, this community includes Heaney and the *Beowulf* poet, giving Heaney rights to the rest of the poem: 'I was ready to translate *Beowulf*', he writes; '*Polian* had opened my right of way' (B, xxvi).

The first element of the right of way Heaney claims in the introduction is asserted forcefully in the first fifteen lines of the poem, where his translation reads:

> He knew what they had tholed,
> the long times and troubles they'd come through   (B, 3)

Given the introduction's ado about 'thole' we should expect to find the 'official' *polian* in the original text, but in fact it is *fyrenðearfe ongeat*— 'he understood their dire distress' (or 'wicked-trouble')—which is rendered with that pregnant Ulsterism. *Polian*, which appears in various inflections nine times in *Beowulf*,[73] is variously translated by Heaney as 'undergo', 'endure', 'last' (as in 'withstand'), 'in deep distress', 'gone through', 'lodge' (as in 'dwell'), 'a hurt', 'nursed', and 'suffered', but never as 'thole'.[74] Having established philologically the 'just'ness of the local word 'thole' to the Anglo-Saxon context, Heaney seems impatient to get it onto the first page of his text. Even the layout of the Faber edition appears to call attention to the word: located at the precise physical centre of the page, the long line nudges 'thole' out beyond the others so it stands uncluttered and obvious. The mark of Heaney is thereby made indelible from the outset. Heaney has said that his *Beowulf* is 'about one-third Heaney, two-thirds "duty to the text"'.[75] In a conversation with Robert Hass, he describes translation in terms which instantly recall the conflicted Irish-English relationship: 'you can enter an oeuvre, colonize it, take it over—but you stay with it, and you change it and it changes you a little bit. . . . I stayed with *Beowulf*.'[76] Thus Heaney performs the postcolonial reading for which his introduction has primed his audience.

To follow Heaney's lead on this question, one way in which the poet 'stays' with *Beowulf* is his occasional use of the word 'bawn' to refer to Hrothgar's dwelling. Some words in poetry are so associated with one poet that they take on metonymic qualities. 'Etherised', for instance, is Eliot; 'gyre', Yeats. For most readers—certainly those for whom it is dialectically unfamiliar—'bawn', like 'guttural' and 'slap' (as a noun), immediately calls to mind the poetry of Seamus Heaney.[77] In *Beowulf*,

---

[73] See lines in *Beowulf*, 3rd edn, ed. Frederick Klaeber (Boston: D. C. Heath, 1950), *polian*, 832; *polað*, 284, 2499; *ðolode*, 131, 1525; *geðolian*, 3109; *geðolianne*, 1419; *geðolode*, 87, 147. These correspond to pages 27, 11, 79, 7, 50, 97, 47, 5, 7, respectively, in Heaney, though the line numbers do not always match.

[74] For reference purposes, these are listed in the same order as pages in the above note.

[75] See Mel Gussow, 'Irish Touch on an Anglo-Saxon Chiller', *The New York Times* (29 March 2000), E1.

[76] Conversation with Robert Hass, 1.

[77] Some commentators, including Heaney, mention 'bawn' in association with Spenser, though his use of the term is limited to letters and a short passage in *A View of the Present State of Ireland*. Of the 350,000 works of English literature stored in the Literature Online database (LION), 31 poems use 'bawn' in the same way, including three by Heaney ('Traditions', 'A New Song', and 'Belderg'; the tally does not include

it is no less replete with significance: 'Putting a bawn into *Beowulf* seems one way for an Irish poet to come to terms with that complex history of conquest and colony, absorption and resistance, integrity and antagonism' (B, xxx). Like 'thole', 'bawn' has divided loyalties—originally an Irish word[78] it was adapted by English and Scottish planters and eventually readopted by the local population. The word participates in Heaney's idea of translation as settling, or settling as translation: both incomer and local are changed in the meeting. By using 'bawn' for the Danish stronghold, Heaney leaves another personal mark on the poem, a mark which affirms its Irish accent.

The most conspicuous of Heaney's inserted terms is 'brehon'—from Old Irish *brithem*, 'judge'—for *ðyle*, an orator or spokesman, a translation which even Heaney would later admit 'went too far' (SS, 440). A *ðyle* in the Anglo-Saxon court is the official orator—the word is also translated as 'spokesman', 'sage', and 'entertainer'.[79] He may also be, as Unferth is, a kind of censor of boasts,[80] the man who makes sure that knights don't vaunt idly or dishonestly in the mead hall. In this sense he is a kind of judge, but certainly not in any capacity as official, or powerful, or respected as that of the Irish *brithem*. And if boast-testing is in fact one of Unferth's official capacities, he discharges it neither honourably nor successfully—Beowulf is quickly proved a man of strength and honour who should be taken at his word. Spenser describes the brehon as the corrupt hand of a barbaric pagan legal system, in which, among other deviant provisions, a murderer may pay a fine rather than suffer some worse form of justice.[81] Abolished by James I and replaced with the Christian law of the realm, Brehon Law is a pagan regime remembered from a Christian context, just as the Christian Beowulf poet tells of pre-Christian rites of retaliation and retribution. In this way the archaic and brutal justice of the poem is brought into momentary focus by the evocation of its Irish concomitant. The

---

Beowulf or the essay 'Mossbawn'). Swift, Yeats, and Tom Paulin have also used the word, but none of these, nor even Spenser, accords as much weight as Heaney.

[78] See n. 15 above.

[79] Klaeber also gives 'poet of note', 'major domus', 'historiologer', 'king's right-hand man', and 'official entertainer' as possible translations (Klaeber (ed.), *Beowulf*, 149).

[80] See Klaeber, *Beowulf*, ll. 499–603, in Heaney, pp. 18–20. Here Unferth challenges Beowulf's reputation as a warrior and is rebuked.

[81] Edmund Spenser, *A View of the Present State of Ireland* (London: Eric Partridge, 1934), 7–8.

semantic gulf between *ðyle* and 'brehon' is narrowed by the latter's associative power in the contemporary postcolonial moment.

Jones has called Heaney's *Beowulf* 'not so much a Troubles as a ceasefire poem', because it describes a society in which 'peace is constantly on the verge of being broken by long-held enmities and suppressed feuds'.[82] In *Wintering Out* and *North*, Heaney established and developed a 'bog people' trope, using self-consciously un-English forms, which allowed him to write about sectarian violence in Northern Ireland while distancing himself and his poetry from the instrumentalism of overtly political verse. This distancing is in fact a safe approach to dangerous subject matter—the danger being as much in the ethics of true representation as in the threat to poetic integrity. In and after *Field Work*, as Heaney grows into a visionary, expansive, literary-allusive mode, this distancing, this approaching, is increasingly achieved via translation. 'Ugolino', in which Archbishop Roger tells that 'hunger killed where grief had only wounded' (FW, 63), is the first such attempt, tracing the words of Dante, with all their cultural and historical authority, to evoke and condemn the conditions which led to the 'dirty protests' of 1978.

Talking about the earlier kind of allegorical writing, in 'Feeling into Words' (1974) Heaney describes poetry as divination, as 'restoration of the culture to itself; poems as elements of continuity, with the aura and authenticity of archaeological finds, where the buried shard has an importance that is not diminished by the importance of the buried city; poetry as a dig' (P, 41). Those words, written just before the publication of *North*, are in reference to his first poem, 'Digging', but apply equally well—perhaps better—to Heaney's latter digging around in the literary traditions of Europe. There is social and ethical value in the 'buried shard'. Speaking of *Beowulf,* Heaney says,

The movement between a deep past and what is going on around us is necessary, I think, if we are to hold on to ourselves as creatures of culture. The literary deep past, I mean, and the historical present.[83]

Heaney is both mindful and bashful about the Eliotic implications of this formulation, continuing: 'I know all that sounds very Eliotesque, very un-post-modern, but it's based on my experience as a reader and as

---

[82] Jones, *Strange Likeness*, 235. Heaney translates about a hundred lines in 1984 or 1985; the rest is done in 1995–9.
[83] Seamus Heaney with Karl Miller, 42.

a writer.'[84] Heaney is just as Eliotic, and more assertively so, when in 1995 he tells the Swedish and sundry dignitaries assembled to laud him that he believes in 'the connection between the construction or destruction of a political order and the founding or foundering of cultural life' (CR, 40).

The connection Heaney asserts may be, as Eliot would have it, 'very diffused, very indirect, and difficult to prove' (OPP, 22), but he prizes it. On translating *Beowulf,* he writes:

I didn't think to myself, 'Ah, here is a story with an ending that matches the sense of an ending we are now experiencing in Northern Ireland. Here is a poet from the remote past whose stoicism and understatement and homiletic power match something in the reticence and staying power and veteran's awareness that prevail in the Ulster sensibility'.... But gradually the adequacy of the poetry to the present time became apparent to me.[85]

In uniting the 'literary deep past' with the historical here-and-now, Heaney establishes and reinforces a continuity of literate tradition which overcomes separations of time and culture, bridging those divides as it does so. In *Wintering Out* the Anglo-Saxon literary tradition was figured as an overpowering bull. In *North* it was like a bone fragment wound in 'the sling of my mind', ready to be pitched at England. Now it is seen as part of a unifying bond among readers, a vital verification of their status as 'creatures of culture'.

Several translations, long and short, have marked the two most recent decades of Heaney's career. In 1990 he translated and staged *The Cure at Troy*, a version of Sophocles's *Philoctetes*. In 1993 he rendered portions of Ovid's *Metamorphoses* and Brian Merriman's *Cúirt an Mheán Oíche* (*The Midnight Court*), which were published together as *The Midnight Verdict*. In 1994 and 1995 he translated Jan Kochanowski's *Laments* (1995), and passages of Aeschylus's *Oresteia*, which were reprinted in *The Spirit Level* (1996) as 'Mycenae Lookout'. The year 1999 saw most of the *Beowulf* translation completed, and the appearance of Heaney's *Diary of One Who Vanished*, originally by Leoš Janáček. In 2002 Heaney translated Sorley MacLean's 'Hallaig',[86] and in 2004 he published a 'retelling' of Robert Henryson's medieval Scots poem, *The Testament of Cresseid* (adding seven of Henryson's fables,

---

[84] Ibid.   [85] Ibid. 42–3.
[86] Appearing in *The Guardian* (30 November 2002), and as a limited bilingual edition (Sleat: Urras Shomhairle/Sorley MacLean Trust, 2002).

three times the length of his *Testament*, for the trade Faber edition of 2009)[87] and returned to Sophocles for a version of *Antigone*, which he entitled *The Burial at Thebes*.[88] In this period the Greek tragedies appealled especially to Heaney in part because, as he says in reference to *Antigone*, 'the choral mode allows for and almost requires a homiletic note that you would tend to exclude from personal lyric' (SS, 421). The 'unrestrained rhetoric' that the choral mode authorizes is audible from the opening lines of *The Cure at Troy*:

> CHORUS
> Philoctetes.
>   Hercules.
>   Odysseus.
> Heroes. Victims. Gods and human beings.
> All throwing shapes, every one of them
> Convinced he's in the right, all of them glad
> To repeat themselves and their every last mistake,
> No matter what.   (CT, 1)

This is yet more faults-on-both-sides, inevitable revenge-cycle stuff, wrought as roughly and directly as the choral mode will allow. Heaney ends the play with a 'glimpse of possibility', holding out hope that 'once in a lifetime | the longed for tidal wave | of justice can rise up, | and hope and history rhyme' (CT, 77), again balancing despair with the chance of an end to desperation. His chorus at the outset announces its function as 'more or less a border line between | The you and the me and the it of it | . . . | And that's the border that poetry | Operates on too, always in between' (CT, 2). *The Cure at Troy*, even in its more direct rhetoric, treads instinctively the same middle ground that the early lyrics keep to. 'Between' is the first word of the first poem in *Death of a Naturalist*,

---

[87] First published as *The Testament of Cresseid: A Retelling of Robert Henryson's Poem* (London: Enitharmon Editions, 2004). The Faber edition appeared as *The Testament of Cresseid and Seven Fables* (London: Faber and Faber, 2009).

[88] To include individual poems in this list is to add translations or versions of Virgil's *Aeneid* ('The Golden Bough', ST, 1–3; 'The Riverbank Field' in *The Riverbank Field*), and *Eclogues* ('Bann Valley Eclogue', EL, 11–12; 'Virgil: Eclogue IX', EL, 31–4; 'Glanmore Eclogue', EL, 35–7); Dante's *Inferno* ('The Crossing', ST, 111–13); Rilke ('Rilke: *After the Fire*', EL, 16; 'Rilke: *The Apple Orchard*', EL, 68); Pushkin ('Arion', EL, 72); Horace's *Odes* ('Anything Can Happen', DC, 13); as well as translations from the Irish: 'Columcille the Scribe', *The Irish Times* (7 June 1997), 45; 'Poet to Blacksmith' (DC, 25).

Heaney's first book. Like several other features of 'Digging', 'between' establishes a paradigm followed throughout the Heaney corpus. Its recurring function is to locate the poet in relation to but equidistant from two social or civic states of mind.[89]

If the pre-ceasefire *Cure at Troy* maintains Heaney's cautious balance between blame and exoneration, between history and hope, post-ceasefire 'Mycenae Lookout' takes an unexpected turn. After the immediate sense of release described in 'Tollund' comes a fresh wash of 'rage at what had gone on in the previous twenty-five years' (SS, 350). In rewriting 'The Tollund Man' Heaney could translate the old despairing claustrophobia into a new sense of open air, a 'new beginning'. But to give free rein finally to suppressed anger, as well as to self-recrimination at having suppressed speech when daily outrages demanded it, Heaney turns to Aeschylus: 'The ox is on my tongue' is the motto Heaney takes from the *Agamemnon*. Or at least Aeschylus is the proximate literary source. Experiencing this unwelcome backward-looking anger instead of the optimism that the moment ought to have implied, Heaney says,

I kept thinking that a version of the *Oresteia* would be one way of getting all of that out of the system, and at the same time, a way of initiating a late-twentieth-century equivalent of the 'Te Deum' . . . Ideally what I needed was the kind of

---

[89] The poem 'Terminus' thematizes this fact autobiographically, linking it to a 'balanced' approach to politics: 'Two buckets were easier carried than one. | I grew up in between. | My left hand placed the standard iron weight. | My right tilted a last grain in the balance' (HL, 5). But even this poem finds a counterweight, in 'Weighing In' (SL, 17–19), which laments holding back 'when I should have drawn blood'. Among the many instances of 'between' are the following: 'Between my finger and my thumb' ('Digging'; DN, 1); 'between bawn and mossland' ('Traditions'; WO, 22); 'between turf-face and demesne wall, | between heathery levels | and glass-toothed stone' ('Bog Queen'; N, 32); 'Socketed between graves, two-faced, trepanned' ('Triptych III'; FW, 14); 'between the cradle and the explosion' ('The Badgers'; FW, 25); 'We toe the line | between the tree in leaf and the bare tree' ('September Song'; FW, 43); 'Between the by-road and the main road' ('Song'; FW, 53); '*I was stretched between contemplation | of a motionless point | and the command to participate | actively in history*', 'somewhere between | balance and inanition' ('Away from it All'; SI, 16–17); 'I stood between them' ('Making Strange'; SI, 32); '*Taught me between the hammer and the block | To face the music*' ('Clearances'; HL, 24); 'between panic and formulae' ('The Mud Vision'; HL, 48); 'An in-between-times', 'between destiny and dread' ('Mycenae Lookout'; SL, 30); 'Between the horizon and the dictionary' ('An Invocation'; SL, 27); 'between the farm and campus' ('The Flight Path'; SL, 24); 'a bright path | Opened between us like a recognition' ('Montana'; EL, 13); 'Between when I was buried and unburied. | Between what happened and was meant to be' ('The Tollund Man in Springtime'; DC, 56).

poem Andrew Marvell wrote on Cromwell's return from Ireland and what I was setting up for was a kind of Jonsonian masque.[90]

As Helen Vendler says, 'Traditions jostle in these remarks.'[91] But she is wrong, I think, to conclude that these traditions give 'access to a pent-up spring of emotion hidden in those apparently monolithic ancestral forms'.[92] The emotion precedes and initiates the recourse to tradition—tradition here is mined for the appropriate form of the expression, not as a source of emotional material. It is precisely because the feeling is there to begin with that so many various traditions are adduced—it is rather as if no one form can on its own do justice to the emotion of moment. Another poet might have decided that, given this, a radically new idiom was required. Heaney, however, wants poetic models that have been adequate to the civic requirements of their own times; he scans the tradition for artworks that are both historically and culturally authorized. Formally, the sequence is—like Heaney's answer to the interviewer's question—simultaneously referentially specific and eclectically agglutinative: the first section is in heroic couplets, the second in long and skinny dimeters reminiscent of *Wintering Out*, the third in rhyming tercets, the fourth in variously rhyming nine-line trimeter stanzas, like truncated Spenserians, the last in unrhymed tercets linked together by terza rima-ish acoustical stitching.

The free speech of 'Mycenae Lookout' is typical of Heaney's post-ceasefire translations, many of which broaden the scope of social engagement, addressing the state of contemporary geopolitics. Heaney may have freed his tongue from ox-weights—and he is even freer in taking sides against American and other non-Irish policies—but he continues to speak through old masters, as if they could never be wrong about suffering. In the twenty-first century, Heaney's public poetry is likely already to have been authored by Sophocles, Virgil, or Horace. The poem that has become known as Heaney's 'September 11th poem' is an adaptation of the thirty-fourth poem in Horace's first book of odes. 'Anything Can Happen', which first appears as 'Horace

---

[90] Seamus Heaney, interview with Henri Cole, 'The Art of Poetry LXXV', *Paris Review* 144 (Fall 1997), 88–138, 136–7.

[91] Helen Vendler, 'Seamus Heaney and the *Oresteia*: "Mycenae Lookout" and the Usefulness of Tradition', *Proceedings of the American Philosophical Society* 143:1 (March 1999), 116–29, 117.

[92] Ibid. 129.

and Thunder' in the *TLS*,[93] registers dread at the idea that a previously inconceivable catastrophe has occurred, but Heaney thinks of it more as a warning about the 'crackdown' that was about to come (SS, 424) than a poem of grief for the American dead, and the term 'crackdown' itself, with its colonial associations, allies Heaney more to the victims of retaliatory violence than those who died in the Twin Towers. There is admonitory detachedness in the lines, 'Anything can happen, the tallest towers | Be overturned, those in high places daunted, | Those overlooked regarded' (DC, 13). This is a public stance that cuts against the grain of global public expressions of sympathy in the late months of 2001. There is nothing unusual, much less culpable, about reacting to the terrorist attack on the United States with antiwar sentiment instead of (for instance) a wish for revenge, but there is something discomforting and uncouth about this poem, the alliances it makes and the lessons that it imparts, or imposes. To some degree tradition permits and underwrites the expression of the commonplace about Fortune's wheel bringing both the weak and the strong their due: it is Horace, not Heaney, who writes, '*hinc apicem rapax | Fortuna cum stridore acuto | Sustulit, hic posuisse gaudet*.'[94] Could Heaney have said 'what goes around comes around' in his own voice at that moment? It is exactly the kind of frontal, outspoken, blaming sentiment Heaney would have suppressed, or sublimated, in response to an outrage committed thirty years earlier and in Northern Ireland. The authorial distance of Horace—the ageless, universal wisdom of the ancient, culturally authorized artwork—combined with Heaney's personal remove from the emotive and psychic trauma of New Yorkers, makes the statement possible.

'Horace and Thunder', before it became 'Anything Can Happen' in *District and Circle*, became *Anything Can Happen: A Poem and Essay with Translations in Support of Art for Amnesty*, which, along with twenty-four translations of Heaney's Horace, includes a prefatory tract in which Heaney explains how he thinks the poem is 'equal to the

---

[93] Seamus Heaney, 'Horace and Thunder', *Times Literary Supplement* (18 January 2002), 40. Perhaps Heaney thought that the original's 'the tallest things' would lose clarity of reference over time. In *District and Circle* he revises the 'things' to 'towers'.
[94] Horace, *Horace: The Odes*, trans. Colin Sydenham (London: Duckworth, 2005), 62. Sydenham's rather close translation reads: 'Fortune now seizes | the crown from one with strident cry, now | Drops it on another as she pleases' (63). Len Krisak's version is more impressionistic, and more effective: 'When hungry, shrieking Fortune claws the heads | of men who thought their crowns were sure.' See Horace, *The Odes of Horace in Latin and English*, trans. Len Krisak (Manchester: Carcanet, 2006), 55.

moment' of post-September 11. Heaney pays his translator's dues to the Roman poet, talking of the 'uncanny soothsaying force' which gives the ode such 'an eerie contemporary resonance' that 'it could have been written yesterday in Baghdad'.[95] Between this and the initial publication, the implicit partiality has been fully realized, with the site of outrage transferred from New York to Iraq, terrorist commuter planes interchanged with B-2 bombers. The insistence on 'contemporary resonance'—or 'relevance', to speak the cliché that is being strenuously avoided here—is pressed further in the translations, which are paired into designated 'languages of conflict': Hebrew to Arabic, Xhosa to Afrikaans, Dutch to Basha Indonesian, and so on. Heaney's English poem is, in a preposterous irony, paired to an Irish translation by Micheál Ó Cearúil. The blunt clarity of the 'message' behind this publication, combined with its public and financial underwriting of an organization whose work is very much in the domain of direct action, bring uneasily to mind Heaney's still recently expressed caution regarding poetry that is 'harnessed to movements which attempt to alleviate [adverse] conditions by direct action' (RP, 2).

Heaney is similarly unembarrassed in his translation of *Antigone*. It is a play that comes pre-loaded with political associations—partly because of its thematic playing out of the conflict between civic duty and family honour (often reinterpreted as standing for 'morality' or 'natural law'), partly because of a performance history strongly allied to the ideal of righteous civil disobedience. Jean Anouilh's version, first performed in Paris in February 1944, was famously inspired by an individual act of political resistance. So the play was, even before liberation, an exemplary narrative of home-front heroism for a French population that had endured the successive humiliations of conquest and collaboration. In the Irish context, Yeats set the civil war reverberating in his chorus from *Antigone*. During the Troubles, Heaney had read Conor Cruise O'Brien's article comparing Antigone to Queen's University's student protesters, seeing then how the play could function as a 'lens that helped to inspect reality more clearly'.[96] Tom Paulin, Marianne McDonald, Brendan Kennelly, Conall Morrison, and Aidan Carl Mathews had all produced translations of the play for the Irish theatre. For Heaney's *Antigone*, the intended allegory is the Bush Administration's War on

---

[95] Seamus Heaney, *Anything Can Happen* (Dublin: TownHouse, 2004), 15.

[96] Quoted in Eileen Battersby, 'A Greek Tragedy for our Times', *Irish Times* (3 April 2004), 55.

Terror, specifically the Iraq conflict, which during 2003 progressed from bellicose rhetoric to invasion to occupation and counter-insurgency campaign. The first of these phases 'resonates' particularly in the figure of the King of Thebes. Heaney writes: 'in 2003 we were watching a leader, a Creon figure if ever there was one: a law and order bossman trying to boss the nations of the world into uncritical agreement with his edicts.'[97] But there is the question, as Eliot might say, of our 'literary values', as well as our political ones. What kind of a figure Creon actually is must be a more complex and a more important question than Heaney's analogy will allow. Reading the present in terms of the past may always entail a certain amount of reading the past in terms of the present, but Heaney's Creon is at times no *more* than an allegorical George Bush. Especially when he is referring to enemies of Thebes, Creon speaks Bushismo rhetoric, calling them 'wrongdoers' who 'terrorised us'. Antigone quotes him derisively: '"I'll flush 'em out", he says. | "Whoever isn't for us | Is against us".'[98] When confronted by his own words in performances of the play, however, Heaney would come to the realization 'that the topical references were a mistake', because 'spelling things out like that is almost like patronizing the audience' (SS, 421). Such topicality actually makes Heaney's version less relevant rather than more—at a distance of only five years, the Bushisms jarred strangely in Derek Walcott's direction of Dominique Le Gendre's opera,[99] using Heaney's play for a libretto, which cast Creon as a black Caribbean dictator.

I have been arguing that Heaney's late engagements in public debates over geopolitics make the mistake of patronizing the audience, and worse, that they fail the criteria of poetic integrity he himself articulated in 'The Redress of Poetry'. Though Heaney adopts the self-distancing, universalizing stratagem of translating the ancients to speak to the present, a tactic consonant both with his early probing instinct and his late drive to forge connections in and through culture, these works are disabled by a

---

[97] Seamus Heaney, 'Search for the Soul of Antigone', *The Guardian* (2 November 2005), Culture: 18.

[98] Seamus Heaney, *The Burial at Thebes* (London: Faber and Faber, 2004), 23, 24, 3. Cf. the address given by the American President to a joint session of Congress on 20 September 2001, in which he declared to the world, 'Either you are with us, or you are with the terrorists': http://www.whitehouse.gov/news/releases/2001/09/20010920-8.html, accessed 17 December 2008. 'Wrongdoers' echoes 'evildoers', a term characteristically used by Bush to characterize America's terrorist enemies abroad. See http://www.sourcewatch.org/index.php?title=Evil-doers, accessed 31 May 2010.

[99] *The Burial at Thebes* (opera) by Dominique Le Gendre, directed by Derek Walcott. Shakespeare's Globe, London (11–12 October 2008).

failure to achieve their intended effect 'by distinctly linguistic means' (RP, 5–6). The Horatian ode, the choral mode, in opening a path through to discursive, instructive speech, turn boldly away from the reticent, reflective intellectual pathways of Heaney's usual, self-controlled lyrics. The 'redress' effected by these translations cleaves too much to the sense of 'reparation' and too little to the sense of setting 'upright again' or finding the 'proper course' (RP, 15); 'poetry' is here too much the active subject of the phrase and too little the passive object.

In this way the late versions and translations serve as valuable test cases for Heaney's defence of poetry, his belief in its capacity to effect redress in the very act of being itself redressed as poetry, 'an eminence established and a pressure exercised by distinctly linguistic means' (RP, 5–6). In terms of authorial motive, they are yet another demonstration of Heaney's active desire to reintroduce the cultural heritage of European literature into the public life. More importantly they ratify, albeit negatively, his idea of the 'redress of poetry'—his version of Eliot's 'integrity of poetry'—as a simultaneously ethical and aesthetic evaluative category. These works fail on that count precisely because 'redress' possesses an integrity of its own, independent of the particular artworks it may be seen to be underwriting. *Beowulf* succeeds better than *Burial* because the text stands on its own, without appeal to relevance: its action, sometimes its diction, is completely alien to the contemporary sensibility well before it becomes oddly familiar. It is a 'strange likeness', to second Jones's quotation of Hill's oxymoron from *Mercian Hymns*. It helps that the specific situation Heaney intends to set echoing in the epic is one that he has thoroughly metabolized—its particulars can be rendered as correspondingly strange and recognizable to the outsider. But Heaney's insistence that the translation be read within a conventional postcolonial critical apparatus hinders instead of furthers this effect, making the universal particular, the resonant still and faint.

Succeeding better than these—perhaps best of all—are the outcomes of Heaney's growing engagement with Virgil, the poet he describes approvingly, and with obvious self-referential overtones, as 'very much the learned poets' poet' who, although he came 'from a country background', had in mind an audience 'very different from the shepherds and goatherds he would have known in his boyhood, on the farm from which his father was eventually expelled'.[100] Heaney comes to know

---

[100] Heaney, 'Eclogues *in Extremis*', 3.

Virgil through Dante at first, especially in the *Station Island* sequence, where it is a Virgilian Joyce who speaks the role of the guiding shade, telling Heaney to 'strike your note' (SI, 93). Heaney's poem is thick with a certain strain of intellectualized, universal poetic tradition, inviting Eliot as well as Joyce and Virgil and Dante into the dense allusive field. More recently, in describing the enduring value of Virgil's *Eclogues* in particular, and the ability of the pastoral more generally to answer to the demands of the moment, Heaney makes two successive allusions that reinforce this alignment: first he claims that the artwork is both a 'revelation and an intervention' that depends on 'how much reality you are ready to accommodate or are accustomed to bear'; next he describes the virtue of Virgil's *Eclogues* as its possessing 'integrity, consonance and radiance'.[101] The first is a direct reference to Eliot's 'Little Gidding'; the second may also summon Eliotic integrity in its multilayered allusion to Joyce, which also invokes the early medieval aesthetics of Dante and St Thomas Aquinas, and, via Thomas, the Greek sources of this scholasticism.[102] When Denis O'Driscoll asks the big question near the end of *Stepping Stones*—'What has poetry taught you?'—Heaney's 'quick response'[103] picks up on his defence of Virgil:

That there's such a thing as truth and it can be told—slant; that subjectivity is not to be theorized away and is worth defending; that poetry itself has virtue, in the first sense of possessing a quality of moral excellence and in the sense also of possessing inherent strength by reason of its sheer made-upness, its *integritas, consonantia* and *claritas*. (SS, 467)

Reflecting on this impromptu answer in an address to the Royal Irish Academy, Heaney sees in it a confirmation of his belief that 'the humanities operate to inform our consciousness as a species and equip us as creatures of memory and reflection', that this cultural memory 'constitutes a basis for the location and different orientations of the self in the world'.[104] So the reference to Joyce's use of Thomas is both the specific articulation of a claim for the value of literary art, and an

[101] Ibid. 7.
[102] See James Joyce, *A Portrait of the Artist as a Young Man* (London: Jonathan Cape, 1968), 216–17; and Thomas Aquinas, *Summa Theologiae* Ia q. 39 a. 8.
[103] Seamus Heaney, 'Holding Patterns: Arts, Letters and the Academy'. Royal Irish Academy (28 January 2008); http://www.ria.ie/news/pdf/Heaney_Discourse.pdf, accessed 21 December 2008, sixth page (n.p.).
[104] Ibid. third page (n.p.).

example and instantiation of that value. What happens to the poet when doing a translation specifically is 'a merging of personal memory with cultural tradition, the working out of a new perspective in the light of inherited matter',[105] but this describes the profit made from every serious encounter with literature.

Heaney's latest translation of Virgil is also a kind of retelling of 'Broagh', written in the same spirit in which 'Tollund' revises 'The Tollund Man'. 'Broagh' is allusively present in the title of 'The Riverbank Field', and the word itself appears, along with 'riverbank' and 'rigs', in the body of the poem. Just as Tollund Moss could be a scene from 'The Townland of Peace', here 'Upper Broagh' is newly observed with its '*domos placidas*', its quiet homes. In this poem Heaney interleaves quotation with translation and commentary, glossing both the original text and the process of translation, or versioning, that his poem is itself enacting:

The Riverbank Field

Ask me to translate what Loeb gives as
'in a retired vale . . . a sequestered grove'
and I'll confound the Lethe in Moyola

by coming through Back Park down from Grove Hill
across Long Rigs on the riverbank—
which way, by happy chance will take me past

the *domos placidas*, 'those peaceful homes'
of Upper Broagh. Moths then on evening water
it would have to be, not butterflies in sunlight,

midge veils instead of lily beds; but *stet*
to all the rest: the willow leaves
Elysian silvered, the grass so full fledged

And unimprinted it can't not conjure thoughts
Of passing spirit-troops, animae, quibus altera fato
Corpora debentur, 'spirits', that is,

'to whom second bodies are owed by fate'.
And now to continue, as enjoined to often,
'in my own words':

'All these presences
Once they have done their turn of a thousand years
Are summoned here to drink the river water

[105] Ibid.

So that memories of life on this side are shed
And soul repines to dwell in flesh and blood
Under the dome of heaven.'
                  after Aeneid VI, 704–15 & 748–51.[106]

The changing and the leaving be (*stet*, the proofer's 'amen'); the conjuring, confounding, and incorporating; the revising, renewing, and remembering—in short, the processes of sounding, crossing, and connecting that help poetry to redress both itself and the social order, are taken up in this poem. It works by roaming the orders of poetic memory and forgetfulness: the deposits of cultural memory whence the poem comes, the poet's 'confounded' memory that transforms it into something known and local, and the forgetfulness that within the original poem permits the reincarnation of souls. In Heaney's version, it is as much to poems that 'second bodies are owed' after a thousand years. There could be no firmer celebration of Heaney's credo, 'I believe poetry dwells in the parish and the universe', than the closing image of Virgil's fated souls gathering in Broagh to drink Moyola water and be reborn.

                              *

Heaney's characterization of his socio-literary, ethical-cultural approach to poetry as 'very Eliotesque' probably has the idea of the 'auditory imagination' foremost in mind, and it is true that Heaney continues, both in his poetry and in his criticism, to be an 'echo-chamber' for the elements he identified in his 1974 exegesis on 'one of the most precise and suggestive of T. S. Eliot's critical formulations'. Behind Heaney's soundings, crossings, connections, and translations also stands the Eliotic idea of linguistic renovation which is a 'perpetual return to the real'. In his self-analysis, however, Heaney displays another 'very Eliotesque' tendency, one which considers literature and the traditions of literature as essential cultural possessions to be preserved and passed on by poets. For Heaney, as for Eliot, being a 'creature of culture' entails the preservation and revitalization of one's own local culture—the 'dialect of the tribe'—as well as fruitful intercultural commerce, which can lead 'beyond the tribe'. When, after the War, Eliot offered two criteria for the renewal of literature to a German radio audience—'First, its ability to receive and assimilate influences from abroad. Second, its ability to go back and learn from its own sources' (NDC, 113)—he was really

---

[106] Seamus Heaney, *The Riverbank Field* (Oldcastle: Gallery Press, 2007), n.p.

insisting that a programme of literary intercommunication could be an agent of peace on a ravaged continent, a way of achieving 'spiritual communication between people and people' (OPP, 23). In terms that recall the subtext of that statement, Heaney speaks of his 'love and trust in the good of the indigenous *per se*', but refuses to limit this local good to the local context from which it springs:

a trust in the staying power and travel-worthiness of such good should encourage us to credit the possibility of a world where respect for the validity of every tradition will issue in the creation and maintenance of a salubrious political space. (CR, 37–8)

The connective, incorporative, allusive style which Heaney gradually adopts after *North* is representative of this double goal of indigenous celebration and intercultural communication.

4

Geoffrey Hill: A 'Question of Value'

Dieu a choisi comme châtiments le travail et la mort. Par consé-
quent le travail et la mort, si l'homme les subit en consentant à les
subir, constituent un transport dans le bien suprême de l'obéis-
sance à Dieu.
God chose work and death as punishments. Consequently work
and death, if man suffers them willingly, are a way into the
supreme good which is obedience to God.

Simone Weil, *L'enracinement,* 1949

The loss of a broad, common religious sensibility, it seems, is no longer
widely regretted, and not because something like art has taken over its
functions, as Arnold predicted it would, but because those who have
found they could do without religion have by and large just done
without, as Eliot recommended. It would be wrong to conclude from
this state of affairs, however, that in a post-religious, postmodern world,
there can be no such thing as a serious religious poem, just as it would be
a nonsense to claim on this basis that religious faith is no longer
justified. Since Eliot wrote his *Four Quartets,* the poet who has most
forcefully and seriously written from a perspective of Christian faith is
Geoffrey Hill. Near the end of his essay 'Language, Suffering, and
Silence' (1999), Hill comes to a conclusion which is as characteristic
in its challenge as it is in its tentativeness:

I would seriously propose a theology of language; and a primary exercise which
might be undertaken towards its establishment. This would comprise a critical
examination of the grounds for claiming (a) that the shock of semantic
recognition must be also a shock of ethical recognition; and that this is the
action of grace in one of its minor, but far from trivial, types; (b) that the art
and literature of the late twentieth century require a memorializing, a memor-
izing, of the dead. (CCW, 405)

The connection between language and deity, what Hill later calls the 'original authorship, the *auctoritas*, of God' (CCW, 263), is already a well-developed concept in Judeo-Christian philosophy and literature, more so than Hill's conspicuous 'seriously' would suggest. The Hebrew God, from the opening verses of the Bible, is a speaking God, creating by declaring ('And God said, Let there be light: and there was light' (Gen 1:3))—creating, verifying, and naming. The Johannine version of Creation is also not *ex nihilo* but *ex verbo*: 'In the beginning was the Word, and the Word was with God, and the Word was God' (John 1:1). From Genesis to John God manifests Himself as Word. The number of books that begin with God in the act of 'speaking' or 'saying' (O.T. אמר—*'amar*; LXX ἔπω, λέγω) or that begin by proclaiming His 'Word' (O.T. דבר—*dabar*; LXX λόγος),[1] including, significantly, all but three of the twenty-one prophetic books (נביאם—*nevi'im*), reflects the extent to which Judeo-Christian tradition conceives of the deity as an entity revealed primarily through language. The fact that men also speak means that language can be directed back towards God: from the moment of the Fall onwards, it is the medium of adoration and supplication (prayer) but also of apostasy and blasphemy (curse). And the Bible tells of the dangers of sharing a language with the divine: in Genesis 11 God confounds the speech of men to restrain the ambition of their imaginations. Cautioning against the converse danger, Paul warns that 'the letter killeth; the spirit giveth life' (2 Cor 3:6). In Paul the Law has been mistaken for the Word, that which is written has overcome that which is meant, the sign has eclipsed the signified. Thus the two directions in which language tempts men—towards hubristic, coercive exercise of language's creative power, and into creative impotence in the face of language's coercive powers—are perilous affronts to the speaking God's will.

In the Bible language saves and damns because human language is somehow *like*, but is not identical to, the divine Word. But the Bible is neither the beginning nor the end of the analogy of language and deity. The theory of the *logos* goes back at least as far as Heraclitus. It permeates Hellenic Judaism, and, once fully Christianized and consecrated in John, remains the subject of elaboration from Augustine to Thomas Aquinas, through the Renaissance, early modernity, and into

---

[1] Of the 66 books of the King James Bible, 29: Gen, Lev, Num, Deut, Josh, Judg, 2 Kgs, Ezra, Isa, Jer, Ezek, Hos, Joel, Amos, Obad, Jonah, Mic, Nahum, Zeph, Hag, Zech, Mal, 1 Cor, 1 Thess, Titus, Heb, John, 1 John, Rev.

the present era. There is, by any measure, extensive literature in almost every century on logology, the language of religion, theology *and* language, and theology *of* language.[2] The surface resemblance of Jacques Derrida's assertion that 'The sign is always the sign of the fall',[3] to Hill's references to the 'grammar that reminds | us of our fall' (OS, 58), and to 'grammar implicated in, interpreting the Fall' (OS, 67), or his 'conviction that the "terrible aboriginal calamity" in the contexture of human life constantly implicates, and is implicated by, the textures of our uttered thought' (CCW, 400–1), underscores the extent to which these different—even antipathetic[4]—writers are drawing from a common well of literary and philosophical tradition.[5]

Nevertheless, Hill's 'seriously' prefix does a certain amount of work to locate his proposal in a context which assumes that it will *not*, or will *no longer*, be taken seriously. This is not, as may be inferred, simply a matter of 'postmodernists' finally having swept away the remainder of a conservative old guard, nor is it only a result of the consummate secularization of society. Responding in 1933 to Matthew Arnold's prediction that poetry would replace 'what now passes for religion and philosophy',[6] Eliot's admonition to a generation of poets, critics, and scholars was that 'if you find that you must do without something, such

---

[2] One measure might use Library of Congress (LC) subject headings to search a university library catalogue. Harvard's HOLLIS, to take the vastest collection, lists 290 volumes under the heading 'Language and languages—Religious aspects' (publication dates from 1655 to 2009), 180 under 'Language and languages—Religious aspects—Christianity' (1483–2010), and 103 under 'Logos—Christian theology' (1550–2010); http://holliscatalog.harvard.edu/, accessed 31 May 2010.

[3] 'Le signe est toujours le signe de la chute.' Jacques Derrida, *De la grammatologie* (Paris: Éditions Minuit, 1967), 401.

[4] Though he hasn't commented on or engaged with his work per se, Hill has called Derrida a 'disastrous influence on modern literary criticism'. See Geoffrey Hill, interview with Anne Mounic, 'Le poème, "moulin mystique": Entretien avec Geoffrey Hill' (19 March 2008); http://www3.sympatico.ca/sylvia.paul/ghill_interview_by_AnneMounic. htm, accessed 31 May 2010.

[5] For a useful and concise discussion of language and the Fall in modern philosophy, see the first chapter of Kevin Hart, *The Trespass of the Sign: Deconstruction, Theology and Philosophy* (New York: Fordham University Press, 2000), 3–39. Coming from a less alien cultural, intellectual, and religious background from Hill (if not ultimately sharing in his approach), and perhaps providing a link to Derridean thought, is recent work on God and language by the 'Radical Orthodoxy' school of Anglican theologians. Especially useful are Chapters 3–6 of John Milbank, *The Word Made Strange: Theology, Language, Culture* (Oxford: Basil Blackwell, 1997), 55–170.

[6] Matthew Arnold, 'The Study of Poetry', in *The Complete Prose of Matthew Arnold*, vol. IX: *English Literature and Irish Politics*, ed. Robert Henry Super (Ann Arbor: University of Michigan Press, 1973), 161–88, 162.

as religious faith or philosophic belief, then you must just do without it' (UPC, 113). For decades before postmodernism put the academy on guard against cultural (including religious) inscriptions in texts and their interpretations, critics were divesting their professional responses to literature of the religious tendencies they may have harboured.

Even in the 'serious' proposition quoted above, Hill's language is tentative; his rhetoric invites 'examination' and critique. This chapter undertakes the examination of Hill's proposal along the lines he himself suggests, first taking up Hill's equation of semantic and ethical recognition, his experience of language as an arena in which our ethical being is both menaced and succoured, though perhaps not secured. Hill's cogitations on this problem begin a career-long investigation into the question of intrinsic value, a concept which he admits has gone out of fashion but which he nonetheless attempts to rescue for his theory of language. (Hill's specification that late-twentieth-century literature ought to memorialize and memorize the dead, while not ruling out the same requirement for earlier literatures, makes the matter more urgent.)Unusually for a Christian and English poet, Hill is a frequent writer of poems about the Shoah and other holocausts, a feature which intersects with other currents in Holocaust literature and thought. Hill does attend to the dead in his poetry, but his scepticism about literature's ability to 'do justice' to its subjects becomes all the more anxious in the elegiac mode. It is an anxiety that drives Hill towards silence—a silence which is at first containable within the poetry, but which seems for a period to overcome it completely.

When Hill finally breaks his silence, after a ten-year publishing hiatus, he does so with a new irruptive, interruptive technique, combined with caustic personae and at times discomforting themes. Hill's late writings assert themselves forcefully as public speech, and increasingly take on questions of what he calls 'civil polity'. This is not exactly a politics, though it concerns itself with the political at some key junctures. It is closer to a civics, and 'civic', 'civil', and 'public' are perhaps the apter adjectives, even if Hill's civil poetry and prose are at times highly *un*civil. Hill's abiding concern is the care and attention an author gives to words in the creation of imaginative writing, and the place of that writing, especially poetry, in the public sphere, even as he despairs of its purchase on civic organization. 'Alienation' becomes a heavy concept in Hill's late corpus, standing at once for the gap between the poet's concerns and the concerns and business of society, and also for the process of artistic creation by which the self produces an art-object which is not-self. In case the public, civic inflection of Hill's late postures suggests a shift in emphasis away from the theological proposal to which I intend to return throughout this chapter, it should be kept in mind that, in the midst of this phase, Hill ventures that, if a truly original work of art could ever be achieved or experienced, the four-teenth-century theologian Thomas Bradwardine's treatise on grace and original sin would be a sufficient refutation of Ralph Waldo Emerson's arguments in favour of 'Self-Reliance'.

THE ENDURANCE OF VALUE

With characteristic rhetorical caution, Hill entitles his first Tanner lecture, given in Oxford in the spring of 2000, 'Intrinsic Value: Marginal Observations on a Central Question', at a stroke claiming import and consequence for his topic while playing down his contribution to it. One is tempted to interchange Hill's adjectives: far from adumbrating the contours of a common or much-discussed issue, the lecture deepens and complicates Hill's long engagement with a question which has been central mainly to his own aesthetic and ethical enterprise. Hill's 'marginal observations' enclose almost fifty years of thought on the value of words, especially when wrought in poetry. When he writes, in the opening sentence, that 'it has never been easy to define the nature of value' (CCW, 465), Hill could as easily be referring to his own career as to intellectual history in general. The phrase 'intrinsic value' is proximately derived from John Ruskin, and first occurs in the earliest of Hill's essays (CCW, 12, 16). In *The Triumph of Love* (1998) he ponders its meaning in verse: '*Intrinsic value* | I am somewhat less sure of. It seems | implicate with active virtue but I cannot | say how, precisely' (TL, 37). It is around the time of *Triumph* that Hill begins to cogitate directly on 'intrinsic value' in his prose, and he is in fact 'less sure of' the phrase. Hill's language is initially tentative: the idea is, in Ruskin, 'at best a promissory note, at worst a semantic relic to ward off the evil eye of commodity' (CCW, 383), which nonetheless 'points in the right direction, towards semantic realizations that have some substance' (CCW, 390). By the late stages of his career, Hill can claim that it is 'a phrase out of which most of my ideas have come'.[7] The dividends

---

[7] Geoffrey Hill, 'Reading and Discussion' (recording), Collège de France (18 March 2008); http://www.college-de-france.fr/audio/hill/ghill_18032008.mp3, accessed 31

have been substantial: 'In my immediate practice as a poet as well as in my critical writings about public language', Hill ventures, 'I have tried to transform the sense of intrinsic value into matters of semantic pitch.'[8]

In *Mercian Hymns* (1971), Hill forges together two kinds of intrinsic value in metaphor:

> Coins handsome as Nero's; of good substance and weight. *Offa Rex* resonant in silver, and the names of his moneyers. They struck with account-able tact. They could alter the king's face.
>
> Exactness of design was to deter imitation; muti-lation if that failed. Exemplary metal, ripe for commerce. Value from a sparse people, scrapers of salt-pans and byres.

(GHCP, 115)

The word 'muti-/lation', illustrating its own dismemberment on the page,[9] also calls attention to its special application to books or texts (OED3, *n.* 3), as well as its etymological Old French sense of a 'partial destruction of a work of art' (OED3, *n. etym*). Similarly, the visual deconstruction of 'account-/able' leaves us with the three distinct sense units which the poem has joined together: 'account' as in the verb meaning 'to reckon for moneys given or received' (OED2, *v.* II.3), 'able' as in 'showing... skill; talented, clever' (OED2, *a.* 7), and 'ac-countable' as in 'answerable, responsible' (OED2, *a.* 1). Here the intrinsic value of art and the intrinsic value of silver coin are combined in the person of the 'moneyer', whose mintage involves as much craft in portraiture as it does in assaying. Value derives equally from 'good substance'—'exemplary metal' of correct weight—and the 'exactness' or integrity of the king's image. These qualities—one inherent, the other assigned—form the basis of the coin's currency in the market,

---

May 2010. The talk was given in English with French phrases frequently and infelici-tously interspersed. The quotation above is my interpretation of Hill's formulation 'une phrase de quoi mes idées pour la plupart déroulent'. Hill might be saying that his ideas (on this subject) derive mainly from Ruskin (as opposed to other sources)—which is also true—but I believe the context authorizes the stronger phrasing I have chosen.

[8] Ibid.

[9] GHCP is faithful to the original lineation in *Mercian Hymns*, whereas the Penguin *Selected Poems* (2006) relineates the poem, doing away with the hyphenation. Whether this is an authorized change or another of the many defects of that edition will be confirmed on publication of Hill's projected *Collected Poems* in 2012.

the 'commerce' for which it is designed and in which it provides a uniform value standard. The mythical-historical setting of the poem is indispensible: the world of modern commerce, in which the value of the coin of the realm is as market-driven as the value of the goods the coin buys, is not up to the same analogy. It is, Hill has said, a 'plutocratic anarchy', one function of which is to 'destroy any sense of intrinsic value'.[10]

Seamus Heaney has imagined Hill's poetry 'as indulging in a morose linguistic delectation, dwelling on the potential of each word with much the same slow relish as Leopold Bloom dwells on the thought of his kidney' (P, 160). If there is a reader's companion to the works of Geoffrey Hill, it must be the *Oxford English Dictionary*, and this applies to the prose as much as the poetry. The OED provides eight headings for the noun 'value' in two main groups. The first sense, encompassing definitions 1–4, is that of equivalence of exchange among things, their material or monetary worth. The second refers to the 'relative status of a thing, or the estimate in which it is held, according to its real or supposed worth, usefulness, or importance . . . the principles or standards of a person or society, the personal or societal judgement of what is valuable and important in life' (OED2, *n*. 6a). Though these two senses of 'value' so defined can be seen to overlap considerably, they are set apart by the degree to which 'value' can be ascertained and how enduring any such assessment may be. As Hill says, 'The matter of intrinsic value carries a distinct referential weight in two particular areas or spheres of activity and discourse: coinage, where it can be assayed, and moral philosophy, where it cannot' (CCW, 465). A third sphere of activity and discourse is the poetic, and the question of whether value can be assayed in words, and to what degree, is what motivates the essays grouped in *Critical Writings* under the title 'Inventions of Value'. One of Hill's 'marginal observations' identifies the source of value in George Eliot's art:

For the author of *Middlemarch*, intrinsic value is not so much in things, or even in qualities, as in a faculty: the faculty of sustained attention; attention conceived of, moreover, as a redemptive power. (CCW, 472)

---

[10] Geoffrey Hill, in conversation with Rowan Williams (Geoffrey Hill and His Contexts, a conference held 2–3 July 2008, at Keeble College, Oxford). 'Plutocratic anarchy' is the polemical phrase that Hill has been using frequently in public appearances and interviews since about 2007 (i.e., after the last piece collected in *Collected Critical Writings* was composed—it does not appear in that volume). It first appears in print in Hill's 'Civil Polity and the Confessing State', *Warwick Review* 2:2 (June 2008), 7–20, 9.

Because it is the *power* to attend—the potential of attention, not acts of attention or the degree of their eventual achievement—that is the first locus of 'value', the attention applied by the author to her work calls her reader to attention, invoking in him his own attentive faculty. Like Ruskin's phrase, this is a pointing 'in the right direction'. When Hill affirms that Eliot's work is the 'moral equivalent of those very qualities it describes' (CCW, 472), or that 'The ethics are right . . . she is happy with the theme and the theme is happy with her' (CCW, 93), he is describing a correspondence between the achieved work and its subject, a kind of authorial faithfulness, an honesty and moral accuracy in artistic representation arrived at through sustained attention to object and to language.

For Hill, honesty and accuracy in representation requires uncertainty, because the reality of our experience is uncertain. Speaking with Michael Berkeley on BBC Radio, Hill amends his host's characterization of his poetry as 'precise':

> It's precision of a certain kind, because it's precision that can't rule out ambiguity. . . . The ambiguities can't come in accidentally, because that's a solecism. You've got to be accurate in your ambiguities.[11]

Calling attention in poetry to the ability of language to confound and mislead makes us all the more aware of the possibility of deception, all the more attentive to the vicissitudes of meaning. This is as much Hill's method in the early poetry, where passives, participles, and particles frequently ambiguate agent and predicate, as in the later poetry, where Hill adopts ever newer techniques of ambiguation. In the fifth episode of *Scenes from Comus* (2005), Hill constructs a poem out of words which find in themselves their own antonyms. The theme is forms of value:

> Add that we're unaccountably [|] held to account;
> that we cannot make our short days add up
> to the sum demanded. Add, that accountancy
>
> is a chartered profession, like surveying;
> that rectitude is a grand directive;
> that righteousness has no known charter
>
> and is not, generally speaking, in demand.
> That there are immoderate measures in plenty;
> that plenty is a term of moderation;
>
> that moderation is by some used to excess.   (SC, 5)

---

[11] *Private Passions*, BBC Radio 3, 25 April 2004.

The beat indicated by the raised vertical bar in the first line extends the time during which 'unaccountably' is expected to apply to 'we', before the passive 'held to account' reverses its direction. We are not acting unaccountably; we *are* accountable, even though we do not measure up. One may add effort or excuse—Hill four times 'add'ing or 'sum'ing in the first stanza—but the final analysis reveals that the valuation of a life is as difficult to fix as the terms of its measurement: that 'plenty' designates an abundance in one context but communicates abstention in another; that contrary to its meaning, 'moderation' can be encountered in the same extremes of paucity and excess as any other quality; that being 'in demand' does not mean a thing is what is 'demanded', or required, by that which holds us to account. Though Hill's diction implies contradiction, this poem does not attempt to ravel up a conundrum or present us with a paradox. Hill's theme is the inveterate uncertainty in which we abide, especially as judgers and assayers of value, once we believe in such a thing as value. He works the semantics of these terms of measure and quantity until they give up their multiplicities of meaning—we are left with an 'account' of their ambiguities, an inventory of prevarications.

In 1984 Christopher Ricks remarked that 'All of Hill's work is concerned . . . with reconciliation.'[12] In the essay on which Ricks was commenting, Hill labours to describe the process of poetic creation as the bridging of epistemological separations and notional divides: 'From the depths of the self we rise to a concurrence with that which is not-self' (CCW, 4). 'Concurrence' belongs to the same lexis as Hill's 'moral equivalent', as does Ezra Pound's 'accord', which Hill is glossing:

For so I read those words of Pound: 'The poet's job is to *define* and yet again define till the detail of surface is in accord with the root in justice'.[13] (CCW, 4)

Pound went on to say that the poet must 'submit to the transient' but that poetry could and should contemplate transience through this

---

[12] Christopher Ricks, *The Force of Poetry* (Oxford: Clarendon Press, 1984), 325.

[13] Pound's words, from a letter to Basil Bunting (December 1935), are often at the tip of Hill's tongue in this period. He quotes them twice in *The Lords of Limit* (1984), and at least once more in an interview with John Haffenden (1984). By 1998, they have been so assimilated that his own publisher in America (Houghton Mifflin) misattributes them in its online promotional blurb for *The Triumph of Love*: 'In Geoffrey Hill's words, "The poet's job is to define and yet again define" '; http://www.houghtonmifflinbooks.com/catalog/titledetail.cfm?titleNumber=681059, accessed 31 May 2010.

process of redefinition.[14] Nevertheless the language—changed and changing, defined and redefined—retains its roots, and the poet's orientation towards that original justice is the first condition for the final accord or concurrence. But 'accord', like 'concurrence', is not one with 'identity'. It suggests agreement, as does 'harmony', but like agreement accord requires some initial difference to be overcome, some separation to be bridged. For Hill, as much as for Pound, there is continuous work to be done to bring poetry into accord.

Hill's lecture on 'Poetry as "Menace" and "Atonement"' was, when he delivered it at the University of Leeds in 1977, the poet's most focused attempt to describe in prose the impulse towards harmony that had been a prime mover of his poetry. He announces his aim with the following statement:

> Ideally my theme would be that the technical perfecting of a poem is an act of atonement, in the radical etymological sense—an act of at-one-ment, a setting at one, a bringing into concord, a reconciling, a uniting in harmony. (CCW, 4)

This etymological rooting—both far-fetched and accurate—discomforts some readers. Because Hill does not disambiguate his retrologism from the current unavoidable religious senses of the word, several critics have accused him of forcing 'at-one-ment' upon 'atonement', offending the integrity of the word with overreaching authorial intent. The inaugurator of this line of critique is Ricks, Hill's friend and colleague (first at Cambridge, then at Boston University), who writes of 'Poetry as "Menace" and "Atonement"' that 'despite the etymology... there can be no atonement of atonement and at-one-ment.... The loss of the ancient concord may be grievous; it must be irrecoverable.'[15] The variation in spelling, the ambiguity of pronunciation, the variety of accompanying prepositions—all these glitches (in an essay about the dangers of grammatical solecism) signal to Ricks that the argument is not coming right 'with a click like a closing box'. But Ricks's essay, despite its title and introduction, is not principally an investigation of Hill's idea of at-one-ment. Ricks is mostly interested in Hill's use of the hyphen, the punctuation which simultaneously unites and divides. The imperfectible unifying of 'atonement' and 'at-one-ment' serves mainly as an illustration of this principle as well as evidence that it is a conscious

---

[14] Ezra Pound, *The Letters of Ezra Pound 1907–1941*, ed. D. D. Paige (London: Faber and Faber, 1951), 366.
[15] Ricks, *The Force of Poetry*, 321.

preoccupation of Hill's. Yet the imperfectability is, at least latently, partially the point. Even in this early essay the recovered sense of 'at-one-ment' is held both together and apart by punctuation, and throughout the argument 'atonement' is notionally hyphenated to the 'menace' housed in language. As Hill's thoughts on this way of seeing things develop, his emphasis shifts towards this gap between real language and perfect language, between object and subject, word and Word. The paradigm of at-one-ing the 'obdurately apart' (CCW, 264) remains the paradigm for ethical art creation, even as the deep difficulty of this is increasingly emphasized.

The bringing together of 'atone' and 'at one' is one of several examples in Hill's work of poetic ideas crossing over into criticism and vice versa. Ricks makes use of instances of 'atone' and 'at one' in Hill's poetry (to which he is more sympathetic) in support of his case against their yoking in prose. Versions of each occur from the beginning: 'By the long barrows of Logres they are made one' ('Merlin', 1953); 'When we revel in our atonement' ('Funeral Music: 5', 1967); to well after Ricks's essay: 'the absolute yet again | atoned with the contingent' ('De Anima', 1992); 'How certainly words are at one with *all* | *corruptible things*' ('On Reading *Milton and the English Revolution*', 2005); 'making our | divorced selves of love still agelessly at one' ('Without Title', 2006). But it is only a few years before 'Poetry as "Menace" and "Atonement"' that Hill writes, in 'Lachrimae Verae',

> the body moves but moves to no avail
> and is at one with that eternal loss.
>
> You are the castaway of drowned remorse,
> you are the world's atonement on the hill.[16]   (GHCP, 145)

The movement from 'at one' to 'atonement' in the poem may span, as Ricks says, an 'unbridgeable distance',[17] but the move is attempted nevertheless. To read 'atonement' counter to Ricks's advice, as layered in the way suggested by Hill's essay, is to gain in meaning. The primary significance is straightforwardly that of expiation—Christ's Calvary is an atonement for the world's sins. But the etymological echoes of the word, amplified by Hill's prose treatment, suggest a secondary and

---

[16] Originally published in *Agenda* 12:4–13:1 (Winter/Spring 1975), 30; collected in *Tenebrae* (1978).
[17] Ricks, *The Force of Poetry*, 322.

complementary reading: that the world is at-oned with itself in the Crucifixion, that the Christian sacrifice is catholic, drawing all men at all times together into Christ's grace. Reformation debates over universal redemption, or 'equal atonement', reverberate here. Is the world 'one' in Christ, or is it divided between damned and elect? This is a minor tremor, but it cannot be disqualified from our attention: the aftershocks are of the utmost consequence.

In *The Orchards of Syon* (2002) XXVII, Hill stages a virtuosic return to the collocation of 'Lachrimae'. The themes are unhurriedly introduced:

> Not all orchards are for carols of death
> and betrayal, the first the final
> coupling, virgin fatality.
>   .   .   .   .   .
> Equalize this if you can. Survivors
> live out their lives as though by will
> and freedom, with or without fulfilment.
> Not that it matters now: such frequencies
> largely dispersed, the myriad-
> faceted black holly of endurance
> itself, keeping sombre-bright clusters
> exilic.   (OS, 27)

Whether or not 'Survivors' and 'will'—chiming eventually with 'dispersed' and 'exilic'—are enough, in a poem by Hill, to bring Leni Riefenstahl's aestheticization of power in *Triumph of the Will* into allusive play, the opening half of the poem foregrounds the Babylonian captivity (the first Jewish 'betrayal') and its twentieth-century analogue (the 'final' solution). As these lines remind us, there are Hanging Gardens and gardens of Gethsemane, but also Gardens of Eden and Promised Lands, the imperative 'equalize this' demanding equal attention to the reward as well as the ordeal. The elements of this equalization are enumerated:

> ... By the way, this
> has to show winter in its bounty,
> Goldengrove laid bare, becalmed,
> lightly sketched in snow; peacock
> and peahen treading the white grass.
> The Master of the Lost Fecundities
> retraces leaf-spoor and hieroglyph,

makes equal atonement.
The hellebore, the Christmas rose, is crowned king.
Yes and we have gifts, at one with the Other.
Such tendernesses to our selves I mean,
perennial, like the ilex.   (OS, 27)

Answering its opening, the poem gives over its attention to the over-
looked bounty of winter, then divides that attention between peacock
and peahen, leaf-spoor and hieroglyph, hellebore and Christmas rose
(the same plant, it has both poisonous and medicinal properties), selves
and Other. If 'coupling' in the poem's third line establishes the topos,
'the first the final' moves binary correspondence towards a broader,
more integrated and cyclical unity. Just as the alpha and omega are
made one in Christ, the Christmas rose, announcing His birth, twists
into a thorny sign of His torment and Crucifixion. The peacock's fan
(symbol of eternal life) is annually refurbished; the holly of endurance
(symbol of the Cross) returns in the final line as 'perennial . . . ilex'. The
poem, rooted in Christian symbolism and proceeding with all the
cyclical resonance of biblical typology, becomes—like the Christian
Bible—the continuing fulfilment of its own prophecy. The prophecy
pointed to, also the biblical *telos*, is that of 'equal atonement', Christ's
sacrifice made for all humanity, which is itself a prefiguration of the
Second Coming and the end of the world. The poem ends, but it ends
on the never-ending, the always-recurring, so that the atonement and
the at-one-ment it both describes and emulates themselves lack finality.

Perhaps this lack of logical finality is the source of the inconsistencies
Ricks identifies in Hill's prose use of 'atonement'/'at-one-ment'. A
poem may end in unfinishedness, but this is against the rules of essay
writing. Whether or not Hill's importation of this poetic conjugation
meets all the lexical and grammatical tests Ricks applies, the more
important question must be the degree to which Hill's idea of the
poem's 'perfection' sustains the collocation of concord and reconcilia-
tion ('at-one-ment'; OED2, †1) with propitiation and reparation
('atonement'; OED2, 4a). When Ricks writes that the 'loss of the
ancient concord . . . must be irrecoverable', his stern tone of forbearance
would not seem out of place on Hill's lips. Hill's frequently attested-to
belief in a 'fallen language' commits him to some version of this
proposition, which is even present in the title—the 'menace' Hill is
counterpoising to 'atonement' is 'a sense of language itself as a manifes-
tation of empirical guilt' (CCW, 9), a result and reflection of original

sin. For Hill, language, like humanity itself, is fallen 'But also splendid. Fallen and noble. Sinewy and funny',[18] so that, even while claiming 'the utmost significance for matters of technique' and bearing witness to 'those rare moments in which the inertia of language . . . seems to have been overcome', Hill must remind us that 'however much a poem is shaped and finished, it remains to some extent within the "imprisoning marble" of a quotidian shapelessness and imperfection' (CCW, 3–4). Because language is part of the originally and irretrievably flawed nature of man, his endeavours in language can never be 'perfected' in the sense of 'made perfect or faultless' (OED2, *v.* 3) however many times they may be brought to completion, completed, finished, or consummated (OED2, *v.* 1). The latter kind of 'perfection' by definition can be achieved; the former, in Hill's axiology, cannot. It serves instead as a goal which must be striven for despite its ultimate unattainability, not a point on the horizon but the horizon itself, towards which the poet must orient himself and his work. This artistic orientation towards 'at-one-ment', combined with the work of constant striving, are what constitute value, both moral and artistic, for Hill. That this ambition is consciously modelled on the Christian spiritual ambition is a vital characteristic.

THE VALUE OF ENDURANCE

Hill may have been stung by Ricks's critique of 'Poetry as "Menace" and "Atonement"'; the care and precision with which the latter prosecutes his argument would at least have given Hill pause. In any case, Hill subsequently drops the word 'atonement' from his prose,[19] recoursing frequently instead to the locution 'at one', which is always used positively.[20] The theme of 'uniting in harmony' is developed, in other words, mainly via the 'radical etymological sense' in the polysemy of 'atonement' that Hill identified and exploited in 'Poetry as "Menace" and "Atonement"'. The most recent incarnation of this theme occurs in

---

[18] Geoffrey Hill, interview with Carl Phillips, 'The Art of Poetry LXXX: Geoffrey Hill', *Paris Review* 154 (Spring 2000), 272–99, 297.

[19] An exception occurs in 'Dividing Legacies', first published in *Agenda* 34:2 (Summer 1996), where Hill tentatively refers to F. H. Bradley's description of 'knowing and being in one' as a version of the atonement imagined or desired by Eliot in 'Marina' and 'Ash-Wednesday', before dismissing this suggestion (CCW, 374).

[20] See CCW, 197, 201, 269, 349, 353, 374, 451, 457.

the last essays collected in *Critical Writings*, where Hill introduces and develops 'eros' as a technical creative principle: 'Eros is the power that can be felt in language when a word or half-finished phrase awaits its consummation' (CCW, 548). Hill thinks of the philosophy of F. H. Bradley and of the early poetry of Eliot as possessing this quality (the later Eliot lacks it completely, according to Hill). Like all yearning, eros is always most powerful when it is unfulfilled, when it retains all its potential of fulfilment. So eros, for Hill, is a 'wanting' in both senses—a desiring and also lack, a presence and a presence of absence. It is anticipated in his description—highly reminiscent, in both its diction and its ecstatic imagery, of 'Poetry as "Menace" and "Atonement"'—of writings in which 'we may receive, at any instant, a sense of things inaccessible suddenly made accessible, where grammar and desire are miraculously at one' (CCW, 349).

Written long after the early cogitation on 'at-one-ment', and just before the late introduction of 'eros', Hill's 'Poetry and Value' (2001) and 'Translating Value: Marginal Observations on a Central Question' (1999) constitute a cautious reprise of the theme of 'uniting'. When Hill identifies George Eliot's success as her 'capacity to represent that actuality of reflection and endurance . . . [which] shows itself the moral equivalent of those very qualities it describes' (CCW, 472), he is describing her orientation towards 'at-one-ment', a *techne* which attempts to bring object into accord with subject, and which, as such, is describable in ethical as well as formal terms. He writes,

In part, what I am attempting to define as 'intrinsic value' is a form of technical integrity that is itself a form of common honesty. . . . Another way of stating the claim is to say that the ethical and the technical are reciprocating forces and that the dimension in which this reciprocation may be demonstrated is the contextual. (CCW, 481–2)

What characterizes Hill's two later reflections on 'value' is not an abandonment of the idea behind 'at-one-ment' but a shift in focus towards this contextual dimension, which Hill calls the 'arena of attention [and] inattention' (CCW, 482). This move allows him to correct and elaborate a lax moment in 'Poetry as "Menace" and "Atonement"', in which he attempted to locate the effecting of 'atonement'/'at-one-ment' in the moment where the 'inertia of language . . . seems to have been overcome'. 'Seems' seems an important qualification, especially in light of Hill's view of language as irreparably flawed, but its potential is vitiated by Hill's approving quotation of Yeats and Eliot, whose images of closing boxes and moments of absolution and annihilation leave the reader with an impression of 'beautiful finality' (CCW, 4). This impression is itself overcome in Hill's later work by an emphasis on the continuous effort required to resist the inertia and coercive force of language.

Although it does not become the object of sustained prose elaboration, the requirement of continuous struggle towards 'atonement'/'at-one-ment', against the flaws and failures of language, is present in the earlier Hill. In 'Lachrimae Verae', partially quoted above, Hill puts into question the central Christian symbol of Christ's atonement for man's sins. Here the endured suffering which is both 'at one' with 'eternal loss' and is 'the world's atonement' itself becomes the object of sceptical attention, bred from human sympathy:

> Crucified Lord, you swim upon your cross
> and never move. Sometimes in dreams of hell
> the body moves but moves to no avail
> and is at one with that eternal loss.
>
> You are the castaway of drowned remorse,
> you are the world's atonement on the hill.
> This is your body twisted by our skill
> into a patience proper for redress.   (GHCP, 145)

The difficulties raised in Hill's meditation on the Cross resist easy resolution because the poem is itself uneasy in its contemplation of Christ's suffering and the translation of that human experience into literary or liturgical artefacts. Hill echoes the central moment of the Christian Mass, the remembrance of Christ's words, 'This is my body which is given for you' (Luke 22:19), as if to retort: no, '*this* is your body', suffering as a body suffers, now pressed into service by the skill of writers (of the Gospels, initially, but also their exegetes, and now by Hill himself). 'Redress' stands against 'twisted', both connotatively and etymologically (see OED2, *v.*[1] †1), but as much as 'redress' reverberates with 'atonement', Christ's body is not twisted into redress, in the sense of reparation—He is already called the world's 'atonement'. His body is twisted into a *patience* proper for redress, where 'patience' cousins the 'passion' in the poem's subtitle ('Seven tears figured in seven passionate Pavans') and epigraph ('Passions I allow, and loves I approve'). Whether 'Passion' should refer to the actual Crucifixion (OED2, *n.* 1a) or the narration of these events in the Gospels or another literary setting (OED2, *n.* 1c) is the difficulty at the centre of the poem. Its crux is in the words 'proper for', which underline the ambivalence of 'redress': is it the skilful twisting into patience that must be redressed, as this poem attempts, or is this new patience the aptest vehicle of redress for a twisted and sinful world? Despite the pessimistic tone of the poem, the question remains open, while the process of questioning, of attending to a difficulty at the heart of the central Christian mystery, is emphasized. Language may have separated us from the truth of the Passion, but it is the only medium through which that truth can be communicated. We must remain unsatisfied in our work towards atonement, but work we must.

The lexis of 'Lachrimae Verae' strongly echoes an earlier piece, the first poem in the long sequence 'The Songbook of Sebastian Arrurruz' (1966):

> Already, like a disciplined scholar,
> I piece fragments together, past conjecture
> Establishing true sequences of pain;
>
> For so it is proper to find value
> In a bleak skill, as in the thing restored:
> The long-lost words of choice and valediction.   (GHCP, 92)

Like the 'pavans' of the later poem, this too is slow and sad music, concerned with pain and loss, and with reparation. 'Restored' comes back in 'Lachrimae Verae' as 'redress', 'long-lost' as 'eternal loss'; 'proper' and 'skill' reappear verbatim. The corrective, penitential connotation of 'discipline' (OED2, *n.* 7a, *v.* 2) resonates with 'redress' and 'restore'; in its other guise, as a synonym for self-mastery, 'discipline' (OED2, *n.* 4) connotes patience and attentive work. The patient and meticulous work of restoration is the theme, but Hill is not here shoring fragments against his ruins. His horizon is an integrity that Eliot decided early on was irrecoverable. The skill may be 'bleak', and the work too, but it has its value: reconstitution, recovery, even remedy. An orientation towards those ends, a devotion to the hard task of advancing them, are themselves proper and valuable undertakings.

The later volume *Speech! Speech!* (2000) begins with the lines, 'Erudition. Pain. Light. Imagine it great | unavoidable work' (SS, 1), the first three sentence-words plotting the course of the disciplined intellectual. In that poem, 'great' sits ambiguously between 'it' and 'work'—the work may indeed end up being great (important, influential), but it is just as likely that the labouring scholar only imagines it so. Or, the scholarly taking of pains which seems a great burden may turn out to be a light one to bear. In either case, there is painstaking work to be done and it cannot be avoided. Later in the collection Hill constructs similar ambiguity through enjambment: 'unstoppable work | schedules can only be envied' (SS, 24). How long the reader chooses to pause at the line break changes the meaning of the words: is it unstoppable work schedules that are to be envied, or are schedules needed to interrupt and order the unstoppable work? In either case, does 'can only be envied' assert that these are enviable, or that they are unattainable? The inbuilt ambiguities of language, which Hill is so fond of exploiting, here hold open multiple possibilities of meaning. Even its parsing is unavoidable, unstoppable work.

Like 'patience', 'endurance' has been a lasting companion to Hill; among its many instances in his work are the two already quoted: the 'actuality of reflection and endurance' to which George Eliot attends, and 'the myriad- | faceted black holly of endurance' which is a sign of the Crucifixion. The proximity of 'endurance' in these two instances, and of 'patience' in 'Lachrimae Verae' to 'atonement'/'at-one-ment' only re-emphasizes the difficult, time-consuming, possibly never-ending nature of the poet's reconciliatory-redemptive orientation. In *The Mystery of the Charity of Charles Péguy* (1983), the link between 'patience' and 'endurance' becomes more than just synonymy. Here the element 'dur' connects the words in a quasi-etymological relationship—the 'hardening' which is linguistically 'built into' the set of 'dur' nouns joining to 'patience':

> Patience hardens to a pittance...   (GHCP, 189)
>
> ... the common 'dur'
> built into duration, the endurance of war;
> blind Vigil herself, helpless and obdurate.   (GHCP, 192)

Later, Hill will write, drawing on Hopkins, 'patience | is hard, reductive' (SS, 12), with 'reduce' understood in the positive (but arcane) sense of 'to bring back, restore' (OED2, *v.* 5), recalling the disciplined patient restoration of 'The Songbook of Sebastian Arrurruz'. However, though 'patience' and 'endurance' reciprocate each other in their primary OED definitions, their synonymy is tempered by connotation and usage. Now 'patience' tends towards its third subheading, 'the calm abiding of the issue of time' (OED2, *n.* 1c), while 'endurance', as in, for instance, 'the endurance of war', can also imply a more directly felt experience of that which is endured. The verb form 'to endure' (the verb 'to patience', though the OED has it, is dead) illustrates this difference: in its intransitive sense it signifies lasting, continued existence (OED2, *v.* II.2); in its transitive sense, it points directly to the hardship undergone, suffered, or submitted to (OED2, *v.* II.3–4). The adjectival forms 'enduring' and 'endurable' flow from this divergence—a feature Hill exploits: 'Piety is less enduring though it endures much' (C, 71)—and the antonyms 'unenduring' and 'unendurable' further demonstrate a connotative distance from each other, and 'impatience'. The distinction between the transitive and intransitive senses of 'endure', which reverberates in the noun form, is one that holds special significance for Hill:

Endurance is one of the great words which lie directly on the active/passive divide... and it is here, on the line, that, through language, value is to be realized, provided that the writer can 'touch ... his mark with a needle's point', 'strike his finger on the place'. (CCW, 387)

By 'realize' Hill means what Hume means by 'fix and ascertain' (CCW, 386), that is, to detect and discern value within a fundamentally unreliable context. The tropes of accuracy Hill quotes to describe the writer's goal are the product of the writer's endurance; by actively enduring the inherent corruption of language, by persevering in that difficult and treacherous medium, the poet manages to discover value in and through language. As readers, we learn to 'realize' and recognize that value, also through endurance and sustained attention. Value endures, and the literary product of endurance itself endures, despite its flawed nature.

In 'Translating Value', it is the hard activity of endurance, of persistence, that meets the intellectual and moral difficulties of the considered life. Hill offers three examples of authors whose attitudes towards 'value' all point in the same direction. The questions persisting in their works have to do with the fundamental ethical unreliability of judgement; the answer Hill gives, which he finds exemplified in the literature, is one of continuous 'working at it':

On Bunyan:

how do you teach yourself to distinguish the treacherous common sense of the reprobate from the faithful knowledge of the elect; the answer is, you work at it. (CCW, 386)

On Wordsworth:

how to confer 'moral existence' on those 'who, according to the classical morality', as Trilling reminds us, 'should have no moral life at all'. The answer is, again, that you work at it. (CCW, 390)

On Hopkins:

the *value* of the 'dream' is authenticated, validated, by the recognition of the difficulty with which purchase is obtained: you work at it, work it through. (CCW, 392)

In a radio talk for the BBC, Hill described his own method of self-verification in nearly identical terms: 'I write very much by intuition and work hard, by means of scholarship and self-criticism, to satisfy myself of the validity of that intuition.'[21] It is the labour, properly oriented, which gives assurance of the moral accuracy of the work.

In his Tanner lectures (2000), Hill argues with some passion that wrought language both harbours and reveals a threat:

Believing, as I have admitted I do, in the radically flawed nature of humanity and of its endeavours entails an acceptance of the fact that, in one way or another, our integrity can be bought; or our honesty can be maimed by some flaw of *techne*; at the same time, however, our cynicism can be defeated, our defeatism thwarted, by processes within the imagination that, as processes, are scarcely to be distinguished from those that discover and betray some flaw in our conceptual structure or hypothesized ideal. (CCW, 481)

This description of the significance of *techne* reinforces Hill's earlier assertion that 'In the act of refining technique one is not only refining emotion, one is also constantly defining and redefining one's ethical and moral sensibility.'[22] This is the poet's job, as Hill was once fond of quoting, to '*define* and yet again define'. But if 'defining' is mainly a linguistic or literary enterprise, for the poet it is also an internal process of making the ethical sense more precise, more accurate, less prone to moral solecism. So the poet, by progressing through this medium, learns to recognize its difficulties. In that 'constant' process of realization, error is corrected, ambiguity is admitted and precised, integrity and honesty are restored.

Writing poetry, for Hill, means working in a medium which is ethically marked at its origin. The ethical is built into the very structure and process of language. The menace of language is against our moral being: the abounding opportunities for inattention to language and

---

[21] *The Living Poet*, BBC Radio 3, 6 August 1979. Quoted in Peter Robinson, *In the Circumstances: About Poems and Poets* (Oxford: Clarendon Press, 1992), 118.
[22] Geoffrey Hill, interview with John Haffenden, in *Viewpoints: Poets in Conversation with John Haffenden* (London: Faber and Faber, 1981), 87.

through language, and for deception and confusion by language, threaten the precision and reliability of our judgements. Poetry is a way of atoning for one's linguistic trespasses, a way of 'at-one-ing' with that from which language separates us. But it is *just* a way, a path which only leads towards, without guaranteeing arrival:

The most painstaking attention to detail does not necessarily preclude the perpetration of 'howlers'; grammatical or referential solecisms. It is arguable that . . . the impulse to persist in writing poetry (and indeed certain kinds of meditative prose) is an impulse to restitution. There is an obligation to get the facts right and when one has failed, one must seek to amend.[23]

'Amend' is another verb which belongs both to the vocabulary of ethics and to that of writing. The act of textual emendation is here conceived of as the making of amends; the 'freeing of faults', done to a text, also absolves the writer. Hill doesn't use 'atone' here, though he is speaking at a distance of only a year and a half from his ' "Menace" and "Atonement" ' lecture. Instead, 'restitution' and 'amend' make the point: that writing ethically entails a continuous expiation of our literary faults, a constant movement towards accuracy and precision in a medium which invites error. This double-edgedness of the linguistic medium supplies the paradox which for Hill has been so productive: that language, recognizing its corrupt state, must be the agent of its own redress. This requires sustained attention, to the object and to the medium, and the endurance to carry through the work without guarantee of achievement.

Diligence is, for Hill, an ethical requirement. It is for lack of diligence, essentially, that he upbraids Eliot in his review of *The Varieties of Metaphysical Poetry*. The stakes are high: in ' "Menace" and "Atonement" ' Hill takes it as 'one of the indubitable signs of Simone Weil's greatness as an ethical writer' that she 'proposes a system whereby "anybody, no matter who, discovering an avoidable error in a printed text or radio broadcast, would be entitled to bring an action before [special] courts" empowered to condemn a convicted offender to prison or hard labour' (CCW, 9–10). Arguing that 'Eliot's metaphysics sometimes require the exquisite pointing of a word or two' (CCW, 373), Hill accuses him of a culpable lack of attention to the shifting meanings of key words: 'To meet with Hooker in significant engagement is . . . to take note that the word "reason" as Hooker deploys it throughout *The*

---

[23] *The Living Poet*. Quoted in Robinson, *In the Circumstances*, 115.

Lawes of Ecclesiasticall Politie has at least seven distinct senses' as much as to notice 'the skill with which Hooker can alter the pitch of the word "common"' (CCW, 375). Hill goes on assiduously to specify each sense and connotation and its context, as if keeping a running tally of Eliot's carelessness. Whether this carelessness would merit Eliot a turn in Weil's proposed author's dock we can only surmise, but Hill's tone is a stern deadpan.

However much diligence may be a condition of ethical writing and carelessness an invitation to disgrace, hard work alone cannot guarantee good ethics. Weil herself is not so much concerned in *L'enracinement* with grammatical solecism or lax expression as with false or misleading content, what she calls 'assaults on the truth'.[24] One can, after all, be as assiduous in evil as in good; one can labour as much in the perpetration of a lie as in the telling of a truth. Work, however hard, however patient, is a means which must be directed towards an end, and the object of the poet's diligence, the focus of his attention, must also be taken into account. Hill finds in the idea of 'workmanship' an apt expression of directed industriousness:

Kenneth Burke has described 'workmanship' as 'a trait in which the ethical and the esthetic are one'. The appeal of this statement rests in the conviction that a formula exists for achieving a consummation of technique which simultaneously 'satisfies the desire of a moral agent' and, in so doing, resolves the 'old difficulty', as it has been called, 'of conceiving ... *an activity with end attained*'. (CCW, 159)

'Workmanship' attaches in some way to a person, but it is observed through a made thing; it refers both to the maker's abilities (OED2, 4) and to the object of creation (OED2, 3). Where 'work' and 'the work' come together, Hill sees the joining of ethical and aesthetic value. He finds another way of expressing the same conjunction in Hopkins. Borrowing from Hopkins's division of 'free will' into 'freedom of

---

[24] 'les atteintes à la vérité'; Simone Weil, *L'enracinement: prélude à une déclaration des devoirs envers l'être humain* (Paris: Gallimard, 1949), 39. Much of Weil's final work turns on the paramount importance of 'truth'—in a strictly historical-empirical sense—within social and cultural milieux: 'Le besoin de vérité est plus sacré qu'aucun autre. ... On a peur de lire quand on s'est une fois rendu compte de la quantité et l'énormité des faussetés matérielles étalées sans honte même dans les livres des auteurs les plus réputés. On lit alors comme on boirait l'eau d'un puits douteux.' ('The need for truth is more sacred than any other. ... We fear reading once we realize the quantity and enormity of material falsehoods spread out shamelessly even in the books of the most reputable authors. So we read as if drinking from a suspect well.') Weil, *L'enracinement*, 38.

pitch' (the determining of choices by the choosing faculty), 'freedom of play' (the way of execution of the choice), and 'freedom of field' (the object of choice),[25] Hill writes, 'The ethical and the aesthetic come together at those points where "freedom of pitch" and "freedom of field" perfectly intersect or perfectly coincide' (CCW, 168). The 'field' is the material which the poet has at his disposal—language and literature; the 'pitch' is how he chooses to use his material. 'Pitch', for Hill, is an instance of *techne*, an artistic determination made by the choosing faculty. The syntax of Hill's locution suggests that 'ethical' belongs to 'freedom of pitch' while 'aesthetic' belongs to 'freedom of field'; in fact 'pitch' itself is determinative of both the ethical and the aesthetic. 'Freedom of field' makes possible the full expression of that conjunction.

In the opening essay of Hill's first prose collection, Hill approves of Weil's juridical scheme as an exemplary yoking of grammatical, orthographic, semantic, or referential rectitude—which is to say authorial rectitude—to ethical rectitude. In the closing essay, which has fared much better among critics (notably Ricks, who lauds it), Hill takes Pound as an example of a poet whose way with words did in fact bring him before the judiciary. 'Our Word is Our Bond' (1983) poises Pound's Shelleyan pronouncement, 'all values ultimately come from [poets'] judicial sentences',[26] against the philosopher J. L. Austin's exclusion of poetic language (along with drama and joke-telling) from his theory of performative utterance. We are here in the thick of the apologetic tradition: Hill begins by quoting Sidney ('the *Poet*, he nothing affirmeth and therefore never lieth'[27]) and has frequent recourse to Donne, Hopkins, Coleridge, and (via Pound) Shelley. Lurking allusively in the background is W. H. Auden, whose presence does not so much assert itself as niggle us by association: 'Time... will pardon Paul Claudel | Pardons him for writing well' feels complicit in Pound's authorial hubris; Hill's reference to the 'dyer's hand' reinforces an Auden connection, though Hill is quoting their common source. Perhaps the most persistent echo is of Auden's most-snippeted line of

[25] Gerard Manley Hopkins, *The Sermons and Devotional Writings of Gerard Manley Hopkins*, ed. Christopher Devlin (London: Oxford University Press, 1959), 148–9.

[26] In a letter to Felix E. Schelling (8 July 1922). Pound, *Letters*, 249.

[27] Philip Sidney, 'A Defence of Poetry', in *Miscellaneous Prose of Sir Philip Sidney*, ed. Katherine Duncan-Jones and Jan Van Dorsten (Oxford: Oxford University Press, 1973), 102; quoted in CCW, 146.

verse, 'For poetry makes nothing happen',[28] which (in its most usual context, which is in fact out of context) might summarize Austin's position in *How To Do Things With Words*. Whereas some words can, by a stated or implied 'hereby', be said to 'do' the things they claim to be doing, Austin says, 'a performative utterance will . . . be *in a peculiar way* hollow or void if uttered by an actor on the stage, or introduced in a poem'.[29] 'Modern poetry', Hill says, 'yearns for this sense of identity between saying and doing . . . but to Pound's embarrassment and ours it discovers itself to possess no "hereby"' (CCW, 163).

Poetry may not possess the 'exercitive' function of a piece of legislation or an executive order—Hill indicts Pound for believing otherwise—but neither is poetry 'hollow or void' in the way that Austin argues. The words poets use matter, and though they may not make things happen in the way a judge or a juror's words can, they do survive, and will hold their authors to account. Hill writes, 'The word-monger, word-wielder, is brought to judgment *by his being the person who does the uttering*" . . . . Our word is our bond' (CCW, 168). Hill divides the semantic field of 'bond' into 'shackle, arbitrary constraint, closure of possibility' and 'reciprocity, covenant, fiduciary symbol' (CCW, 161), insisting that the promise of our words is one to which we will be held, that our words, once said or written, commit us to their intents.

MEMORIZING, MEMORIALIZING

Part of the reason why solecism, grammatical or referential, is anathema to Hill is because words actually matter, empirically and verifiably, and this is most urgently the case when they are issued in the public sphere and survive on public record. Hill's comment to George Steiner that 'Centuries before the Nazis made it a hideous actuality, the crime of Christianity was to speak grammatically of Judaism in the past tense'[30] follows from his assertion that 'Language . . . is not "the outward sign" of a moral action; it is the moral action' (CCW, 123). The linguistic

---

[28] W. H. Auden, *The English Auden: Poems, Essays and Dramatic Writings 1927–1939*, ed. Edward Mendelson (London: Faber and Faber, 1977), 242.

[29] Quoted in CCW, 147. Cf. J. L. Austin, *How To Do Things With Words*, ed. J. O. Urmson (Oxford: Clarendon Press, 1965), 88.

[30] Reported in Eric McHenry, 'UNI Lecturer Steiner Looks to the Future of Futurity', *BU Bridge News* 2:29 (2 April 1999); http://www.bu.edu/bridge/archive/1999/04-02/features2.html, accessed 31 May 2010.

feature of tense may in this case betray a wicked state of mind or a collective consciousness steeped in venality, but it is not just the state of mind or the collective consciousness which is culpable. Hill's indictment of Christianity on this count draws an arc from centuries of grammatical obliteration directly to physical annihilation.

The public world, the 'real world' where poetry, once printed or uttered, endures for a time, is a world in which 'things (and people) regularly "get done"' (CCW, 147). Poets who are 'oblivious of, or indifferent to' this fact ignore it at their peril. Hill's early poem, 'Ovid in the Third Reich', aims at this culpable indifference with a euphemism akin to 'get done': 'I love my work and my children. God | Is distant, difficult. Things happen' (GHCP, 61). The outrage of Pound's anti-Semitism is intensified by orders of magnitude by 'things' that were happening at the time of his broadcasts, by the pressing demands of the 'real world' not only on writers but on all ethical beings. Pound, or what reputation of his survives, is still held to account for those words in unofficial courts of the mind, in classrooms and in books, even if 'traitor' was eventually revised to 'unfit' by the official courts that tried him. It is his words and his work, together with the circumstance in which he worked on his words, that makes Pound's offence against Jews unpardonable. Hill is right to condemn the phrase 'stupid suburban prejudice' as inexcusably self-indulgent (CCW, 164). The intense regularity with which the Jews of Europe were 'getting done' implicates to some degree each instance of that particular prejudice (once possible to pass off, à la Pound, as just another expression of a naturally but inconsequentially prejudiced society) in the Nazi atrocities. The field becomes morally perilous; to pitch one's words as Pound did becomes a grievous crime.

Words exist in the 'real world'; words represent and refer to things in the 'real world'. When Hill writes, in his note towards the establishment of a 'theology of language', that 'the art and literature of the late twentieth century require a memorializing, a memorizing, of the dead' (CCW, 405), he is directing diligence, endurance, and attention—the ethical attributes of attitude and process—towards an ethical end. By 'late twentieth century' we understand the post-Holocaust world; by 'the dead' we understand in particular the victims of the Jewish Shoah. But Hill also has a more general, comprehensive and methodical memorializing in mind, a memorializing mode for or approach to the writing of poetry. The appeal of Paul Ricoeur's observation in *Temps et récit* that the victims of Auschwitz are as representatives elected by the victims of history to the parliament of our memory[31] is that the conceit accords a central place in the history of victimhood to what we feel is one of history's worst incidences of victimization without denying or diminishing the victims of other crimes. That 'Auschwitz' itself, in Ricoeur's formulation as much as in common parlance, synecdochically refers to the Europe-wide extermination project, to the business of the more or less remembered place names Dachau, Bergen-Belsen, Buchenwald, Birkenau, Treblinka, Belzec, Sobibór, Majdanek, Chelmno, etc., as well as the torching of the Warsaw ghetto and other less-named and nameless Nazi atrocities (which, despite its inclusive intention, the supposed catch-all *et cetera* incorporates less well than just 'Auschwitz'), is a further illustration of how one horror can be 'representative'—in Ricoeur's politically analogous sense—of another. In the same passage, Ricoeur argues on behalf of the *tremendum horrendum*, that the intense horror associated with events that it is necessary *never to forget* (for which the Holocaust, metonymized as 'Auschwitz', stands as the prime example) motivates us ethically to memorialize victims and victimization in narratives, be they of the historical or fictional genre.[32] Thus, for Ricoeur, horror is a 'reverse veneration' (*vénération inversée*), the Holocaust a 'negative revelation' (*révélation négative*) which by its necessary *un*forgettableness pushes us towards a more general and comprehensive remembrance, an ethic of memory which is our responsibility to the murdered.

This is an ethic for Hill, and a work ethic. The ethics of diligence and attention, of difficult and time-consuming labour in and on the linguistic medium, is related to the ethics of responsibility, of debt:

> By understanding I understand diligence
> and attention, appropriately understood
> as actuated self-knowledge, a daily acknowledgement
> of what is owed the dead.   (TL, 63)

---

[31] 'Les victimes d'Auschwitz sont, par excellence, les délégués auprès de notre mémoire de toutes les victimes de l'histoire.' ('The victims of Auschwitz are, par excellence, representatives in our memory of all of history's victims.') Paul Ricoeur, *Temps et récit*, vol. 3 (Paris: Seuil, 1985), 273.

[32] 'L'horreur s'attache à des événements qu'il est nécessaire de ne jamais oublier. Elle constitue la motivation éthique ultime de l'histoire des victimes.' ('Horror attaches itself to those events which it is necessary never to forget. It constitutes the ultimate ethical motivation for [writing] the history of victims.') Ibid.

Ricoeur writes of a debt of recognition of the dead which places the writer (of history and of fiction) in a position of infinite obligation.[33] Like the labour towards rectitude in a fallen and sinning world, or the labour of writing in a deficient and threatening medium, the repayment of the debt to the dead can never be accomplished, but must nevertheless be worked on continuously and dutifully. The integrity of the struggle lies in submitting to the labour without prospect of accomplishing the goal.

Hill's requirement of a formal 'memorializing, a memorizing, of the dead' in literature, made late in his career, is one which he had been exerting himself towards from the very beginning. His acts of memor-(ial)ization are unremittingly sceptical of their own methods, but Hill persists in representing the dead. His first collection, *For the Unfallen* (1959), calls up the converse of its title (as well as its specific biblical sense, 'fallen' describes both 'those who have died in battle' (OED2, 4) and that which has 'lost purity or innocence' (OED2, 5a)); it is a collection possessed by the dead and murdered. In 'Merlin' Hill turns to face his subject: 'I will consider the outnumbering dead' (GHCP, 19), he begins, not only taking account of but also counting the dead, as if realigning the living–dead relationship into one in which the living hold a position of calculable subordination. The poem's field is layered with generations of dead, with 'pinnacled corn' growing on top. The growing corn, conventional symbol of continuity and regeneration, here also foreshadows the communion of the living and the dead (the dead 'are husks of what was rich seed'), the death moment when the living will join the greater number and be 'made one' with their host. But the poem is suspicious of its own familiar elegiac topos. The transition between life and death is marked by inevitable degradation: however much 'considered', the dead cannot finally be 'numbered', as the living can, by naming or census. 'By the long barrows of Logres they are made one', Hill writes, as the numbered living add their numbers to the homogenous, anonymous dead. The growing corn, hackneyed sign (it is already showing signs of wear when Eliot uses it in 'East Coker' (CP, 183); all the more so in Heaney's 'Requiem

---

[33] 'Il a une dette à l'égard du passé, une dette de reconnaissance à l'égard des morts, qui fait de lui un débiteur insolvable.... Dette pour dette, lequel, de l'historien ou du romancier, est le plus insolvable?' ('[The historian] has a debt to the past, a debt of recognition towards the dead, debts that make him an insolvent debtor.... Debt for debt, who is the most insolvent, the historian or the fiction writer?') Ibid. 204, 279.

for the Croppies'), if still perhaps serviceable, of the natural and proper continuum of death and regeneration (memento mori), in this poem also conceals the dead from easy consideration by the living. The corn is still alive, still husk, seed, and stalk, and though it may have sprung from the 'rich seed' of the dead, as it grows it covers the dead-populated earth: 'over their city stands the pinnacled corn' the poem ends, leaving the reader with the image of expansive tranquil wheat fields below which the dead have vanished. This is food for the living that, though it draws its nutrients from the dead, also puts them out of sight and mind. Are men similarly distracted from the reality of death, from the presence of the dead, by this poetry's easy tokens of cyclical regeneration?

Nineteen of the twenty-nine poems in *For the Unfallen* have death and/or the dead in mind.[34] In many of these the dead are deep under earth, as in 'Merlin', or (more often) under water, obscured by the processes of time or the machinations of men and revealed only partially, indirectly, or by accident to the poet:

> Though in close shrouds their bodies lie
> Under the rough pelt of the sea;
>
>   ('Genesis'; GHCP, 16)
>
> Those varied dead. The undiscerning sea
> Shelves and dissolves their flesh as it burns spray
>
>   ('Metamorphoses: 4. Drake's Drum'; GHCP, 25)
>
> Each day the tide withdraws; chills us; pastes
> The sand with dead gulls, oranges, dead men.
>
>   ('Wreaths'; GHCP, 37)

The sea buries, changes, and may expose its dead. Often in its indifferent violence it leaves them unrecognizable. At other times the sea 'evacuates its dead' ('Requiem for the Plantagenet Kings'; GHCP, 29) onto 'disturbed shore' ('The Guardians'; GHCP, 39). The poet, as much as nature, buries, changes, and exposes the dead—the literal, physical reposes of the dead do to them literally what poets do to them literarily. But this is not always the case; where the dead are a party to the relationship complexities multiply. Sometimes nature and men find themselves at odds over the fate of the dead. So, in 'The White Ship' Hill imagines the sea as an indifferent protector of the drowned:

---

[34] The word 'dead' occurs on twenty-four of forty-six pages; 'death' on five; 'die' on three.

This does not much matter.
They are put down as dead. Water
Silences all who would interfere;

Retains, still, what it might give
As casually as it took away:
Creatures passed through the wet sieve
Without enrichment or decay.   (GHCP, 40)

Contrasted to the sea's vast, disinterested exertion of force on the dead is poetry's effect on them, which varies according to the skill of the poet, its interestedness determined by his motives.

Language in 'The White Ship' is an interference which must be 'silenced'; writing is an act of turning one's back on the dead, a closing of the books: 'They are put down as dead.' Here the sea preserves the dead against artful, egotistical handling by the living. In a later poem, the poet is again a self-interested trespasser in resting places:

The tongue's atrocities. Poetry
Unearths from among the speechless dead

Lazarus mystified, common man
Of death. The lily rears its gouged face
From the provided loam.   (GHCP, 84)

'The tongue's atrocities': does poetry represent atrocity with the tongue (i.e., language), or is poetry itself an atrocity committed by the tongue? Either way it is transgressive—in this poem, as in 'The White Ship', poetry is interference. Where nature has provided, the poet takes away. The poem ends, 'Thus laudable the trodden bone thus | Unanswerable the knack of tongues'. Unanswerable, because the dead cannot answer. They are 'speechless' and/or 'mystified' (both bewildered (OED3, 2) and imbued with mystery (OED3, †1)), trodden on, perhaps once downtrodden, material now for the 'knack' of tongues. Unanswerable, too, in the sense of 'irresponsible' (OED2, 3). Hill uses 'knack' to describe poetic skill more than once—in *The Orchards of Syon* he describes 'a knack, a way | with broken speech' (OS, 21) and in *A Treatise of Civil Power* (Clutag, 2005) he fusses that some kinds of poetry are 'beyond my knack'.[35] Here too 'knack' is art-skill, an 'acquired faculty' (OED2, *n.*[2] 2), but it also retains its negative connotation, 'a

---

[35] Geoffrey Hill, 'A Treatise of Civil Power XII', in *A Treatise of Civil Power* (Thame: Clutag, 2005), n.p.

trick... a deceitful or crafty device' (OED2, $n.^2$ 1), while digging up, if only briefly, the obsolete seventeenth-century sense of 'an ingeniously contrived literary composition; a quaint device or conceit in writing' (OED2, 3†c). Going hand-in-hand with artful human ingenuity and all its creative potential is the equally common human knack for atrocity.

Poets may preserve or rouse the dead in poetry, may incur or pay their debts there. Hill has abhorred what he considers 'one of the major outrages of modern life':

the neglect of the dead, and a refusal to acknowledge what we owe to them, and a refusal to submit ourselves to the wisdom of the dead and, indeed, to the folly of the dead and the criminality of the dead—simply a refusal to accept that the dead are as real as we are, probably more so.[36]

For Hill the obligation is felt personally as well as generally: 'Not a day passes without my thinking of the dead of my own family, and my pride in them, and my gratitude to them.'[37] But whereas personal recognition of a debt to the dead is, presumably, mainly an unspoken and private exercise, the writer's professional acknowledgement is dauntingly, almost forbiddingly, public. The more Hill's poetry acknowledges horror's victims, the more it questions its rights to speech. For, as Ricks observes, 'atrocity may get flattened down into the casually "atrocious"' or it may 'get fattened up into that debased form of imagination which is prurience'.[38] The command to 'do justice' compels caution—the poet must be circumspect of his motive and his means.

So, preparing to broach the word 'Auschwitz' in poetry, Hill begins with self-suspicion and misgiving:

> Statesmen have known visions. And, not alone,
> Artistic men prod dead men from their stone:
> Some of us have heard the dead speak:
> The dead are my obsession this week
> But may be lifted away....
> ('Of Commerce and Society: 4'; GHCP, 49)

The opening treats both politicians and artists casually, almost indifferently, as if their brief and serviceable interest in the dead could end guiltlessly, as simply and completely as the full stop after 'lifted away' ends the sentence. But 'artistic men' are meant to have different and

---

[36] Hill, interview with Carl Phillips, 298.   [37] Ibid.
[38] Ricks, *The Force of Poetry*, 285.

more noble ambitions than statesmen. Atrocity owes much to the grand 'visions' of politicians—by comparison the reputation of artistic men has had it good. The illusion of indifference without consequence is lifted mid-line by a sharp change of tone:

> ... In summer
> Thunder may strike, or, as a tremor
> Of remote adjustment, pass on the far side
> From us: however deified and defied
>
> By those it does strike. Many have died. Auschwitz,
> Its furnace chambers and lime pits
> Half-erased, is half-dead; a fable
> Unbelievable in fatted marble.   (GHCP, 49)

Whereas 'may be lifted away' is nonchalant, 'may strike' is serious and menacing. Even if it happens not to strike us, calamity is occurring 'on the far side' to others; its reverberations can be felt by the attentive. Or, as happens, the vibrations of misfortune may diminish towards insensibility. On first reading, 'Many have died' appears to continue to refer to those struck down by tragedy. But when we arrive at 'half-dead', referring to 'Auschwitz', the antecedent of 'many' becomes ambiguous. It is not just victims who die; the record of their murder dies as well. 'Many' thunder-claps have passed from our memories; the Jewish Holocaust is on its way to joining them. The poet or statesman whose concern for the dead is but a week-long 'obsession' (long enough, perhaps, to write the inscription for the next 'fatted marble' monument) is an accomplice after the fact, and worse, the perpetrator of a second, final victimization. Hill ends the poem,

> There is, at times, some need to demonstrate
> Jehovah's touchy methods that create
> The connoisseur of blood, the smitten man.
> At times it seems not common to explain.   (GHCP, 49)

The God of Israel requires a regular blood-sacrifice (O.T. עלה—*'olah* and כליל—*kaliyl*; LXX ὁλοκαύτωμα—'holocaust') as a sign of man's submission to Him.[39] His primacy over other gods must continually be attested to; His Law must be obeyed. Worshippers of the jealous God,

---

[39] The holocaust was generally a sacrifice of devotion, a sign of obeisance. The other kinds of blood-sacrifice were either in expiation of sin (חטאה—*chata'ath* and אשם—*'asham*), or in thanksgiving or recognition (שלם—*shelem*).

the Jews of the Old Testament did not know the redemptive blood of Christ but were well acquainted with the blood of retribution and punishment, their enemies' and their own. The poem's last stanza, illustrating the distance between 'demonstrate' and 'explain', terrifies not because God's vengeance is inexplicable or difficult to explain, but because circumstances arise in which it *needs to be* demonstrated. One question that has animated post-Holocaust thought is whether 'Auschwitz' can be 'explained' by reason. Hill gestures towards this problem without attempting to answer it. Instead he allows that the mystery of human suffering is part of the divine mystery, and may be implicated in the mysterious relationship between man and God. Does this 'need to demonstrate' arise out of the character of God, or is it a result of the actions of statesmen and artistic men?

The verdict that 'after Auschwitz, poetry is impossible', attributed to Theodor Adorno, is almost always invoked in order to refute it. In English quotation it most often appears out of context and is reformulated with varying degrees of textual fidelity, from Steiner's liberal, '"No poetry after Auschwitz", said Adorno' to Brodsky's summary paraphrase, '"How can one write poetry after Auschwitz?" inquired Adorno' (GR, 55) to Ricks's correct but incomplete reference to 'Adorno's cry that to write poetry after Auschwitz is barbaric'.[40] The passage to which all three are referring reads as follows:

Cultural criticism finds itself faced with the final stage of the dialectic of culture and barbarism. To write poetry after Auschwitz is barbaric. And it corrodes even the knowledge why it has become impossible to write poetry today.[41]

Steiner's attribution misreports the letter and perverts the spirit of Adorno's statement. However much the text may insist against it, Adorno is most often reduced (in casual and scholarly discourse alike) to the 'impossibility thesis' that Steiner attributes to him. Ricks, though he quotes faithfully and is correct to imply Adorno's despair at the proposition, does nothing to recover its original context and significance. Only Brodsky can be said to represent the 'impossibility thesis' as

[40] George Steiner, *Language and Silence: Essays on Language, Literature, and the Inhuman* (New York: Athenaeum, 1967), 53; Ricks, *The Force of Poetry*, 287.

[41] Theodor W. Adorno, *The Adorno Reader*, ed. Brian O'Connor (Oxford: Basil Blackwell, 2000), 210. The original text reads: 'Kulturkritik findet sich der letzten Stufe der Dialektik von Kultur und Barbarei gegenüber: nach Auschwitz ein Gedicht zu schreiben, ist barbarisch, und das frißt auch die Erkenntnis an, die ausspricht, warum es unmöglich ward, heute Gedichte zu schreiben.'

a component of a broader and tentative inquiry, and in so doing comes closest to Adorno's intent.[42]

What Adorno actually describes, in *Kulturkritik und Gesellschaft* as well as in other writings, is an aporia in which the traditional 'dialectic' between culture and barbarism is no longer able to produce a synthesis. This traditional dialectic, as Klaus Hofmann describes it, of 'poetry set against barbarism, critique uncovering the barbarism into which culture sends its roots in order to overcome it',[43] collapses once the truths of Auschwitz are realized and acknowledged, so much so that even the cultural and intellectual processes whereby these truths are realized are themselves affected. Adorno does not declare the empirical impossibility of ethical poetry (those who quote him tend to refute him as Johnson refuted Berkeley, by submitting evidence of poetic creation since 1945), nor does he proscribe its writing on ethical or aesthetic grounds, as Steiner would have it. As Hofmann argues, even as Adorno announces that the traditional dialect has entered its final stage, he 'retains . . . the term "dialectic", which promises the persistence of negation and opposition. . . . The barbarity of writing a poem after Auschwitz stands in strict opposition to the barbarity of not writing poetry after Auschwitz.'[44] Negation and opposition constitute a dialectic when they exist in a process of cyclical resolution; when the negative and positive propositions are equally true (and equally false), the term is aporia. The aporetic state in which poetry is both essential and impossible is in many ways descriptive of the current disagreements over Holocaust representation, debates in which Adorno's phrase is transplanted from its nourishing and necessary context to represent only one of the extremities it proposes. When Steiner invokes Adorno in order to write, 'I am not saying that writers should stop writing. This would be fatuous',[45] he is beating back the phantasm of a radical dictum—a phantasm of his own making—in order to take up a position which, as it protests its own moderation, reveals itself to be more proscriptive in fact than Adorno's.

---

[42] The subsequent '*inquired* Adorno' suggests that Brodsky's 'How can one' is meant unrhetorically as an honest interrogation of a possibly solvable problematic, rather than pointedly, as cancelling the validity of the proposition.

[43] Klaus Hofmann, 'Poetry After Auschwitz—Adorno's Dictum', *German Life and Letters* 58:2 (April 2005), 182–94, 188.

[44] Ibid. 190.

[45] Steiner, *Language and Silence*, 53.

The ethical requirement of witness and the role that recounting plays in *never forgetting* the victims of atrocity always exist in necessary tension with the admission that artistic representation often does violence to its subject, whether it means to or not, that the art-object consumes and comes to replace that which it represents. Implicated in this debate are Ricoeur's requirement that history and literature memorialize the dead, as well as Steiner's question of whether the poet should stay silent in a post-Holocaust civilization which may have 'forfeited its claims to that indispensable luxury which we call literature'.[46] That the two apparently conflicting positions (one calling for speech, the other for silence) emerge from the same ethical impulse—essentially, an orientation of recognition and respect towards the dead—reflects the aporetic character of post-Holocaust culture that Adorno first described. But the conflict also suggests a way in which this aporia can be a productive instead of a paralysing one. Poetry *is* possible after Auschwitz, empirically and ethically, because the partial and difficult recognition of its impossibility (the 'knowledge' which Auschwitz 'corrodes') itself stems from the ethical. What *kind* of poetry it will turn out to be is another, perhaps far more nebulous, numinous, question. It may even be, as Primo Levi would have it, that after Auschwitz, poetry on anything other than Auschwitz is impossible,[47] meaning that all poetry will be forced to acknowledge the impossibly high ethical threshold that Auschwitz presents for it, all the while striving for it.

SILENCE AND SUFFERING

So we must agree as much with Ricoeur's ethics of narration as with Steiner's insistence that the 'question of whether the poet should speak or be silent, of whether language is in a condition to accord with his needs, is a real one'.[48] Steiner does not make the distinction, which must nevertheless be made, between the two kinds of silence with which the poet must contend: the silence of the unspeakable and the silence of the unsayable, also called the unutterable and the ineffable. The unspeakable requires an ethical choice in favour of silence when to name or describe would offend or cause injury. It is within the possibilities of

[46] Ibid.
[47] Primo Levi, interviewed in *Corriere della Sera* (28 October 1984), 3.
[48] Steiner, *Language and Silence*, 53.

language, though it lies outside the bounds of ethical language. The unsayable is a metaphysical apprehension of that which cannot be expressed in language even if desired, of what lies beyond language, to which language (and especially poetry) aspires. Steiner is conflating these two frontiers of language and silence, to the detriment of his analysis. Though he does not seem to see it, when Steiner describes the Nazi genocide as 'outside speech' and when he describes the divine as beyond language, it should be clear that we are dealing with two very different kinds of silence.[49] Two kinds which put equal and opposite ethical pressure on the poet.

What I'm calling the unsayable is for Steiner, as much as for Hill, a consequence of the divine source of language, the original presence of a speaking God: 'it is decisively the fact that language does have its frontiers—light, music, and silence—which gives us proof of a transcendent presence in the fabric of the world.'[50] So the poet's labour, unless he despairs of it, is to penetrate to what Eliot called 'unnamed feelings', to push language against the boundaries of the unsayable, towards light, music, and silence. Hill has attempted this in his poetry, testing his language against the divine in the 'Lachrimae' sequence:

> You are beyond me, innermost true light,
>
> uttermost exile for no exile's sake
> king of our earth not caring to unclasp
> its void embrace, the semblance of your quiet.

> (4. Lachrimae Coactae; GHCP, 148)

'Where the word of the poet ceases, a great light begins',[51] writes Steiner of the theological and literary trope (e.g., *passim* Dante) that would have language transcended by the light of God. Within the long tradition of negative theology, silence, listed by Steiner as the most important mode of linguistic transcendence in literature, is the consum-

---

[49] In a later essay collected in the same volume, Steiner appears aware enough of this distinction to attempt its conflation: 'The world of Auschwitz lies outside speech as it lies outside reason. To speak of the *unspeakable* is to risk the survivance of language as creator of and bearer of humane, rational truth' (123). That which lies outside speech and reason is not just *unspeakable*—insofar as language is an extension of reason, it is *unsayable*. Steiner's movement from 'reason' to 'humane, rational truth' is unsatisfactory. The perpetrators of Auschwitz may not have been 'reasonable' or even reasonably 'humane', but they were reason*ing*. Their reasons can be and are known to us, even as our reason rejects them. Acts that lie 'outside reason' are also outside proof, guilt, and justice.

[50] Steiner, *Language and Silence*, 39.

[51] Ibid.

mation of apophatic approach to the divine. Richard Hooker's exaltation of silence as the 'safest' kind of worship is perhaps the nearest to Hill:

> Dangerous it were for the feeble brain of man to wade far into the doings of the most High . . . our soundest knowledge is to know that we know him not as in deed he is, neither can know him: and our safest eloquence concerning him is our silence, when we confess without confession that his glory is inexplicable, his greatness above our capacity and reach.[52]

Where language seeks to be eloquent of God, Hill finds light and silence. The 'capacitie and reach' of reason, too, come up against their limits; the juxtapositions that in 'Lachrimae 4' only gesture towards paradox—beyond/innermost and uttermost (not, but nearly, outermost), exile for no exile's sake, void embrace—in the next poem become consummately paradoxical:

> Your silence is an ecstasy of sound
> And your nocturnals blaze upon the day.
> I founder in desire for things unfound.
> I stay amid the things that will not stay.
>
> (5. Pavana Dolorosa; GHCP, 149)

Paradox, light-vision, music, and silence are the transcendent modes of the mystical tradition. They broach the unsayable, unseeable, and inconceivable. Each is thematically and methodologically important to Hill's poetry. Hooker rejects language and rationality as means of adoration, but his call to 'confess without confession' is not a demand for dumb silence. Hooker's silence brims with intention and desire. It is an 'ecstasy of sound', a placing outside of sound but also a rapturous verging on the beyond-sound of God's Word.

The unsayable exists above language; the unspeakable beneath. To approach either is precarious—the reckless or inattentive may commit hubris or blasphemy, may offend the god(s) or the dead. Nevertheless the unsayable continues to be the aspiration of language, while the unspeakable remains its basest incarnation. For Hill, and even for Steiner, it is not the un*sayable* but rather the un*speakable* state of the world post-Auschwitz that pushes the poet ethically out of language. When Steiner writes despairingly of culture forfeiting its 'claims to that

---

[52] Richard Hooker, *Of the Laws of Ecclesiastical Polity*, ed. Arthur Stephen McGrade (Cambridge: Cambridge University Press, 1989), 55.

indispensable luxury which we call literature', when Adorno calls poetry after Auschwitz 'barbaric', they are referring to things which *must not* be uttered, not to that which *cannot*. This 'unutterable' lies forebodingly behind Hill's poems of tribute to and recognition of the dead, his approximations to atrocity, as he attempts to reconcile the ethics of witness and acknowledgement with the ethics of respect. The unsayable suffuses Hill's psalmic poetry, the poems of worship, adoration, confession, and contrition.

Ricks has written with especial sensitivity on the 'contained silence' of Hill's parentheses, which serve to 'indict prurience' and maintain 'compassionate separateness' between 'the sufferer's feelings and the poet's'.[53] If poetry lives precariously on the boundary between the recognition/memorialization of suffering and the consumption/exploitation of it, Hill's tendency in the direction of silence must be read as scrupulous vigilance, a careful alertness to this danger. Ricks writes, 'the brackets lower the words within them down into the silent depths... they intimate an irreducible recalcitrance, of the kind which any true poem on such atrocities ought to intimate.'[54] Ricks's 'ought' articulates the tacit imperative followed in Hill's poetry not to trespass beyond the ethical limits of language. This impulse towards caution, this 'recalcitrance', intensifies as language broaches atrocity, because it is there that the ethical demand that language be 'accurate' and 'attentive' to its subject reaches the extreme of necessity just as it tests the limits of possibility. The crisis triggered by the ineluctable ethical imperative to 'do justice', set against the inadequacy of language to that end, slows Hill's poetry into a compulsively self-aware and self-questioning manner the nearer his language comes to the horrific. The hushing prophylaxis that Ricks recognizes in Hill's parentheses is one early example. Another is a distinct use of parenthesis which Ricks ignores: parenthesis as insertion, interruption, and self-correction—not the poet setting apart his sufferings from his subject's; rather the inclusion of second, typically affronted, voice. In *King Log* (1968), 'The Humanist' indicts the aesthete, then names itself as co-accused:

> Virtue is virtù. These
> Lips debate and praise

---

[53] Ricks, *The Force of Poetry*. 'contained silence', 312; 'indict prurience', 314; 'compassionate separateness', 'the sufferer's feelings and the poet's', 316.
[54] Ibid. 300.

> Some rich aphorism,
> A delicate white meat.
>
> The commonplace hands once
> Thick with Plato's blood
> (Tasteless! Tasteless!) are laid
> Dryly against the robes.   (GHCP, 69)

Confusing moral and artistic value (virtue–virtù) is the error of the dilettante.[55] Blood on the hands is difficult to wash away; the tang of it is not easily masked by bland suppers of fashionable cliché (for 'rich', used of food, is 'sumptuous' (OED2, 6d); used of speech it is 'preposterous, outrageous' (OED2, 7d)). But how much can a poem condemn vacuous artiness before it invites its own denunciation? The bracketed '(Tasteless! Tasteless!)', while punning internally on the 'tastelessness' of the previous stanza's 'white meat', protests as if from the outside the gruesomeness of the blood-image. This ostensible audience smudges the line between poet and real audience: are they (and we), along with the aesthete, censured for preferring the one kind of tastelessness (insipidness) to the other (unpleasantness)? Or does this audience of alter-poet(s)/alter-reader(s) (the persona contains both) object with good cause to the poet's performance as it becomes clear where it is leading—to an indictment of values which poets and poetry-lovers (including the 'audience') aspire to, or from which they derive a benefit? That would indeed be 'rich'—haughty snobbery compounded by smug hypocrisy. The round brackets shield the interjection from further narration, protecting the ambiguity, allowing each incompatible interpretation to amplify the other.

The heckler's 'Tasteless! Tasteless!' joltingly reminds us of two things: first, that there are those who would prefer to leave unsaid certain things that must be said; second, that saying those necessary things ethically and responsibly is difficult. *Taisez-vous donc*, jeers the crowd and the conscience. If Ricks's examples of parenthesis lower the tone of their inclusions to a forbearing whisper, here the inclusion boisterously and

---

[55] And may be the error of Pound (who sought to rescue 'dilettante' from its pejorative sense in 'The Serious Artist') in his essay 'On Virtue': 'It is artist's business to find his own *virtù*'. See Ezra Pound, *Selected Prose 1909–1965* (London: Faber and Faber, 1973), 29. Hill later tells an audience that 'the particular problem with Machiavellian *virtù* is that, while in the main it is a value word suggesting wit and subtlety applied to good, it may also indicate a courage or strength of malign energy'. Geoffrey Hill, 'Milton as Muse' (recording), Christ's College, Cambridge (29 October 2008); http://www.christs.cam.ac.uk/milton400/podcasts/hill.mp3, accessed 31 May 2010.

righteously demands a quiet. We sense the upper and lower ethical bounds of language—prurience and blitheness (Ricks's 'fatness' and 'flatness'), hubris and blasphemy, the consuming word and the word that consumes—constricting; the margins narrow. Whether retiring or irrupting, Hill's use of parentheses tends ethically away from language towards silence. Steiner's reflections on language and silence lead him to prescribe 'two essential courses' to the poet who 'feels that the condition of language is in question, that the word may be losing something of its humane genius': he 'may seek to render his own idiom representative of the general crisis, to convey through it the precariousness and vulnerability of the communicative act; or he may choose the suicidal rhetoric of silence'.[56] The thematic and technical tendency towards silence in Hill's early poetry seemed to arrive at a 'suicidal' consummation in the decade of quiet that followed *The Mystery of the Charity of Charles Péguy* in 1983. The publication in 1985 of *Geoffrey Hill Collected Poems*, which included only one new poem, confirmed to some that Hill had had his last word.

He had not. Thirteen new poems appeared in *New and Collected Poems 1952–1992* (1994), and these were subsequently revised and included among the seventy-two pages of new poetry in *Canaan* (1996). In the seventeen years from 1996 to 2012, Hill will have published eight new collections of poetry,[57] far surpassing the corpus accumulated in his first forty years of publication. From Hill's long quiet emerged a recognizable but recognizably different poetry, both on the page and in the ear and mind. Gone were the firm rhyming quatrains that had lent architectural solidity to Hill's former work. The first pages of *Canaan* present poems of distended lineation and spasmodic interruption. In eight poems Hill does away with all punctuation save the forward-leaning colon and dash.[58] Full stops, commas, inverted commas, and even, most awkwardly, possessive apostrophes have been taken

---

[56] Steiner, *Language and Silence*, 49–50.

[57] Not counting current *Collecteds* and *Selecteds*, but counting separately—though they include some of the same poems—the Yale/Penguin edition of *A Treatise of Civil Power* (2007) and the 48-page pamphlet of verse, *A Treatise of Civil Power*, published in 2005 by Clutag Press, of Thame, Oxon. With the first two collections, *Canaan* in 1996 (9,300 words long) and *The Triumph of Love* in 1998 (10,700 words long), Hill surpassed the length of all of his previous collections combined (19,000 words). In all, Hill's output since 1996 is about three times that of his first four decades. Hill's projected *Collected Poems* of 2012 will include a significant number of new poems.

[58] 'That Man as a Rational Animal Desires the Knowledge Which is his Perfection', 'Of Coming into Being and Passing Away', 'De Anima', 'Whether the Virtues are

away,[59] so that the effect approaches that of stream-of-consciousness writing—each thought, each image giving way to the next without time for elaboration, reflection, or conclusion. The rigid titles of these poems, which read like those of seventeenth-century Latin act verses or the disputation theses they elaborated ('That Man as a Rational Animal Desires the Knowledge Which is his Perfection'; 'Whether Moral Virtue Comes by Habituation') become contrasting containments of apparently disordered thought fragments. In 'Psalms of Assize', the same contrast is achieved by austere Latin epigraphs (e.g. *'Homini autem nulla umbra sapientie* [*sic*] *magis in promptu est sua ignorans natura'* in the sixth 'Psalm'). But these poems are ruminations and revelations, not expostulations. The stakes are set by the titles and epigraphs—this is weighty stuff of the utmost importance—but the style is ecstatic, or prophetic, not discursive. In the last of the 'Psalms of Assize', Hill turns to the Last Judgement, the final 'assize':

> even so
> God of miracles the crying
> even so
> this is how it ends
> how it goes at the last day
> spargens sonum
> the day of bitten tongues
> say what you like   (C, 66)

The second line of the poem (just 'cum sibylla', centred in the verse-column) chimes twenty lines later with 'spargens sonum': Hill is drawing a vision of the apocalypse from the *Dies Irae*, in places correcting Eliot's vision of the Day of Wrath in 'The Hollow Men'. Present are Eliot's half-saids and said-agains, but the eerie cadence of his nursery-rhyme derivation, 'This is the way the world ends', is here emptied of its sing-song. This *Dies Irae* describes not a whimper but a bang—fulminations and detonations announce the arrival of the End Times. The lacuna before 'spargens sonum' is just long enough to accommodate the original *tuba mirum*. In Hill's version, 'spargens' lacks a subject—

Emotions', 'Whether Moral Virtue Comes by Habituation', 'Ritornelli', 'Psalms of Assize', and 'Of Constancy and Measure'.

[59] These are sometimes interpretable as poetic elisions of the copula ('the souls [are] images', 'her natures [are a] ripped hardihood') but unambiguous instances confirm that it is in fact the apostrophe that has been elided: 'humankinds heaviness', 'florists roses', 'the bloods | haphazard fatalities'.

the discharging of sounds now become a general overpowering noise. The damned are silenced (*confutatis maledictis*), the humble are lost for words (*Quid sum miser tunc dicturus?*); whether tongues are bitten (off?) or unleashed ('say what you like'), it seems men will not be suffered to plead at their judgement. What will we say in our defence? 'Say what you like' can be either genuine or dismissive, an invitation to free speech or an assertion of its futility.

In the second to last of the 'Psalms of Assize', Hill approaches speaking and not speaking by way of Hooker's recommendation to silent worship:[60]

> we cannot know God
> > > we cannot
> deny his sequestered
> power
> > in a marred nature
> if eloquent at all
> > > it is
> with the inuring of scars
> and speechlessness
> it does not improve Sion
> it has no place
> > > among psalms
>
> > .   .   .   .
>
> > > it is not
> the almond branch prophetic
> > > > wakefulness
> nor is it any kind of blessing
> > > > given this people   (C, 65)

The almond branch, biblical emblem of the priestly caste (Num 17), confers the right to take the Word of God to the people. It is, for instance, a sign of vocation to Jeremiah, in whose mouth God puts His own words (Jer 1:9–11). The prophetic mode having long since lost traction on the world, what form of revelation will now bring us closer to God? The poem is pessimistic. Speechlessness can be a kind of eloquence—perhaps, as Hooker suggested, the 'safest' kind—but it cannot be of shared benefit or lead to civic improvement. So the poem laments speechlessness while admitting that it may be the only articulation possible.

---

[60] See p. 194, n. 52, above.

How far can a poem go in condemning both eloquence and speech-lessness before it must shut its own damned mouth? How much can a psalm sing of things that have 'no place | among psalms' before it demands its own silence? For the poet who gravitates towards silence as a consummation of aesthetic, ethical, and religious aspirations, these are questions which must be negotiated continuously. The presence of the unsayable and the unspeakable in poetry courts either paradox or transgression, for a poem by its nature cannot be silent. Hill comes up against this fact in *Scenes from Comus*:

> profuse expediency that leaves us speechless,
>
> wordless, even. Their words attack my throat
> wordlessly. If it were silence to silence!
> Silence is shown defending a loved child
>
> against | incorrigible fact. Mute
> suffering's a factor of countless decibels.
> I see the pristine hammer hammer alarm.
>
> I see it but I can hear nothing.   (SC, 6)

To call for silence is to break one's own silence—one cannot silence silently—and here the poet is forced to voice his demand for quiet. But if his are words that aspire to a silence, they are here set against a meaningless expression that pretends to be speech. The 'profuse expediency' that Hill critiques is a lightness of tongue that does violence to the language it speaks, reduces it to incoherence, speechless speech, wordless word. This 'wordlessness' of unexamined, unreflective speech is contrasted to 'silence' in the second half of the poem: just as words can be empty, silence can be full. The silence that emanates from those that suffer, from 'suffering' abstractly considered, is full: its decibels are off both ends of the scale, they are both nil and over-loud. Surrounding this are the possibilities for ethical silence: silence that defends, silence that rings alarm.

With respect to suffering, silence can be that of unheard pleading, or that of stoic endurance, or else, if either is too prolonged, that eternal silence of the dead. Speaking of suffering, like speaking of silence, is risky: 'Suffering is real, but "suffering" is a sing-song, that is to say, cant' (CCW, 405), Hill writes in 'Language, Suffering, and Silence'. Better at times to mind one's tongue, but to do so to excess would mean the death of the poet's art. The middle way requires a governing of silence as much as of speech:

when we speak we are to speak advisedly; our taciturnity, or silence, must be able to moderate itself. Weigh More's 'esteemed very light of your tonge' against [Donne's] 'it is a desperate state, to be speechlesse.' Both are true. (CCW, 395)

The imperative to weigh, to balance one injunction against its opposite, guides the follower of the middle way. Hill's counter-propositions, exhortations to speech and to silence, exert equal and opposite ethical force on him, and the space between them is narrow and difficult to travel. The plane on which speech and silence are not ethically at odds can be located in responses to the extremes of human suffering:

The silence of the Shoah is the silence of total obliteration, the eradication of history, nothingness.... A Jew of the Shoah, an Iraqi opponent of Saddam Hussein, must elect to write and to speak on the same plane at which Thomas More and Margaret Clitheroe elected to be silent. (CCW, 399)

Clitheroe and other sixteenth-century Catholic martyrs (Hill also mentions Southwell and Ingram) were able to avoid seizure of their property by refusing to answer the charges laid against them. These acts of 'witness', of martyrdom, were the direct result of a refusal to bear witness against one's own self within a justice system that could not convict in the absence of a plea. This form of silence, silence as 'forensic equivocation—a position that is neither assent nor refusal of assent, a strategy for assuring personal salvation, even though it cannot save one's life', is the final resistance of the persecuted. It is 'desperate' indeed, but it is also a sign of 'human potentiality' (CCW, 398).

More often than not for the poet, writing is not done on the plane of martyrs' silence. How is the poet who is not a Jew of the Shoah and isn't otherwise implicated either in the silence of final resistance or in the silence of survival to assure his personal salvation? How can this poet, at a remove from the experience of atrocity, acknowledge his debt to the dead without encroaching on them; how can he contain the unspeakable and the unsayable in poetry without causing offence? Hill is, in the final analysis, deeply sceptical that he can. In 'Language, Suffering, and Silence', he ultimately concludes, following Hopkins, that actions and not words are the proper expression of concern for the 'oppressed'. Yet Hill holds out a hope, against hope, of the possibility of ethical language that meets its own demands for justice:

> Even now, I tell myself, there is a language
> to which I might speak and which

> would rightly hear me;
> responding with eloquence; in its turn,
> negotiating sense without insult
> given or injury taken.
> Familiar to those who already know it
> elsewhere as justice,
> it is met also in the form of silence.   (TL, 19)

'Even now', meaning late in his career and life, against all evidence of experience; 'I tell myself' the last shaky brace of the unreassured. But 'even now' can also refer to the present time, a time in which the 'debasement of words'[61] continues apace—even now perfect communication may exist, in some or another form. In *Canaan* Hill wrote 'I imagine singing I imagine || getting it right' (C, 2), aspiring to the unsayable. Here the ideal, no less imagined perhaps, is for a corresponding language to 'rightly hear me'. The unspeakable, too, is contained within this language that does not give insult or take offence. Ultimately, inescapably, the ideal of language must remain 'elsewhere' (as thunder strikes 'on the far side | From us'); in this world it is encountered in the form of another frequently trespassed ideal ('justice') or else as the silence that transcends language.

WEIGHT OF THE WORD

As an alternative to the 'suicidal rhetoric of silence', Steiner suggests that the poet who mistrusts the ability of language to do justice adopt an 'idiom representative of the general crisis'. Hill's late idiom, from *Canaan* onwards, is an ethically troubled transformation. On the one hand Hill's continuous reflexive turns, his ventriloquized 'editor' and 'audience' who emend, amend, and castigate, are partially the result of an ethical stance which refuses to excuse the poem from its own censure, instead submitting to self-interruption, self-correction, and self-indictment. On the other hand the later volumes rail against their social contexture, seething with contempt for editors and audience, and (especially) for the general public, the dumb masses, the vulgar, the proud, the lazy, the avaricious, and the

---

[61] 'In handling the English language the poet makes an act of recognition that etymology is history. The history of the creation and the debasement of words is a paradigm of the loss of the kingdom of innocence and original justice.' Hill, interview with John Haffenden, 88.

stupid. The dust jacket of *Speech! Speech!* depicts an applauding audience, their faces stretched in stupefied adulation. *On dit que les Parisiens sont difficiles à satisfaire* is the sardonic title of the Daumier lithograph Hill uses for the front cover—clearly the *poet* is genuinely hard to please, if also sometimes hard to get pleasure from. The first word of Hill's first poem is 'against' ('Against the burly air I strode'; GHCP, 1) and like Heaney's 'Between', the preposition has been a constant and versatile companion. Certainly Hill finds much in the culture to be against, to cry out against, but he also hopes against hope, hopes to rub up against, finds something still to defend 'against incorrigible fact'.

I say Hill's late public persona alienates and is alienated from the 'general public', not the 'common reader'. William Logan, reviewing *A Treatise of Civil Power* (Yale/Penguin, 2007) in the *New York Times Book Review*, is I think describing this feature of Hill's work when he opines that 'Hill has made brutally plain that the common reader is of no interest to him. Indeed, he believes that sinking to common ground betrays the high purpose of verse.'[62] Since the review appeared, in his public appearances Hill has often quoted Logan's judgement, once calling it 'a plain libel' which 'I can refute ... directly.'[63] The problem is that 'common' is a heavy word in Hill's lexicon, and Logan uses it lightly. We remember that it is for failing to register the alterations Hooker can make to the 'pitch of the word "common"' that Hill castigates Eliot, going on to enumerate eleven instances: '"common received error", "common sense or phancy", "a common opinion held by the Scribes", "the common sorte of men", "common discretion, and judgement", "in every action of common life", "the common good", "common miserie", "the mindes of the common sorte", "for common utilities sake"' (CCW, 375). Many other writers are quoted in *Collected Critical Writings*, pitching the word up and down: John Whitgift: 'common persons and private men' (345); Henry Peacham: 'common vtterance' (199); Robert Burton: 'the gullish commonalty' (302, 307), 'that which is common' (303); Clarendon: 'the common practice of men' (209, 210, 219, 224, 269), 'the Common apprehension' (212); Hobbes: 'common use of speech' (195, 196, 204), 'common Conversation and Commerce' (202), 'the common people' (307); Henry Wotton: 'You Common people of the Skies' (219, 224); Dryden: 'common

---

[62] William Logan, 'Living With Ghosts', *The New York Times* (20 January 2008), BR1.
[63] Geoffrey Hill, 'Reading and Discussion' (recording), 18 March 2008.

Libellers' (227), 'custom and common use' (232), 'common Humours' (232), 'One common Note' (235), 'the common Track of Business, which is not always clean' (241); Joseph Butler: 'common Language . . . common Behaviour' (483); Hume: 'the common sentiments of human nature' (386); Kant: 'common element' (113); Coleridge: 'a common well-educated thoughtful man' (97–8); T. H. Green: 'the charlatanry of common sense' (117); Cardinal Newman: 'common measure of minds', 'common measure of arguments' (120); Hopkins: 'common repute' (91), 'common prose' (106); James Murray: 'common words' (270, 293); A. C. Bradley: 'as we commonly understand' (140); F. H. Bradley: 'the common essence' (418); Hilaire Belloc: vanquished 'common life' (429); Pound: 'the common Italian' (187), 'the common fate of all things rare' (247); J. C. Ransom: 'common usage' (132), 'the common barbarian reader' (144); Christopher Ricks: 'generous common humanity' (378).

For Hill, the semantic field of 'common' brings together the orders of thought and belief to which he continuously returns—the political, the religious, and the linguistic—laying bare as it does so the central problematic of value common to all three. 'Common' can signify that which is of enough value and rarity that it must be shared by the citizenry (OED2, *a.* 5a, 5b), or that which is usual, frequent, undistinguished, or ordinary (OED2, *a.* 10a, 11a, 12a), or else again that which is so base it must be eschewed (OED2, *a.* 14a, 14b, 15). For the sixteenth- and seventeenth-century writers Hill quotes, 'common' is a term vital to questions of civil polity: who is the common man, what the common weal? Related to this, it is a contested term in the theological problems of the emergent Church of England. Of the early Anglicans' 'resonant' and 'ambiguous' deployments of the word, Hill writes with emulating precision and variation, 'When common supplications are made to God out of the midst of common sufferings, we forget the "gullish commonalty", and the sufferings themselves are reduced (in comely theory) from extortionate private musings to the comfortable words of common confession and absolution' (CCW, 302). Throughout the range of Hill's quotations, from Peacham's 'common vtterance' to Ransom's 'common usage', 'common' is implicated in choice of language, and it implicates language in the public spheres of civic and religious conscience. Here again 'common' can be played at a varying pitch: public speech may take the form of 'comfortable words of common confession', of Butler's 'common Language' or Hume's 'common sentiments', which rest on the moral faculty common to all human persons, and therefore be implicated in the various generous references to the 'common life', 'common good', or 'common humanity'; or language may be just 'common parlance', a comfort only to the 'gullish commonalty', to Ransom's 'common barbarian reader'.

Hill praises Ivor Gurney for his subtle playing of this semantic range between the 'common' that values the good in things and draws men together, and the 'common' that ranks men apart and despises low qualities:

Gurney has 'the dearness of common things', 'beauty | Of common living', 'the common goodness of those soldiers shown day after day', 'the day's | Common wonder'. But against this wondrous and dear commonness we have to set those other occurrences in his poetry, where 'common' is as common parlance would have it, a word that imposes extrinsic 'standards' upon the intrinsic qualities of the thing described: 'the commonness of the tale', 'To be signallers and to be relieved two hours | Before the common infantry', 'Casual and common is the wonder grown—', 'a Common Private makes but little show', 'How England should take as common their vast endurance'. (CCW, 429)

In Hill's relation of kinds of commonness to his persisting meditations on the question of intrinsic value, we begin to see the common thread emerging. We recall that in *Péguy* Hill wrote about 'the common "dur" | built into duration, the endurance of war', and that as far back as *King Log* he described 'Lazarus mystified, common man | Of death', and, earlier still, 'Man's common nature suddenly too rare' (GHCP, 44). If 'Endurance is one of the great words which lie directly on the active/ passive divide', the contrast between Gurney's 'take as common their vast endurance' and Hill's 'common "dur" | built into . . . endurance' illustrates neatly the difference between extrinsic standards and intrinsic qualities, as well as the relation of this divide to the spheres of language, words, and etymology on one hand, and social contexture and civil polity on the other. Hill has said that 'Democracy . . . exists along some kind of active-passive divide.'[64] The 'common man', 'Man's common nature', as ways of expressing man's intrinsic qualities, are locutions which lie on the active side of this divide, unwilling to submit passively to common opinion or a confectioned common standard of taste.

Surprisingly, perhaps, one of Hill's clearest made expositions of the various pitches of 'common' comes not from the context of Reformation anxiety over civic organization (though a civil war is perhaps a

---

[64] Hill, 'Civil Polity and the Confessing State', 9.

meaningful common element), but from nineteenth-century America, from the poet who could loudly and unreservedly 'utter the word Democratic, the word En-Masse' and yet imagine 'One common indivisible destiny for All'.[65] In coming to terms with Walt Whitman's 'polemic of civil polity', Hill finds his own 'key-word' levied in precisely the sense he favours:

Grand, common stock! to me the accomplish'd and convincing growth, prophetic of the future; proof undeniable to sharpest sense, of perfect beauty, tenderness and pluck, that never feudal lord, nor Greek, nor Roman breed, yet rival'd.[66]

To Hill, this usage contrasts perfectly with another of Whitman's 'common's:

To-day, in books, in the rivalry of writers, especially novelists, success, (so-call'd), is for him or her who strikes the mean flat average, the sensational appetite for stimulus, incident, persiflage, &c, and depicts, to the common caliber, sensual, exterior life.[67]

Hill writes, 'a "grand common stock" shall not find its destiny realized in the "common caliber", the "mean flat average"', a view he believes he holds in common with Whitman, if not with 'most Whitmanites of the succeeding century and a half' (CCW, 525).

By 'common reader', Logan means something like Ransom's 'common barbarian reader', though he won't take responsibility for implying 'barbarian', imputing that to Hill. In order to refute Logan's 'plain libel', Hill recourses to his essay on Isaac Rosenberg, where he writes,

The 'common readership', like the 'common standard of taste' is more often than not a confection of literary middlemen. The true common reader is a natural aristocrat of the spirit, and is far more necessary, far more valuable, to a culture such as ours than are the majority of its writers. (CCW, 459)

This may be taken either as refutation or confirmation of Logan's point. Hill wishes to exclude the *average* reader from the *common* stock, wishes to split away the low pitch of 'common' and retain the high. His reference to 'literary middlemen' unfairly verges onto the literary 'middlebrow', an implication confirmed by the hierarchy of spirit

---

[65] Walt Whitman, *Complete Poetry and Collected Prose* (New York: Library of America, 1982), 165, 348.
[66] Ibid. 946, quoted in CCW, 524.
[67] Ibid. 974–5, quoted in CCW, 524–5.

introduced in the next sentence. It is fair to believe, or at least to allow, that those who deal in books know something about what books get purchased, that such business is not a mere 'confection' made up to promote mediocrity for profit. However it is also fair to relieve the poet of any duty to such 'postulated readership' if he thinks it a 'gullish commonalty'. (But who thinks it so? Hill or Logan? Each, in his way.) Hill's idea of public utterance, of common speech, is directed to the 'natural aristocrat of the spirit', to the 'hierarchical democrat', as Hill has described himself,[68] to the commonwealth if not to the common barbarian reader. What passes for democracy in today's civil polity is, according to Hill, no more than a 'plutocratic anarchy' which 'poisons and rots the entire body of political, ethical, and aesthetic thought'.[69] The back-cover blurb for the 2003 paperback edition of *Speech! Speech!* locates that volume within a social context where 'our minds and ears' are 'relentlessly fouled by degraded public speech', in 'a time when our common language has been made false and ugly'. It seems the 'enemy's country', which in the title of Hill's second prose collection signified the 'vast apparatus of Opinion' (CCW, 173) through which one's written works must travel, has greatly enlarged its borders. Hill's 'hierarchical democrat', his 'natural aristocrat of the spirit', against the plutocratic anarchist, reclaims common language to a common purpose, for a common good which is at once political, ethical, and aesthetic.

It is a despairing effort. 'Intrinsic value', Hill says, 'is for the defeated'; the poet, much less the poem, has no real 'purchase' on polity.[70] The tone of the late work is that of one who constantly expects to be disappointed by the 'common caliber': 'Trust Dad | to find the wrong wavelength . . . Trust the Old Man | to pawn his dentures . . . Trust Sandy | MacPherson to blow us to Kingdom Come' (SS, 9). Hill cannot bring himself to trust the world around him to get things right, as he imagines he might in *Canaan*—the minutiae of stress, pause, and emphasis in the poetry are dictated via diacritical accents and raised vertical bars. This feature of enhanced authorial control, borrowed mainly from Hopkins, both adds and takes away. In *The Orchards of Syon*, for instance, when Hill first quotes and then re-accents Barnes—

---

[68] On many occasions, including his 'Reading and Discussion' at Collège de France (18 March 2008), and his dialogue with Rowan Williams in Oxford (2 July 2008).

[69] Geoffrey Hill, 'Sermon: Balliol College' (11 November 2007); http://www.trin. cam.ac.uk/show.php?dowid=520, accessed 31 May 2010.

[70] Hill, 'Civil Polity and the Confessing State', 10.

'Our people, | where áre they?—cranky old BARNES—But óh, | our peóple, whére are théy?' (OS, 59)—we are fairly guided to a new stress and a new interpretation. Similarly, when Hopkins accents 'Their ránsom, théir réscue, ánd first, fást, last friénd',[71] he is ruling out what would be the more natural reading: 'Their ránsom, their réscue'. Less clear is how Hill's adopted markings add to these lines from Speech! Speech!:

> that THEATRE OF VOICES, nóble | íf nót
> ridiculous. Forsaken in the telling –   (SS, 52)

Stressing 'if' may be warranted, though not strictly necessary; the remaining diacritics are gratuitous. The first syllable of 'noble' is always stressed, whether or not it carries an accent; the comma preceding it doubles this emphasis. The pause must be the linguistic feature covered by the richest variety of punctuation—what does the vertical bar here achieve that a comma, colon, semicolon, full stop, dash (en or em), space, parenthesis, ellipsis, or enjambment would not? How is the pause mark to be not-uttered differently from the conventional signs when it replaces them, such as at the place of enjambment:

> Are you serious? Well I'm |
> not JOKING exactly.   (SS, 14)
>
> INORDINATE | wording of Common Prayer |
> find here dilated.   (SS, 26)

or in a quotation where, as can be intuited from the text, the original has a comma:

> LÓRD |
> THOÚ HAST BEEN OUR DWELLING PLÁCE...   (SS, 26)

In these last two examples the 'beat' punctuation first surrounds and finally penetrates the liturgical text, suggesting a possible source for it. In his review of the new Yale edition of Tyndale's New Testament, Hill quotes a Tyndale scholar's observation that 'the old punctuation of bars drawn across at the end of the rhythmical clause' go together with 'sense and rhythm' (CCW, 287). Hill claims that the 'modern re-interpretation' of this punctuation, which claims that it 'pulls the reader along', is antithetical to the original sensibility, which was

---

[71] Gerard Manley Hopkins, 'The Lantern out of Doors', in The Poetical Works of Gerard Manley Hopkins, ed. Norman H. Mackenzie (Oxford: Clarendon Press, 1990), 140.

ruminative: 'To be "pull[ed] along" is to be passive, helpless' (CCW, 287). Is the resuscitated bar, defining and containing Hill's 'rhythmical clauses', an attempted rescue of the 'old punctuation' from postmodern imputation? Perhaps. Certainly it slows the reader instead of pulling him along, forces pause in the place of alacrity. But Hill's late punctuation, beginning with *Canaan* and arriving at an irruptive climax in *Speech! Speech!*, if it won't be accused of pulling along, is open to the charge of pushing around.

Hill's late textual markings, though they appear to add complexity, and are discomfiting at first, are in reality simplifications of the poetry. Though they can look strange, they are but additional precisions of stress, pace, and metre. In places they direct the reader towards a counterintuitive reading; in others they exclude readings which would introduce ambiguity. In others still they precise a way of reading which does not necessarily add or subtract from the meaning that would be derived from any number of the tonal variations normally within a reader's licence. This additional inscription must be read, at least in part, as a result of Hill's anxiety over 'solecism'—misunderstanding, misquotation, and misattribution—and also as stemming from his distrust of the 'common barbarian reader'. But, as Hill himself asks, 'Why does poetry have to address us in simplified terms...?'[72] It is enough of a menace that the language be fundamentally deficient without typography further troubling sense. Part of Hill's defence of 'difficulty' over the years has been his claim that work and applied attention are positive, even ethically necessary elements of the literary experience, that 'genuinely difficult art is truly democratic' and only 'tyranny requires simplification'.[73] Hill's fussy typography, as much as it intends accuracy, must also admit its tyrannical side.

Why would Hill adopt and expand on a technique which seems, at least on first analysis, to demand less and not more of the reader, which instead of precising ambiguity, cancels it? One reason has to do with the idea of 'pitch' that Hill develops in his prose collection of 2003, but which has its origins in a much earlier analysis of Hopkins on free will:

If, however, language as medium is a prime manifestation of 'freedom of field' and the right-keeping of the will manifests 'freedom of pitch', Hopkins's theological crux is necessarily a linguistic crux. The abrupt and

---

[72] Hill, interview with Carl Phillips, 276.
[73] Ibid. 277.

ugly phrasings . . . excessively, even absurdly, concentrate the sense of pitch. (CCW, 167)

Increasingly in his late writings Hill turns to Hopkins's idea of 'pitch' as a critical category encompassing the minute specificities of an author's linguistic choices. 'Pitch' signifies the author's sensitivity to words and his skill in deploying them. It is a question of intrinsic value, of intrinsic word-value valued above the extrinsic values 'imposed on words by various forms of cultural pressure'.[74] Having near-perfect pitch means 'hearing words in depth' and therefore 'hearing, or sounding, history and morality in depth'.[75] So, in Hill's *Collected Critical Writings*, 'pitch' merits twenty-two index entries (grouped into eight subheadings: . . . and Eliot, . . . and Emerson, etc.) appearing in nineteen of the thirty-four essays. Hooker is lauded for the aforementioned pitching of 'common', Clarendon for his 'politic grasp of associational pitch-values' (CCW, 329), Hobbes for raising 'ordinary words . . . to an extraordinary pitch of signification' (CCW, 273), and so on. But 'pitch' is not just a way with words. Hopkins's own gloss, which Hill quotes, makes more of it than simple linguistic choice: '*pitch* is ultimately simple positiveness, that by which being differs from and is more than nothing and not-being' (CCW, 267).[76] Even for Hopkins, who was not writing on language but on the theological question of free will, 'pitch' is a kind of authorship, an exercise of the will which brings into being. What Hill senses in Hopkins's 'abrupt and ugly phrasings' is the incontrovertible sign of their authorship—words which by their very awkwardness announce the absent presence of the writer. When Hill writes, for instance, 'That | Gospel? Súre that Gospel! Thát sure Gospel music in my head . . . | this mý Gospel, thís sure músic in mý head' (OS, 7), the poet's presence is affirmed by the accents, even as we resist their assertiveness, briefly or obdurately, or puzzle over their effectiveness, or else do both, as in this last example.

There is no denying that 'abrupt and ugly phrasings' punctuate Hill's later work. Hopkinsian diacritics and cumbersome turns of phrase are only a contributing element of this intended awkwardness. Most jarringly, 'awkwardness' (in the several senses of 'awkward'—ungainly and untoward, embarrass*ed* and embarrass*ing*, Tasteless! Tasteless!) is

---

[74] Hill, 'Reading and Discussion' (recording), 18 March 2008.
[75] Geoffrey Hill, 'The Conscious Mind's Intelligible Structure', *Agenda* 9:4–10:1 (Fall/Winter 1971–2), 14–23, 21.
[76] The quotation is taken from *Sermons*, 151.

incorporated in the form of interjection and interruption. In *The Triumph of Love*, Hill's 'serious' ruminations ('Even now, I tell myself, there is a language') are routinely interrupted by a restless and irrepressible voice:

> Boom-boom! Obnoxious chthonic old fart,
> boom-boom, boom-boom! (TL, 18)

> Shameless old man, bent on committing
> More public nuisance. Incontinent
> fury wetting the air. (TL, 19)

> Rancorous, narcissistic old sod—what
> makes him go on? We thought, hoped rather,
> he might be dead. Too bad. (TL, 20)

> This is quite dreadful—he's become obsessed. (TL, 21)

We recognize in these (unbracketed) interjections the voice that cried '(Tasteless! Tasteless!)' in 'The Humanist', a voice also related to the one that calls for *Speech! Speech!* in the collection of that name. It is an alter-audience as well as an alter-poet, an incorporation of outside voices which is also a setting free of inner voices. Freed of its original parentheses, sometimes in the later volumes the voice runs rampant. But in its various late containments, in the guise of heckle, joke, quotation, allusion, stage-direction, self- or editorial correction, this voice is rhetorically incorporated from a distance: when '—ED' complains 'Phew, what a "prang"' (TL, 24), when verses call for '(*cat-calls, cheers*)' and '(*laughter, cries of "shame"*)' (SS, 13) from the alter-audience or hear them cry '(*show-off!*)' (SS, 39), when Hill continually interpellates a 'you' which is sometimes himself, imploring, 'say what you like' (C, 66), 'Dón't say' (SS, 33), 'Say again —' (SS, 43), 'Don't | say that' (TL, 81), 'Say something' (OS, 9), 'Say what you will' (OS, 43), 'What did you say?' (SC, 66), and 'Say it again' (WT, 10), or asks, 'Did you then say . . . ?'[77], the poet is both saying and not saying, incorporating speech while still holding speech at a distance. In presenting this content as it were in the voice of an 'other', in distancing himself from his own authorship, Hill finds a way of saying which does not speak the unspeakable, or make a mockery of the unsayable. Hill hears 'voicing' in *The Orchards of Syon* as an openness to the suffering of others, an opening into speech for the otherwise speechless:

> voicing means hearing, at a price a gift,
> affliction chiefly, whereas despair
> clamps and is speechless. (OS, 2)

---

[77] Geoffrey Hill, *A Treatise of Civil Power* (2007), 24.

'It is a desperate state, to be speechless', writes Hill, following Donne. In his late work, Hill attempts to 'give voice' by writing verse in which 'saying' is punctuated, often punctured, by 'hearing'. That this 'voicing'/ 'hearing' ranges in tone from the jocular to the acerbic, from the ironic to the dyspeptic, from the critical to the vituperative, accentuates its distance from the authorial hand. In 'Translating Value', Hill writes that 'where the imperfection of the man is nakedly realized in the speech, integrity and value are affirmed' (CCW, 386). Admixing adorned and as it were spontaneous, 'heard' inclusions heightens the 'naked'ness of the outburst, affirming its particular kind of honesty.

Clearly the self-distancing Hill practises in the late volumes of poetry is related to the distance he puts between his poetic persona and the 'mean flat average' of civil society. This is a matter of aesthetic value as well as civic stance: Hill finds there is 'verbal power rooted in a kind of rift between self-recognition made public (on the one hand) and public non-acceptance (on the other)' (CCW, 562). He rails against the majority opinion of the 'enemy's country', but he also knows that his own loud noises are also open to censure. If in real terms Hill alienates the 'common caliber', if as 'an hierarchical democrat' he is himself alienated by the 'plutocratic anarchy' in which he finds himself, he is also self-alienating in his own work and is self-alienated by it. This points to what Hill sees as the 'bifold nature of alienation, of alienation as both estrangement and artistic distancing' (CCW, 510). In 'A Treatise of Civil Power', these two kinds of alienation turn on a point about intrinsic value:

> There is genius in money,
> and hazard, but not immanence, exactly—
> not Beethoven's vexed erasures or Brahms'
> self-haul through the obvious. Not Hugo
> Wolf's alien majesty of invention.[78]

This coin is not the 'good substance' or 'Exemplary metal' Hill wrote about in *Mercian Hymns*. Its moneyers are as tactless as they are unaccountable. This is currency, the lifeblood of plutocratic anarchy, worth just what the hazards of the market economy determine. Hill contrasts this extrinsic determining of worth to the immanence he identifies with artistic invention, an innerness which is also an 'alien

---

[78] Geoffrey Hill, 'A Treatise of Civil Power III', in *A Treatise of Civil Power* (2005), n.p.

majesty'. Here it is not silence but music—'Music, arguably | not implicated in the loss of Eden' (OS, 7)—the second mode of linguistic transcendence that has been important to Hill, that reveals this intrinsic worth which is so alien.

It is in *The Triumph of Love* that the source of Hill's 'alien majesty', Ralph Waldo Emerson's phrase, 'alienated majesty',[79] first appears in Hill's writings:

> If I were to grasp once, in emulation,
> work of the absolute, origin-creating mind,
> its *opus est*, conclusive
> otherness, the veil
> of certitude discovered as itself
> that which is to be revealed,
> I should hold for my own, my self-giving,
> my retort upon Emerson's 'alienated majesty',
> the *De Causa Dei* of Thomas Bradwardine.   (TL, 3)

Hill's 'retort upon Emerson' is pursued in prose over almost one hundred pages in the final section of the *Critical Writings*, which takes Emerson's phrase for its title, though not his sense. Hill is doing something similar here in poetry: artworks are not, for Hill (as they are for Emerson), ratifications of the self's self-certainty, but appear as radically different from the self, different even from the very self that has made them, if it has made them well. The work is a 'conclusive otherness', which confronts us with the fact of our *in*certitude in our self, its thoughts and its possessions. 'Revealed' is the etymological cousin of 'un-veiled' and a synonym of 'dis-covered'; the self-discovery provoked by the origin-creating mind is that our selves are not in themselves capable of discovery or revelation.

Hill's retort is not exactly Bradwardine, though the analogy holds, since Bradwardine also was arguing against an ethos of self-reliance or self-responsibility based on the denial of original sin. Hill's idea of original sin as it applies to language, and to one's work in language, completes that analogy. 'Poetry can be in, or out of grace' (CCW, 563), Hill says. On the 'sense of creative isolation and autonomy' that goes with work in and on the fallen language, he writes that 'We are talking about a wounding of spirit that is at the same time a wounding of

---

[79] The phrase is from Emerson's essay 'Self Reliance'. See Ralph Waldo Emerson, *Essays and Lectures* (New York: Library of America, 1983).

language, and about language's capacity for self-healing' (CCW, 562). Early in *The Orchards of Syon*, which takes a quotation on divine grace from *De Causa Dei* for one of its epigraphs, Hill describes 'creation'—the word left unmodified so as to tend towards artistic creation while not ruling out divine creation—in similar terms:

> I believe
> creation is self-healing, a self-stanched
> issue of blood. It is also
> furtherance of slow exile, but enjoy—   (OS, 5)

The slow exile is furthered by the alienating power of language itself, its tendency to make strange the product of the poet's work even as he is exercising his will on the language. Language and poet are not exactly brought into conflict by this trope; rather they are put into a converse relation, since the poet also is labouring to distance something immanent, to bring it into creation by alienating it from himself, to create from within the self that which is not-self.

In his late critical writings Hill thinks hard about poetic creation in terms of alienation. He writes,

Whenever we have made anything of our own and made it well—a poem, say—our words come back to us with a certain alienated majesty. In the act of creation we alienate ourselves from that which we have created, or, conversely, the genius of language alienates us from itself. (CCW, 565)

The quotation is from the final essay in *Collected Critical Writings*. In the first essay of that volume, written twenty-seven years earlier, Hill described how the rare successful poem effects 'at-one-ment' of language and subject, and his subsequent essays argued that poetic 'coming right' is an ethical as well as an aesthetic achievement. This meantime has seen the problem of at-one-ment radicalized at both extremities. There is no longer much hope, if there ever had been, in rising 'From the depths of the self . . . to a concurrence with that which is not-self'; the object of at-one-ment has, as Ricks says of the word 'at-one-ment', become irrecoverably, irretrievably alien. Yet Hill writes in *Scenes from Comus*:

> That weight of the world, weight of the word, is.
> Not wholly irreconcilable. Almost.
> Almost we cannot pull free; almost we escape
>
> the leadenness of things. Almost I have walked
> the first step upon water. Nothing beyond.
> The inconceivable is a basic service.   (SC, 12)

'Not wholly irreconcilable. Almost.' The great poet 'can reconcile what is irreconcilable', Hill later says.[80] In *The Triumph of Love* he refers to the 'Angel of self-alienation' and 'the loud- | winged Angels of Equal Sacrifice, the sole | Angel standing in for hope and despair' (TL, 77). 'Equal sacrifice' means 'equal atonement'. The one angel representing both hope and despair guards the artistic as well as the civic enterprise.

And this may be what makes the achieved poem, when successful, so alien. In its successes it brings together the irreconcilable, thinks the inconceivable, recovers for a moment the irrecoverable, or else, in failing this task, nakedly admits and illustrates its failure. Hill's 'but enjoy—' is sardonic. Encountering a great poem, Hill says, results not in enjoyment—he is attacking Eliot for saying so—but is rather 'like being brushed past, or aside, by an alien being' (CCW, 567). Whether this being is (that rare thing) language self-perfecting, encountered in a state of dogged recognition of its own obduracy, or (that rarest, almost inconceivable thing) language finally perfected, in a state of accord with the world, it sequesters itself apart from the common experience of language. The first case may be an instance of artistic distancing, of authorial self-distancing, of attempting to say what cannot or must not be said. The second, despite its negative inflection, is absolutely continuous with an accord between atonement and at-one-ment.

*

Introducing the essays grouped together as *Style and Faith*, Hill writes that the equation of the title words meant, for the sixteenth- and seventeenth-century authors he treats, imitating 'the original authorship, the *auctoritas* of God, at least to the extent that forbade them from being idle spectators of their own writing' (CCW, 263). To 'pitch' as Hooker, Hobbes, and Clarendon 'pitched', then to concentrate that care with words through awkward and difficult phrasings, as Hopkins did, is to aspire to just this sort of 'original authorship', to be not idle but active in the creation of one's writing, to work at aligning one's style with one's faith. With apparent reference to his own late style, Hill writes,

[80] Hill, interview with Anne Mounic. Hill is talking about the reconciliation of aesthetics and ethics in poetry, but he explicitly distances his answer from Wittgenstein's parenthetical claim that 'ethics and aesthetics are one and the same'. See Ludwig Wittgenstein, *Tractatus Logico-Philosophicus*, trans. D. F. Pears and B. F. Guinness (London: Routledge, 1974), 6.421.

> I pitch
> and check, balanced against hazard,
> self-sustained, credulous; well on the way
> to hit by accident a coup de grâce.
> Intolerable stress on will and shall,
> recovery of sprung rhythms, if not rhythm;
> test of creation almost to destruction—   (OS, 58)

Hill's late style is certainly a 'test' of creation, and of the created work, so much so that it does, at times, put the poetry in jeopardy. His late stress-marks may be 'intolerable' to some; they may put 'intolerable stress' on the meaning and movement of the work. 'Hazard' itself balances between 'venture' and 'peril, jeopardy' (OED2, *n.* (*a.*) 2, 3), and the ways in which 'coup de grâce', so pitched, can be taken underscore this. Taken figuratively it is 'a finishing stroke', a settling of some matter, the final word on a subject. Otherwise it is a mercy killing, a putting out of one's misery (his or ours?), a final word heard or uttered before death. But *grâce* is also grace, and Hill's view that in Hopkins 'the determining of grace necessitates at times a graceless articulation' (CCW, 167), that 'the genius of language alienates us from itself', extends the range of what might be achieved in poetry, either *par hazard* or by the deliberate process of pitch and check, check and balance.

The segment ends with an image of vatic rapture:

> Cosmic flare-wind
> with our ears singing, our eyes back,
> mute, Atlantean.   (OS, 58)

'Atlantean', which is to say, as if supporting the weight of the world on one's shoulders. Here it is in a 'mute' state; in *Scenes from Comus*, Hill characterizes writing as essentially 'Atlantean': 'But weight of the world, weight of the word, is' (SC, 12). Fallen world, fallen word. Prelapsarian perfection cannot be achieved, or hoped for. The 'necessitating principle', a term Hill borrows from Baxter in a review-essay called 'The Weight of the Word' (1991),[81] is the 'natural "pondus"' (CCW, 362), a result of the Fall and original sin, which draws both man and his language into error. It is a condition of the world, a weight in the world, which the world, and also the word, strive against.

---

[81] Originally entitled 'Style and Faith' and published in the *TLS* (27 December 1991).

That Hill's striving is always 'almost' does not take away from its integrity. On the contrary, integrity is gained and secured in the striving. The 'theology of language' that Hill proposes, quoted at the beginning of this chapter and returned to throughout, is referred to again in 'The Weight of the Word'. Early in his career Hill wrote about the hard and patient work of 'atonement' within the fundamentally 'menacing' context of language; here we are again on the topic of intrinsic value, where 'goodness' is detected in a grammatically continuous 'reconciling', and 'malignity' is housed within a conclusive and concluding 'finality'. The religious and ethical writings of the late-seventeenth-century, according to Hill, form

the nexus of a different order of theological understanding, inherent in etymology and the contextures of grammar and syntax, clamped to a paradox that the 'one solid coherent body' of the work may be its 'Intrinsic Goodness', its reconciling of style and faith, or an abandoned finality of mind and soul, an intrinsic malignity 'as it were heavy as lead'. (CCW, 365)

The elements of Hill's changing style, from the early containments to the late fulminations, are the enactments of a poetic conscience determined to continue the hard work of reconciliation, of at-one-ment of word and world, an artistic self-distancing which also may result in radical self-alienation. This happens in the assiduous plying of words, the working of their 'etymology . . . grammar and syntax', especially of the words that have meant the most to Hill—'value', 'atonement', 'endurance', 'patience', 'attention', 'justice', 'grace', 'pitch', 'common', 'alienation'. And it recognizes that ethics may require silence of language even as ethics calls for speech, that ethical language must find a way of speaking silence. This 'reconciling' of writing and ethics, of word and world, of style and faith, is just as forcefully manifested in the recognition that 'in most instances style and faith remain obdurately apart' (CCW, 264), that language is inveterate, that the work is ongoing.

Bibliography

CITED WORKS BY T. S. ELIOT

Eliot, T. S. 'The Post-Georgians', *The Athenaeum* 4641 (11 April 1919), 171–2.

——. 'The Beating of a Drum', *The Nation and The Athenaeum* 34:1 (6 October 1923), 11–12.

——. 'Note sur Mallarmé et Poe', trans. Ramon Fernandez, *Nouvelle revue française* 15:158 (November 1926), 524–6.

——. *The Sacred Wood* (London: Methuen, 1928).

——. *The Use of Poetry and the Use of Criticism* (London: Faber and Faber, 1933).

——. *After Strange Gods: A Primer of Modern Heresy* (London: Faber and Faber, 1934).

——. 'A Chorus', *The Norseman* 1:6 (November 1943), 458.

——. 'The Responsibility of the Man of Letters in the Cultural Restoration of Europe', *The Norseman* 2:4 (July/August 1944), 243–8.

——. 'Cultural Diversity and European Unity', *The Adelphi* 22.4 (July–September 1945), 149–58.

——. *Notes Towards the Definition of Culture* (London: Faber and Faber, 1948).

——. *Selected Essays* (London: Faber and Faber, 1951).

——. *On Poetry and Poets* (London: Faber and Faber, 1957).

——. *Collected Poems 1909–1962* (New York: Harcourt Brace, 1963).

——. *To Criticize the Critic* (London: Faber and Faber, 1965).

——. *The Varieties of Metaphysical Poetry*, ed. Ronald Schuchard (New York: Harcourt Brace, 1993).

CITED WORKS BY JOSEPH BRODSKY

Brodsky, Joseph. *Joseph Brodsky Selected Poems*, trans. George Kline (Harmondsworth: Penguin, 1973).

——. Остановка в пустыне (*Ostanovka v pustyne*) (Ann Arbor: Ardis, 1978).

——. Interview with Sven Birkerts, 'The Art of Poetry XXVIII', *Paris Review* 83 (Spring 1982), 82–126.

——. 'December in Florence', trans. George Kline and Maurice English, *Shearsman* 7 (1982), 19–21.

——. 'Why Milan Kundera is Wrong about Dostoyevsky', *The New York Times* (17 February 1985), BR31.

——. *Less than One: Selected Essays* (Harmondsworth: Viking, 1986).

——. Interview with Noel Russell, *Literary Review* (January 1986), 10–12.

——. 'Joseph Brodsky: poésie et dissidence', *L'infini* 21 (Spring 1988), 55–9.

——. Interview with David Montenegro, in David Montenegro, *Points of Departure: International Writers on Writing and Politics* (Ann Arbor: University of Michigan Press, 1991), 132–48.

——. *On Grief and Reason* (London: Penguin, 1996).

——. *Collected Poems in English*, ed. Ann Kjellberg, trans. Anthony Hecht et al. (Manchester: Carcanet, 2001).

——. *Joseph Brodsky: Conversations*, ed. Cynthia L. Haven (Jackson: University Press of Mississippi, 2002).

CITED WORKS BY SEAMUS HEANEY

Heaney, Seamus. *Death of a Naturalist* (London: Faber and Faber, 1966).

——. *Door into the Dark* (London: Faber and Faber, 1969).

——. 'Intimidation', *Malahat Review* 17 (1971), 34.

——. 'Nocturne', *Malahat Review* 17 (1971), 35.

——. *Wintering Out* (London: Faber and Faber, 1972).

——. *North* (London: Faber and Faber, 1975).

——. *Stations* (Belfast: Ulsterman Publications, 1975).

——. *Field Work* (London: Faber and Faber, 1979).

——. Interview with James Randall, *Ploughshares* 5:3 (1979), 7–22.

——. *Preoccupations: Selected Prose 1968–1978* (London: Faber and Faber, 1980).

——. Interview with Frank Kinahan, *Critical Inquiry* 8:3 (Spring 1982), 405–14.

——. *Among Schoolchildren* (John Malone Memorial Committee, 1983).

——. *Sweeney Astray* (London: Faber and Faber, 1983).

——. 'Envies and Identifications: Dante and the Modern Poet', *Irish University Review* 15:1 (Spring 1985), 5–19.

——. *Station Island* (London: Faber and Faber, 1985).

——. 'Brodsky's Nobel: What the Applause Was About', *The New York Times* (8 November 1987), BR1.

——. *The Haw Lantern* (London: Faber and Faber, 1987).

——. *The Government of the Tongue: The 1986 T. S. Eliot Memorial Lectures and Other Critical Writings* (London: Faber and Faber, 1988).

——. *The Cure at Troy: A Version of Sophocles's Philoctetes* (London: Faber and Faber, 1990).

——. *Seeing Things* (London: Faber and Faber, 1991).

——. Interview with John Breslin, *The Critic* 46:2 (Winter 1991), 26–35.

——. *The Redress of Poetry* (London: Faber and Faber, 1995).

Heaney, Seamus. 'The Singer of Tales: On Joseph Brodsky', *The New York Times* (3 March 1996), BR31.

——. *Crediting Poetry: The Nobel Lecture* (New York: Farrar, Straus and Giroux, 1996).

——. *The Spirit Level* (London: Faber and Faber, 1996).

——. 'Columcille the Scribe', *Irish Times* (7 June 1997), 45.

——. Interview with Henri Cole, 'The Art of Poetry LXXV', *Paris Review* 144 (Fall 1997), 88–138.

——. Translation and introduction, *Beowulf* (London: Faber and Faber, 1999).

——. *The Midnight Verdict* (Oldcastle: Gallery Press, 2000).

—— and Robert Hass. *Sounding Lines: The Art of Translating Poetry* (Berkeley: Townsend Center, 1999).

—— and Karl Miller. *Seamus Heaney in Conversation with Karl Miller* (London: Between the Lines, 2000).

——. *Electric Light* (London: Faber and Faber, 2001).

——. 'Lux Perpetua: Seamus Heaney on the Making of his Recent Collection, Electric Light', *The Guardian* (16 June 2001), 9.

——. 'Horace and Thunder', *Times Literary Supplement* (18 January 2002), 40.

——. 'Hallaig', *The Guardian* (30 November 2002).

——. *Hallaig* (Sleat: Urras Shomhairle/The Sorley MacLean Trust, 2002).

——. *Finders Keepers: Selected Prose 1971–2002* (London: Faber and Faber, 2002).

——. 'Linked Verses', *AGNI* 57 (2003), 8.

——. 'Eclogues in Extremis: On the Staying Power of the Pastoral', *Proceedings of the Royal Irish Academy* 103C:1 (2003), 1–12.

——. *The Testament of Cresseid: A Retelling of Robert Henryson's Poem* (London: Enitharmon Editions, 2004).

——. *The Burial at Thebes* (London: Faber and Faber, 2004).

——. *Anything Can Happen: A Poem and Essay with Translations in Support of Art for Amnesty* (Dublin: TownHouse, 2004).

——. 'Search for the Soul of Antigone', *The Guardian* (2 November 2005), Culture: 18.

——. *District and Circle* (London: Faber and Faber, 2006).

——. 'One Poet in Search of a Title', *The Times Online* (25 March 2006); http://www.thetimes.co.uk/tto/arts/books/article2450529.ece, accessed 31 May 2010.

——. *The Riverbank Field* (Oldcastle: Gallery Press, 2007).

—— and Dennis O'Driscoll. *Stepping Stones* (London: Faber and Faber, 2008).

——. 'Holding Patterns: Arts, Letters and the Academy', *Royal Irish Academy* (28 January 2008); http://www.ria.ie/news/pdf/Heaney_Discourse.pdf, accessed 21 December 2008.

——. *The Testament of Cresseid* (London: Faber and Faber, 2009).

CITED WORKS BY GEOFFREY HILL

Hill, Geoffrey. 'The Conscious Mind's Intelligible Structure', *Agenda* 9:4–10:1 (Fall/Winter 1971–2), 14–23.

——. *Collected Poems* (Harmondsworth: Penguin, 1985).

——. *Canaan* (London: Penguin, 1996).

——. *The Triumph of Love* (London: Penguin, 1998).

——. *Speech! Speech!* (London: Penguin, 2000).

——. Interview with Carl Philips. 'The Art of Poetry LXXX', *Paris Review* 154 (Spring 2000), 272–99.

——. 'A Matter of Timing', *The Guardian* (21 September 2002).

——. *The Orchards of Syon* (London: Penguin, 2002).

——. *Style and Faith* (New York: Counterpoint, 2003).

——. Interviewed on Private Passions, BBC Radio 3, 25 April 2004.

——. *Scenes from Comus* (London: Penguin, 2005).

——. *A Treatise of Civil Power* (Thame, Oxon: Clutag, 2005).

——. *Without Title* (London: Penguin, 2006).

——. *A Treatise of Civil Power* (London: Penguin, 2007).

——. 'Sermon: Balliol College', Oxford (11 November 2007); http://www.trin.cam.ac.uk/show.php?dowid=520, accessed 20 January 2009.

——. *Collected Critical Writings* (Oxford: Oxford University Press, 2008).

——. 'Reading and Discussion' (recording), Collège de France (18 March 2008); http://www.college-de-france.fr/audio/hill/ghill_18032008.mp3, accessed 31 May 2010.

——. Interview with Anne Mounic, 'Le poème, moulin mystique' (19 March 2008); http://www3.sympatico.ca/sylvia.paul/ghill_interview_by_AnneMounic.htm, accessed 31 May 2010.

——. 'Civil Polity and the Confessing State', *Warwick Review* 2:2 (June 2008), 7–20.

——. 'Milton as Muse' (recording), Christ's College, Cambridge (29 October 2008); http://www.christs.cam.ac.uk/milton400/podcasts/hill.mp3, accessed 31 May 2010.

OTHER WORKS CITED

Adorno, Theodor W. *The Adorno Reader*, ed. Brian O'Connor (Oxford: Basil Blackwell, 2000).

Allen, Michael (ed.). *Seamus Heaney: Contemporary Critical Essays* (New York: St Martin's, 1997).

Altieri, Charles. 'Lyrical Ethics and Literary Experience', in Todd F. Davis and Kenneth Womack (eds), *Mapping the Ethical Turn: A Reader in Ethics,*

Culture, and Literary Theory (Charlottesville: University Press of Virginia, 2001), 30–58.

Anonymous (Frida Vigdorova). Русская Мысль (*Russkaia Mysl'*) (5 May 1964).

——.'Poezja przed sądem w Leningradzie', *Kultura: szkice, opowiadania, sprawozdania* 7:201–8:202 (July–August 1964), 3–28.

——.'The Trial of Iosif Brodsky: A Transcript', *The New Leader* (31 August 1964), 6–17.

——.'Trial of a Young Poet', *Encounter* 23:3 (September 1964), 84–91.

——.'Заседание суда Дзержинского района города Ленинграда' ('Zasedanie suda Dzerzhinskogo raĭona goroda Leningrada'), Воздушные пути: альманах (*Vozdushnye puti: al'manakh*) 4 (1965), 279–303.

Anonymous (Geoffrey West). 'Mr Eliot's New Essays', *Times Literary Supplement* (6 December 1928), 953.

Anonymous 'Poetry of W. B. Yeats; Mr Eliot's Critical Assessment', *Irish Times* (1 July 1940), 6.

——.'Tributes by Mr T. S. Eliot', *Irish Independent* (1 July 1940), 8.

——.'"Yeats the Greatest Poet of Our Time"—Mr Eliot', *Irish Press* (2 July 1940), 9.

——.'Soviet-Born Poet Awarded Nobel Prize for Literature', *Toronto Star* (23 October 1987), A3.

Aquinas, St Thomas. *Summa Theologiae* (London: Blackfriars, 1964–81).

Arendt, Hannah. *Between Past and Future: Eight Exercises in Political Thought* (New York: Viking, 1968).

Armitage, Simon, and Robert Crawford (eds). *Penguin Book of Poetry from Britain and Ireland since 1945* (London: Viking, 1998).

Arnold, Matthew. *The Complete Prose of Matthew Arnold*, vol. IX: *English Literature and Irish Politics*, ed. Robert Henry Super (Ann Arbor: University of Michigan Press, 1973).

Astell, Anne, and Justin Jackson (eds). *Levinas and Medieval Literature: The Difficult Reading of English and Rabbinic Texts* (Pittsburgh: Duquesne University Press, 2009).

Attridge, Derek. *The Singularity of Literature* (London: Routledge, 2004).

Auden, Wystan Hugh. *The English Auden: Poems, Essays and Dramatic Writings 1927–1939*, ed. Edward Mendelson (London: Faber and Faber, 1977).

Austin, J. L. *How to Do Things with Words*, ed. J. O. Urmson (Oxford: Clarendon Press, 1965).

Baker, Peter (ed.). *Onward: Contemporary Poetry and Poetics* (New York: Peter Lang, 1996).

Baratynskiĭ, Evgeniĭ Abramovich. *Selected Poems of Yevgeny Abramovitch Baratynsky*, trans. Jill Higgs (Spalding: Hub Editions, 2004).

Barber, Tony. 'Brodsky Prize Recalls Past Sensitive Awards to Soviet Writers', *Reuters News* (22 October 1987).

Barry, Randall K. (ed.). *ALA-LC Romanization Tables: Transliteration Schemes for Non-Roman Scripts* (Washington, DC: Cataloging Distribution Service, Library of Congress, 1997).

Bateson, F. W. 'Criticism's Lost Leader', in *The Literary Criticism of T. S. Eliot: New Essays*, ed. David Newton-de Molina (London: Athlone, 1977), 1–19.

Battersby, Eileen. 'A Greek Tragedy for our Times', *Irish Times* (3 April 2004), 55.

Begunov, IUriĭ Konstaninovich. Правда о суде над Иосифом Бродским (*Pravda o sude nad Iosifom Brodskim*) (St Petersburg: Izdatel´stvo imeni A.S. Severina/Sojuz pistaelej Rossii, 1996).

Bennett, Alan. *Writing Home* (London: Faber and Faber, 1994).

'Biblegateway.com'. 1995–2010. http://www.biblegateway.com.

Birkerts, Sven. 'A Subversive in Verse', *The New York Times* (17 September 2000), 7.10.

Bland, Robert, and John Merivale (eds). *Collections from the Greek Anthology: A New Edition* (London: Longman etc., 1833).

Booth, Wayne C. *The Company We Keep: An Ethics of Fiction* (Berkeley: University of California Press, 1988).

——. 'Why Ethical Criticism Can Never be Simple', in Todd F. Davis and Kenneth Womack (eds), *Mapping the Ethical Turn: A Reader in Ethics, Culture, and Literary Theory* (Charlottesville: University Press of Virginia, 2001), 16–29.

Bowie, Andrew. *From Romanticism to Critical Theory* (London: Routledge, 1997).

Boym, Svetlana. 'Estrangement as Lifestyle: Shklovsky and Brodsky', *Poetics Today* 17:4 (Winter 1996), 511–30.

——. 'Poetics and Politics of Estrangement: Victor Shklovsky and Hannah Arendt', *Poetics Today* 26:4 (Winter 2005), 581–611.

Brandes, Rand, and Michael Durkan (eds). *Seamus Heaney: A Bibliography 1959–2003* (London: Faber and Faber, 2008).

Brinkley, Tony, and Raina Kostova. '"The Road to Stalin": Mandelstam's Ode to Stalin and "The Lines on the Unknown Soldier"', *Shofar: An Interdisciplinary Journal of Jewish Studies* 21:4 (2003), 32–62.

Buell, Lawrence. 'What We Talk about When We Talk about Ethics', in Marjorie Garber, Beatrice Hansen, and Rebecca L. Walkowitz (eds), *The Turn to Ethics* (New York: Routledge, 2000), 1–14.

Bugan, Carmen. 'Poetics of Exile: East European Poetry in Translation and Seamus Heaney's Ars Poetica'. Dissertation, University of Oxford, 2004.

Burke, Kenneth. *The Philosophy of Literary Form*, 3rd edn (Berkeley: University of California Press, 1973).

Burnett, Leon. 'Galatea Encore', in Lev Loseff and Valentina Polukhina (eds), *Joseph Brodsky: The Art of the Poem* (New York: Palgrave, 1999).

Burns, Robert. *The Canongate Burns: The Complete Poems and Songs of Robert Burns*, ed. Andrew Noble and Patrick Scott (Edinburgh: Canongate, 2003).

Bush, George W. 'Address to a Joint Session of Congress and the American People' (20 September 2001); http://www.whitehouse.gov/news/releases/2001/09/20010920-8.html, accessed 17 December 2008.

Butler, Judith. 'Ethical Ambivalence', in Marjorie Garber, Beatrice Hansen, and Rebecca L. Walkowitz (eds), *The Turn to Ethics* (New York: Routledge, 2000), 15–28.

Cavanagh, Michael. *Professing Poetry: Seamus Heaney's Poetics* (Washington, DC: Catholic University of America Press, 2009).

Cavell, Stanley. *Disowning Knowledge in Six Plays of Shakespeare* (Cambridge: Cambridge University Press, 1987).

Celan, Paul. *Collected Prose*, trans. Rosmarie Waldrop (Manchester: Carcanet, 1986).

Chaucer, Geoffrey. *The Riverside Chaucer*, ed. Larry D. Benson (Boston: Houghton Mifflin, 1987).

Cicero. *De Oratore*, trans. E. W. Sutton (London: William Heinemann, 1959).

Cohen, Ralph (ed.). *New Literary History* 15:1 (Autumn 1983).

Coleridge, Samuel Taylor. *The Collected Letters of Samuel Taylor Coleridge*, vol. 1, ed. Earl Leslie Griggs (Oxford: Clarendon Press, 1966).

——. *Biographia Literaria II*, in *The Collected Works of Samuel Taylor Coleridge*, vol. 7, ed. James Engell and W. Jackson Bate (Princeton: Princeton University Press, 1983).

Corcoran, Neil. *Seamus Heaney: A Critical Study* (London: Faber and Faber, 1998).

Covington, Richard. 'A Scruffy Fighting Place', *Salon.com*, (1996); http://archive.salon.com/weekly/heaney2.html, accessed 31 May 2010.

Coyle, Michael. '"This Rather Elusory Broadcast Technique": T. S. Eliot and the Genre of the Radio Talk', *ANQ* 11:4 (Fall 1998), 32–42.

Crawford, Robert. *The Savage and the City in the Work of T. S. Eliot* (Oxford: Clarendon Press, 1987).

'Crosswalk.com'. 1995–2010. http://bible.crosswalk.com/.

Davie, Donald. *Czeslaw Milosz and the Insufficiency of the Lyric* (Cambridge: Cambridge University Press, 1986).

Davis, Todd F., and Kenneth Womack (eds). *Mapping the Ethical Turn: A Reader in Ethics, Culture, and Literary Theory* (Charlottesville: University Press of Virginia, 2001).

Day Lewis, Cecil. *A Hope for Poetry* (Oxford: Blackwell, 1947).

——. *Collected Poems* (London: Jonathan Cape, 1954).

de Man, Paul. *Allegories of Reading: Figural Language in Rousseau, Nietzsche, Rilke and Proust* (New Haven, CT: Yale University Press, 1979).

de Petris, Carla. 'Heaney and Dante', in Robert F. Garrat (ed.), *Critical Essays on Seamus Heaney* (London: Prentice Hall, 1995), 161–71.

de Tocqueville, Alexis. *De la démocratie en Amérique*, vol. 2 (Paris: Gallimard, 1993).

Derrida, Jacques. *L'écriture et la différence* (Paris: Seuil, 1967).

——. *De la grammatologie* (Paris: Éditions Minuit, 1967).

Dolan, Terence Patrick (ed.). *Dictionary of Hiberno-English* (Dublin: Gill and MacMillan, 1998).

Dostoevsky, Fyodor. *The Brothers Karamazov*, trans. Constance Garnett (London: Heinemann, 1968).

Eaglestone, Robert. *Ethical Criticism: Reading after Levinas* (Edinburgh: Edinburgh University Press, 1997).

——. 'One and the Same? Ethics, Aesthetics, and Truth', *Poetics Today* 25:4 (Winter 2004), 595–608.

Eaton, Marcia Muelder. 'Aesthetics: The Mother of Ethics?', *Journal of Aesthetics and Art Criticism* 55:4 (Fall 1997), 355–64.

Eskin, Michael. *Ethics and Dialogue in the Works of Levinas, Bakhtin, Mandel'-shtam, and Celan* (Oxford: Oxford University Press, 2000).

——. 'On Literature and Ethics', *Poetics Today* 25:4 (Winter 2004), 573–94.

Etkind, Efim. *Notes of a Non-Conspirator*, trans. Peter France (Oxford: Oxford University Press, 1978).

——. *Brodski, ou, Le procès d'un poète* (Paris: Librairie Générale Française, 1988).

——. Процесс Иосифа Бродского (*Protsess Iosifa Brodskogo*) (London: Overseas Publications Interchange, 1988).

Freidin, Gregory. *A Coat of Many Colors* (Berkeley: University of California Press, 1987).

Frost, Robert. *Collected Poems, Prose, and Plays* (New York: Library of America, 1995).

Gallup, Donald. *T. S. Eliot: A Bibliography* (London: Faber and Faber, 1969).

Garber, Marjorie, Beatrice Hansen, and Rebecca L. Walkowitz (eds). *The Turn to Ethics* (New York: Routledge, 2000).

Garrat, Robert F. (ed.). *Critical Essays on Seamus Heaney* (London: Prentice Hall, 1995).

Gibson, Andrew. *Postmodernity, Ethics and the Novel: From Leavis to Levinas* (London: Routledge, 1999).

Gorky, Maxim, et al. *Soviet Writers' Congress, 1934: The Debate on Socialist Realism and Modernism in the Soviet Union*, trans. and ed. H. G. Scott (London: Lawrence and Wishart, 1977).

Gubar, Susan. 'Poets of Testimony: C. K. Williams and Jacqueline Osherow as Proxy Witnesses of the Shoah', in Todd F. Davis and Kenneth Womack (eds), *Mapping the Ethical Turn: A Reader in Ethics, Culture, and Literary Theory* (Charlottesville: University Press of Virginia, 2001), 165–91.

Guillory, John. 'The Ethical Practice of Modernity', in Marjorie Garber, Beatrice Hansen, and Rebecca L. Walkowitz (eds), *The Turn to Ethics* (New York: Routledge, 2000), 29–46.

Gussow, Mel. 'Irish Touch on an Anglo-Saxon Chiller' (Review of *Beowulf*), *The New York Times* (29 March 2000), E1.

Haffenden, John. *Viewpoints: Poets in Conversation with John Haffenden* (London: Faber and Faber, 1981).

Hand, Seán (ed.). *Facing the Other: The Ethics of Emmanuel Levinas* (Richmond: Curzon, 1996).

——. 'Shadowing Ethics: Levinas's View of Art and Aesthetics', in Seán Hand (ed.), *Facing the Other: The Ethics of Emmanuel Levinas* (Richmond: Curzon, 1996), 63–90.

Hart, Henry. 'What Is Heaney Seeing in Seeing Things?', *Colby Quarterly* 30:1 (March 1994), 33–42.

Hart, Kevin. *The Trespass of the Sign: Deconstruction, Theology and Philosophy* (New York: Fordham University Press, 2000).

Harvard University Libraries. 'HOLLIS Catalog'. The President and Fellows of Harvard College, 2010. http://holliscatalog.harvard.edu/, accessed 31 May 2010.

Havel, Václav. *Open Letters: Selected Writings 1965–1990*, trans. and ed. Paul Wilson (New York: Vintage, 1992).

Heidegger, Martin. *Being and Time*, trans. John Macquarrie and Edward Robinson (Oxford: Basil Blackwell, 1967 [1962]).

——. 'The Origin of the Work of Art', in *Off the Beaten Track*, trans. and ed. Julian Young and Kenneth Haynes (Cambridge: Cambridge University Press, 2002).

Hofmann, Klaus. 'Poetry After Auschwitz—Adorno's Dictum', *German Life and Letters* 58:2 (April 2005), 182–94.

Hooker, Richard. *Of the Laws of Ecclesiastical Polity*, ed. Arthur Stephen McGrade (Cambridge: Cambridge University Press, 1989).

Hopkins, Gerard Manley. *The Sermons and Devotional Writings of Gerard Manley Hopkins*, ed. Christopher Devlin (London: Oxford University Press, 1959).

——. *The Poetical Works of Gerard Manley Hopkins*, ed. Norman H. Mackenzie (Oxford: Clarendon, 1990).

Horace. *The Art of Poetry*, ed. Burton Raffel (Albany: SUNY Press, 1974).

——. *Horace: The Odes*, trans. Colin Sydenham (London: Duckworth, 2005).

——. *The Odes of Horace in Latin and English*, trans. Len Krisak (Manchester: Carcanet, 2006).

Howe, Irving. 'Writing and the Holocaust', in Berel Lang (ed.), *Writing and the Holocaust* (New York: Holmes and Meier, 1988), 175–99.

James, Stephen. *Shades of Authority: The Poetry of Lowell, Hill and Heaney* (Liverpool: Liverpool University Press, 2007).

Johnson, Barbara. *A World of Difference* (Baltimore: Johns Hopkins University Press, 1987).

Jones, Chris. *Strange Likeness: The Use of Old English in Twentieth Century Poetry* (Oxford: Oxford University Press, 2006).

Joyce, James. *A Portrait of the Artist as a Young Man* (London: Jonathan Cape, 1968).

Kahn, Andrew. 'First Person: The Great Brodsky', *Times Literary Supplement* (4 May 2007), 3.

Kant, Immanuel. *Critique of Aesthetic Judgement*, trans. James Creed Meredith (Oxford: Clarendon Press, 1911).

Kearney, Richard. *Poetics of Modernity: Towards a Hermeneutic Imagination* (New Jersey: Humanities Press, 1995).

Klaeber, Frederick (ed.). *Beowulf,* 3rd edn (Boston: D. C. Heath, 1950).

Lang, Berel (ed.). *Writing and the Holocaust* (New York: Holmes & Meier, 1988).

Levi, Primo. 'Levi: l'ora incerta della poesia', interview, *Corriere della Sera* (28 October 1984), 3.

Levinas, Emmanuel. 'La réalité et son ombre', *Les Temps Modernes* 38 (November 1948), 771–89.

Levy, Alan. 'Think it Over Brodsky, but Decide Now', *Saturday Review* (8 July 1972), 6–8.

Logan, William. 'Living with Ghosts', *The New York Times* (20 January 2008), BR1.

Loseff, Lev, and Valentina Polukhina (eds). *Brodsky's Poetics and Aesthetics* (London: Macmillan, 1990).

——. 'Politics/Poetics', in Lev Loseff and Valentina Polukhina (eds), *Brodsky's Poetics and Aesthetics* (London: Macmillan, 1990), 34–55.

—— (as Lev Losev). Иосиф Бродский: Опыт литературиой биографии (*Iosif Brodskiĭ: Opyt literaturnoĭ biografii*) (Moscow: Molodaia gvardiia, 2006).

Lowell, Robert. 'Books of the Year', *The Observer* (December 1975).

——. 'Two Controversial Questions', in Robert Giroux (ed.), *Robert Lowell: Collected Prose* (New York: Farrar, Straus and Giroux, 1987), 48–52.

Macafee, C. I. (ed.). *Concise Ulster Dictionary* (Oxford: Oxford University Press, 1996).

MacFadyen, David. *Joseph Brodsky and the Baroque* (Liverpool: Liverpool University Press, 1998).

McHenry, Eric. 'UNI lecturer Steiner Looks to the Future of Futurity', *BU Bridge News* 2:29 (2 April 1999); http://www.bu.edu/bridge/archive/1999/04-02/features2.html, accessed 31 May 2010.

MacIntyre, Alasdair. *Whose Justice? Which Rationality?* (Notre Dame: University of Notre Dame Press, 1988).

MacIntyre, Alasdair. *A Short History of Ethics: A History of Moral Philosophy from the Homeric Age to the Twentieth Century* (London: Routledge, 1998).

Mallarmé, Stéphane. *Œuvres complètes: Poésies* (Paris: Gallimard, 1998).

Manganaro, Marc. "'Beating a Drum in a Jungle": T. S. Eliot on the Artist as "Primitive"', *Modern Language Quarterly* 47:4 (December 1986), 393–421.

Massa, Anna, and Alistair Stead (eds). *Forked Tongues? Comparing Twentieth Century British and American Literature* (New York: Longman, 1994).

Meffan, James, and Kim L. Worthington. 'Ethics Before Politics: J. M. Coetzee's Disgrace', in Todd F. Davis and Kenneth Womack (eds), *Mapping the Ethical Turn: A Reader in Ethics, Culture, and Literary Theory* (Charlottesville: University Press of Virginia, 2001), 131–50.

'Megalithomania.com'. 2001–2010. http://www.megalithomania.com/, accessed 31 May 2010.

Milbank, John. *The Word Made Strange: Theology, Language, Culture* (Oxford: Basil Blackwell, 1997).

Molino, Michael R. *Questioning Tradition, Language, and Myth: The Poetry of Seamus Heaney* (Washington, DC: Catholic University of America Press, 1994).

Montenegro, David. *Points of Departure: International Writers on Writing and Politics* (Ann Arbor: University of Michigan Press, 1991).

Moore, Marianne. *Complete Poems* (New York: Penguin, 1994).

Mouffe, Chantal. 'Which Ethics for Democracy?', in Marjorie Garber, Beatrice Hansen, and Rebecca L. Walkowitz (eds), *The Turn to Ethics* (New York: Routledge, 2000), 85–94.

Newey, Adam. 'A Scratchy Woollen Jumper That Doesn't Quite Fit: Adam Newey Finds Too Much Romanticised Oirishness in Seamus Heaney's Poetry' (Review of *Electric Light*), *New Statesman* (16 April 2001), 53.

Nussbaum, Martha. *Love's Knowledge: Essays on Philosophy and Literature* (Oxford: Oxford University Press, 1990).

——. *Poetic Justice: The Literary Imagination and Public Life* (Boston: Beacon, 1995).

O'Donoghue, Bernard. *Seamus Heaney and the Language of Poetry* (London: Harvester Wheatsheaf, 1994).

Ozick, Cynthia. 'T. S. Eliot at 101', *New Yorker* (20 November 1989), 119–54.

Paterson, Don. *Landing Light* (London: Faber and Faber, 2003).

'Perseus Digital Library Project', ed. Gregory R. Crane (Tufts University, 2006). http://www.perseus.tufts.edu, accessed 4 September 2006.

Pickstock, Catherine. *After Writing: on the Liturgical Consummation of Philosophy* (Oxford: Basil Blackwell, 1998).

Pinsky, Robert. *Democracy, Culture and the Voice of Poetry* (Princeton: Princeton University Press, 2002).

Plato. *Dialogues of Plato: Translated into English with Analyses and Introductions by B. Jowett*, 4th edn, trans. Benjamin Jowett (Oxford: Clarendon Press, 1953).

Plutarch. *Plutarch's Morals*, translated by several hands, ed. William W. Goodwin (Boston: Little, Brown, 1878).

Polukhina, Valentina. *Joseph Brodsky a Poet for our Time* (Cambridge: Cambridge University Press, 1989).

——. *Brodsky through the Eyes of his Contemporaries*, vols 1 and 2 (Boston: Academic Studies Press, 2008).

Posner, Richard. 'Against Ethical Criticism', *Literature and Philosophy* 21:1 (1997), 1–27.

Potts, Robert. 'The View from Olympia: Seamus Heaney's Poetic Procedures are Beginning to Look Like Mannerisms' (Review of *Electric Light*), *The Guardian* (7 April 2001), 8.

Pound, Ezra. *The Letters of Ezra Pound 1907–1941*, ed. D. D. Paige (London: Faber and Faber, 1951).

——. *Literary Essays*, ed. T. S. Eliot (London: Faber and Faber, 1954).

——. Interview with Donald Hall, 'The Art of Poetry V: Ezra Pound', *Paris Review* 28 (Summer–Fall 1962), 22–51.

——. *Selected Prose 1909–1965*, ed. William Cookson (London: Faber and Faber, 1973).

Raine, Craig. 'A Reputation Subject to Inflation', *Financial Times* (16 November 1996), Books: 19.

Ravvin, Norman. 'Have You Reread Levinas Lately?', in Andrew Hadfield et al. (eds), *The Ethics in Literature* (London: Macmillan, 1999).

Reid, Christopher. 'Great American Disaster', *London Review of Books* (8 December 1988), 17–18.

Remnick, David. 'Soviet Exile Wins Nobel for Literature', *Washington Post* (23 October 1987), A1.

Retallack, Joan. *The Poethical Wager* (Berkeley: University of California Press, 2003).

Rich, Elisabeth. 'Joseph Brodsky in Memoriam: The Russian Perspective', *South Central Review* 14:1 (Spring 1997), 10–31.

Ricks, Christopher. *The Force of Poetry* (Oxford: Clarendon Press, 1984).

——. *True Friendship: Geoffrey Hill, Anthony Hecht, and Robert Lowell under the Sign of Eliot and Pound* (New Haven, CT: Yale University Press, 2010).

Ricoeur, Paul. *Temps et récit*, vol. 3 (Paris: Seuil, 1985).

Rilke, Rainer Maria. *Selected Works: Volume II – Poetry*, trans. J. B. Leishman (London: Hogarth, 1960).

Robbins, Jill. *Altered Reading: Levinas in Literature* (Chicago: University of Chicago Press, 1999).

Robinson, Peter. *In the Circumstances: About Poems and Poets* (Oxford: Clarendon Press, 1992).

Rorty, Richard. *Contingency, Irony, and Solidarity* (Cambridge: Cambridge University Press 1989).

Rushing, Conrad L. '"Mere Words": The Trial of Ezra Pound', *Critical Inquiry* 14:1 (Autumn 1987), 111–33.

Shakespeare, William. *The Riverside Shakespeare*, ed. G. Blakemore Evans (Boston: Houghton Mifflin, 1997).

Shelley, Percy Bysshe. *Shelley's Poetry and Prose*, ed. Donald H. Reiman and Sharon B. Powers (New York: Norton, 2002).

Shentalinsky, Vitaly. *Arrested Voices: Resurrecting the Disappeared Writers of the Soviet Regime*, trans. John Crowfoot (New York: Free Press, 1993).

Sherry, Vincent. *The Uncommon Tongue: The Poetry and Criticism of Geoffrey Hill* (Ann Arbor: University of Michigan Press, 1987).

Shtern, Liudmila. Бродский: Оси́а, Иосиф, Joseph (*Brodskiĭ: Osia, Iosif, Joseph*) (Moscow: Izd-vo Nezavisimaia Gazeta, 2001).

——. *Brodsky: A Personal Memoir* (Fort Worth: Baskerville, 2004).

Sidney, Philip. 'A Defence of Poetry', in *Miscellaneous Prose of Sir Philip Sidney*, ed. Katherine Duncan-Jones and Jan Van Dorsten (Oxford: Oxford University Press, 1973).

Simpson, J. A., and E. S. C. Weiner (eds). *OED Online*. Oxford University Press. http://dictionary.oed.com/, 1989–(ongoing).

——. *The Oxford English Dictionary*, 2nd edn (Oxford: Clarendon Press, 1989).

Sourcewatch.org. 'Evil-doers' (11 August 2008); http://www.sourcewatch.org/index.php?title=Evil-doers, accessed 31 May 2010.

Spenser, Edmund. *A View of the Present State of Ireland* (London: Eric Partridge, 1934).

Steiner, George. *Language and Silence: Essays on Language, Literature, and the Inhuman* (New York: Athenaeum, 1967).

Strawson, Galen. 'Against Narrativity', *Ratio* 18:4 (4 December 2004), 429–52.

Taylor, Charles. *Sources of the Self: The Making of the Modern Identity* (Cambridge: Cambridge University Press, 1989).

US Newswire, 'Poetry Foundation, Library of Congress Co-sponsor Poet Laureate's "American Life in Poetry" Project Brings Poetry Back to Newspapers' (31 March 2005).

Vendler, Helen. *Soul Says: On Recent Poetry* (Cambridge: Harvard University Press, 1995).

——. 'The Booby Trap', *New Republic* 215:15 (7 October 1996), 34–40.

——. 'Seamus Heaney and the *Oresteia*: "Mycenae Lookout" and the Usefulness of Tradition', *Proceedings of the American Philosophical Society* 143:1 (March 1999), 116–29.

Volkov, Solomon. *Conversations with Joseph Brodsky: A Poet's Journey through the Twentieth Century*, trans. Marian Schwartz (New York: Free Press, 1998).

von Schlegel, Friedrich. *The Aesthetic and Miscellaneous Writings of Frederick Von Schlegel*, trans. E. J. Millington (London: Bohn, 1849).

Wainwright, Jeffrey. *Acceptable Words: Essays on the Poetry of Geoffrey Hill* (Manchester: Manchester University Press, 2005).

Wehrs, Donald, and David Haney (eds). *Levinas and Nineteenth Century Literature: Ethics and Otherness from Romanticism through Realism* (Newark: University of Delaware Press, 2009).

Weil, Simone. *L'enracinement: prélude à une déclaration des devoirs envers l'être humain* (Paris: Gallimard, 1949).

Weisberg, Richard. *Poethics and Other Strategies of Law and Literature* (New York: Columbia University Press, 1992).

Weissbort, Daniel. *From Russian with Love: Joseph Brodsky in English* (London: Anvil, 2004).

West, Robin. *Narrative, Authority, and Law* (Ann Arbor: University of Michigan Press, 1993).

Whitman, Walt. *Complete Poetry and Collected Prose* (New York: Library of America, 1982).

Wilde, Oscar. *The Artist as Critic: Critical Writings of Oscar Wilde*, ed. Richard Ellmann (New York: Random House, 1969).

Williams, Bernard. 'The Women of Trachis: Fictions, Pessimism, Ethics', in R. B. Louden and P. Schollmeier (eds), *The Greeks and Us* (Chicago: University of Chicago Press, 1996).

Winters, Yvor. 'T. S. Eliot or the Illusion of Reaction', in *T. S. Eliot: Critical Assessments*, vol. 4, ed. Graham Clarke (London: Christopher Elm, 1990), 68–98.

Wittgenstein, Ludwig. *Tractatus Logico-Philosophicus*, trans. D. F. Pears and B. F. Guinness (London: Routledge, 1974).

Wordsworth, William. 'Preface to Lyrical Ballads', in *Lyrical Ballads, and Other Poems, 1797–1800*, ed. James Butler and Karen Green (London: Cornell University Press, 1992).

Worm-Müller, Dr Jacob S. 'Editorial', *The Norseman: An Independent Literary and Political Review* 1:1 (January 1943), 5–6.

—— (ed.). 'Notes on Contributors', *The Norseman: An Independent Literary and Political Review* 1:6 (November 1943), back leaf.

Wyschogrod, Edith. 'The Art in Ethics: Aesthetics, Objectivity, and Alterity in the Philosophy of Emmanuel Levinas', in Adriaan T. Peperzak (ed.), *Ethics as First Philosophy: The Significance of Emmanuel Levinas for Philosophy, Literature and Religion* (New York: Routledge, 1995), 138–48.

Yeats, W. B. *The Complete Poems*, ed. Richard J. Finneran (New York: MacMillan, 1983).

Zabel, M. D. 'T. S. Eliot in Mid-Career', in B. C. Southam (ed.), *T.S. Eliot, 'Prufrock', 'Gerontion', 'Ash-Wednesday' and Other Shorter Poems: A Casebook* (London: Macmillan, 1978), 71–80.

Index